MAIMONIDES

THE GUIDE
OF THE PERPLEXED

ISBN-13: 978-0-87220-325-9 (cloth)
ISBN-13: 978-0-87220-324-2 (pbk.)

Originally published in 1952
by East and West Library

Copyright 1952 by
The Horovitz Publishing Co. Ltd

MAIMONIDES
THE GUIDE
OF THE PERPLEXED

AN ABRIDGED EDITION
WITH INTRODUCTION AND COMMENTARY
BY JULIUS GUTTMANN

TRANSLATED FROM THE ARABIC
BY CHAIM RABIN

NEW INTRODUCTION
BY DANIEL H. FRANK

HACKETT PUBLISHING COMPANY, INC.
INDIANAPOLIS/CAMBRIDGE

Moses Maimonides: 1135–1204

Copyright © 1995 by Hackett Publishing Company, Inc.

17 16 15 14 13   4 5 6 7 8 9

For further information, please address
Hackett Publishing Company, Inc.
P.O. Box 44937
Indianapolis, Indiana 46244-0937

www.hackettpublishing.com

Cover design by Listenberger & Associates

Library of Congress Cataloging-in-Publication Data

Maimonides, Moses, 1135–1204.
    [Dalālat al-ḥāʾirīn. English. Selections.]
    The guide of the perplexed/Maimonides; an abridged edition with
introduction and commentary by Julius Guttmann; translated from the Arabic
by Chaim Rabin; new introduction (1995) by Daniel H. Frank.
       p.   cm.
    Previously published: London: East and West Library, 1952.
    Includes bibliographical references.
    ISBN 0-87220-325-5 (cloth).   ISBN 0-87220-324-7 (pbk.)
    1. Judaism—Works to 1900.   2. Philosophy, Jewish—Early works to
1800.   3. Philosophy, Medieval.   I. Guttmann, Julius, 1880–1950.
II. Rabin, Chaim.   III. Frank, Daniel H., 1950–   IV. Title.
BM545.D3413   1995
181'.06—dc20   95-31544
                                          CIP

ISBN-13: 978-0-87220-325-9 (cloth)
ISBN-13: 978-0-87220-324-2 (pbk.)

CONTENTS

New Introduction   vii

Editor's Introduction   1

Translator's Preface   37

Abbreviations   40

Maimonides' Introduction   41

Selections from Book I

CHAPTER I	51
CHAPTER II	53
CHAPTER XXXI	55
CHAPTER XXXII	58
CHAPTER XXXIV	58
CHAPTER XXXV	63
CHAPTER L	65
CHAPTER LI	66
CHAPTER LII	68
CHAPTER LIV	71
CHAPTER LVII	77
CHAPTER LVIII	79
CHAPTER LXIX	83

Selections from Book II

Propositions   89

CHAPTER I	90
CHAPTER XIII	94
CHAPTER XIV	99
CHAPTER XVI	101
CHAPTER XVII	102
CHAPTER XVIII	106
CHAPTER XIX	109
CHAPTER XXII	110
CHAPTER XXV	114
CHAPTER XXVII	117
CHAPTER XXIX	118
CHAPTER XXXII	126

vi CONTENTS

Selections from Book II—*contd.*

CHAPTER XXXV   129
CHAPTER XXXVI   130
CHAPTER XXXVII   135
CHAPTER XXXVIII   137
CHAPTER XXXIX   139
CHAPTER XL   142
CHAPTER XLII   146

Selections from Book III

CHAPTER XII   149
CHAPTER XIII   151
CHAPTER XVI   157
CHAPTER XX   160
CHAPTER XXI   164
CHAPTERS XVII-XVIII   165
CHAPTER XXIII   170
CHAPTER XXVII   173
CHAPTER XXIX   175
CHAPTER XXXII   180
CHAPTER LI   184
CHAPTER LII   195
CHAPTER LIV   197

Commentary   203
Index I. *Names and Subjects*   227
   II. *Hebrew words*   230
   III. *Quotations*   231

NEW INTRODUCTION

My Goal in this introduction to Julius Guttmann's and Chaim Rabin's abridgment of Maimonides' *Guide of the Perplexed* is to introduce the reader to the *Guide* and its interpretation and to indicate some directions in recent scholarship on Maimonides. That not a great deal needs to be done to render this edition current is testimony to the clarity and good sense which pervaded the entire project, a project begun by Guttmann in the mid-1940s and completed by Rabin in the early 1950s. This edition of the *Guide* was conceived by Guttmann, was abridged and annotated by him, and was translated by Rabin from the Arabic text of Munk (Paris, 1856–66) as edited by Joel (Jerusalem, 1931). The final revision of the entire manuscript was overseen by Rabin before publication in London in 1952.

This volume is one of a very small number in the *Philosophia Judaica* series, a series published under the imprint of East and West Library. This venture, the brainchild of Bela Horovitz (1898–1955), the founder of the renowned Phaidon Press, was short-lived, and the series in question included only about a half dozen volumes of Jewish philosophical classics, representing such preeminent thinkers as Philo (d. 50?), Saadiah Gaon (d. 942), and Judah Halevi (d. 1141). The intended audience of the series, of which the Guttmann-Rabin edition of the *Guide* is an essential part, is perhaps best indicated by Rabin's remarks about the *Guide* itself: "The *Guide of the Perplexed* was intended for the educated public, not for the specialist" (p. 37). Thus, what you hold before you is a school edition of Maimonides' *Guide*, aiming to help (guide!) the reader coming to the work for the first time.

I presume most readers today will not be approaching the *Guide* as did Joseph, the addressee of the *Guide* and an erstwhile student of Maimonides—in perplexity as to how to live one's life and whether or not to engage in deep reflection about the foundations of one's tradition. Rather, we (nontraditionalists) approach the *Guide* with interests in medieval philosophy or theology, in philosophy of religion, or in the history of philosophy. In other words, we come to the text as exegetes, from a vantage point outside the tradition. Joseph's perplexity is not ours, and in this sense the *Guide* is not addressed to us. Nevertheless, the contemporary reader, though distant from Joseph's crisis, should not overlook the *practical* nature of the *Guide,* simply the fact that it was written for those perplexed as to how to live their lives, in particular lives defined by traditional religious norms.[1] And, once again, though I presume that most readers of these words live lives defined by nonreligious, secular categories, even they will surely recognize the genre of philosophical literature into which the *Guide* falls, normative and prescriptive in its own way. The *Guide* is of a piece with, say, Plato's *Republic,* Aristotle's *Nicomachean Ethics,* and Spinoza's *Ethics* in being a treatise in practical philosophy, with the good life as its goal, which helps one understand the foundations of the life one ought to lead. So even if the *Guide* is addressed to one beset with problems not our own, and even if we perforce come to the text from outside the tradition, let us try to accept and read the work in the spirit in which it was written, as a work in practical philosophy which moves one toward the human good by virtue of clarifying it.

To view the *Guide* from this perspective has important ramifications. The *Guide* is a large and sprawling work of approximately 180 chapters, excluding introductions. (This abridgment presents about one fourth of the whole work.) No wonder that scholars, intent on explicating particular passages and points of detail, lose sight of the whole and, thus, the overarching practical purpose of the work. Again, the focus on particular 'theoretical' points in semantic theory, epistemology, cosmology, prophetology, legal theory, and so forth tends to obscure the overall nontheoretical telos of the treatise. Nevertheless, however conventional the literary form of the *Guide* may be, an epistle to a beloved and disturbed student, one must take the topos seriously. Maimonides is not writing for himself, nor is the *Guide* to be understood as a patchwork of theoretical minitreatises on the aforementioned topics. This is, of course, not in the least to deflate or to overlook the brilliance of Maimonides' contributions to a variety of deep and difficult philosophical and scientific topics, but rather to contextualize those discussions in the appropriate way. In sum, everything in the *Guide* subserves the end of showing the addressee, Joseph, that, properly understood, his religion—his traditional way of life, one circumscribed by halakhic (legal) norms—is philosophically defensible. And *this* point is not a theoretical

---

1. My audience thus is different from K. Seeskin's audience in his fine 1991 book, *Maimonides: A Guide for Today's Perplexed.* Nevertheless, we both agree about the *practical* nature of the *Guide,* for whomever it is addressed.

one, offered for its own sake, but manifestly a moral and even political one. The *Guide* assuages Joseph's perplexity and thereby (re)positions him squarely within the community, from which as an 'intellectual' he is temporarily estranged.[2]

As one influenced by Kant and the neo-Kantianism of Hermann Cohen (1842–1918), Julius Guttmann was well-positioned to understand the 'primacy of the practical,' that even theory is goal-directed and value-laden, presupposing norms. Perhaps this comes out best in the final section (viii) of his introduction (pp. 29–36). Guttmann repeatedly (and rightly) emphasizes the role Maimonides gives to knowledge in his hierarchy of human perfections: "The belief in knowledge as the supreme ideal of human life runs like a red thread through the entire *Guide*" (p. 29). Knowledge of God is the summum bonum. But before one succumbs to this Aristotelian ideal of 'detached theory' as the goal, Guttmann forces us to carefully attend to the very end of the *Guide* (3.54) and its quotation from Jeremiah (9:22–23): "Thus saith the Lord, Let not the wise man glory in his wisdom, neither let the mighty man glory in his might, let not the rich man glory in his riches; but let him that glorieth glory in this, that he understandeth and knoweth me, that I am the Lord which exercise lovingkindness, justice, and righteousness in the earth; for in these I delight, saith the Lord." Guttmann comments: "Knowledge of God is here raised above all other human perfections . . . but its subject is not the metaphysical existence of God but His moral government" (p. 34; cf. *Guide* 1.54, pp. 71–77). The comment is apposite, for it indicates not only that the summum bonum must be understood as a philosophically grounded moral wisdom, but that such a wisdom is a limiting condition upon the human intellect—an intellect by its very nature incapable of discerning God's (metaphysical) essence. Whatever may be the real nature of

---

2. Cf. Kellner 1990, p. 64: "Maimonides' book [the *Guide*] is transformative and not simply expository, subsuming throughout a practical aim." To give but one example of a practical dimension embedded in a 'theoretical' discussion: Maimonides' semantic theory, presented in his celebrated discussion of divine attributes (1.50–60, pp. 65–82), is offered, in large part I would suggest, to deflate Joseph's impetuosity concerning the (unlimited) scope and powers of human knowledge, the very cause of his initial perplexity and estrangement. In teaching, via the ('theoretical') discussion of divine attributes, that human knowledge is perforce limited, Maimonides hopes to curb Joseph's impetuosity, his naive epistemological optimism. And this latter desideratum is a practical point, requiring a change in Joseph's *character*. In sum, for Maimonides the doctrine of divine attributes entails humility as its desired outcome.

God and the purpose of his creation, humankind can only discern the end result of God's intentions, his actions. The finitude of the human intellect entails that one understands God to the extent that one understands his creation, the divine hand in history. And for Maimonides, the divine handiwork is good, the product of a beneficent creator who exercises "lovingkindness, justice, and righteousness in the earth." Reciprocally, our goal as humans, as images of God, is to return God's beneficence through love of him and imitation of his ways, his actions. In this way, then, the summum bonum for Maimonides is an imitatio Dei grounded in a knowledge of God in his role as a beneficent creator and judge. Human knowledge of God ultimately cannot be construed as 'detached theory' in an Aristotelian sense; it must always be contextualized against the background of an amor Dei which entails moral and political action.[3]

Guttmann seems to understand this moral spin on the summum bonum as the final victory of the Bible over Greek philosophy. He writes: "Under the influence of the Biblical conception of God [sc. as a moral agent], morality finally regains the position which it had lost at an earlier stage" (p. 34). This way of putting things needs revision. Indeed, I think it is *internally* inconsistent with remarks Guttmann makes earlier in his introduction: ". . . Maimonides does not see his task [in the *Guide*] in creating a harmony between philosophy on the one hand and the Bible on the other, but in demonstrating the philosophical content of the Bible itself" (p. 9). If this latter is true, and I think it is, then Guttmann ought not to be trumpeting the victory of religion over philosophy at the end of the *Guide*. To do so would be to give the lie to the Maimonidean project as initially conceived. It would perhaps be better to stress a non-*Aristotelian* but nonetheless *philosophical* moment in Maimonides' thought. Much recent work since Guttmann wrote has been devoted to just such a salutary muddying of the relevant philosophical *Quellen;* pride of place surely belongs to Shlomo Pines's introduction ("The Philosophic Sources of *The Guide of the Perplexed*") to his own translation of the *Guide* (Chicago: University of Chicago Press [1963], pp. lvii–cxxxiv). Leaving aside many details not important for present purposes, it should be noted that the *Platonic* legacy, inclusive of neo-Platonism and the Platonic

---

3. S. Pines's 1979 article, "The Limitations of Human Knowledge according to Al-Farabi, ibn Bajja, and Maimonides" (reprinted in Buijs [ed.], 1988), is the classic discussion for this reading of the end of the *Guide* and the moral-political dimension of imitatio Dei.

political philosophical tradition in Islam, must be accounted as central to any fair estimate of the philosophical influences upon Maimonides. Given this, such strains in the *Guide* which Guttmann tended to see as evincing tensions between the Bible (religion) and philosophy ought rather to be understood as manifesting a *philosophical* tension between (neo-)Platonic and Aristotelian elements within Maimonides' thought.

In conceiving of the *Guide* in this way, as striving to clarify "the philosophical content" of the tradition in which Joseph lives, Guttmann staked out a position diametrically opposed to that of Leo Strauss (1899-1973). For Strauss, an unbridgeable gap exists between Athens and Jerusalem, between philosophy and revealed religion. Given this dichotomy, the apparent harmonization of opposites in the *Guide* is no more than appearance, hiding a deep discordancy. For Strauss, "the *Guide* . . . is not a philosophic book . . . but a Jewish book." ("How to Begin to Study *The Guide of the Perplexed*," in Pines's translation of the *Guide*, op. cit., p. xiv). By this Strauss underscores the aforementioned opposition he sees between religion (the Law) and philosophy. Strauss's and Guttmann's respective positions concerning Maimonides' thought and the nature of the *Guide* could not be more opposed. This is not the place to adjudicate the dispute, but merely to note it. (The interested reader may refer to items 34-38 in the bibliography at the end of this introduction.) This much, however, can be said: If Strauss is right that Maimonides is committed to an irreconcilable opposition between religion and philosophy (between 'law' and 'necessity,' as he puts it elsewhere), then the *Guide* itself is a massive deception on the part of its author. The *Guide* certainly appears to be a philosophic work in defense of Judaism, replete with dialectical and demonstrative argumentation. But for Strauss, such a project of 'reconciliation' is (and must be) illusory, undertaken to hide the truth from those, like Joseph, not prepared to understand it.

A troublesome difficulty attends Strauss's line of interpretation. One may well wonder what the 'hidden' truth is supposed to be. It cannot be that the *Guide* is a philosophic work devoted to a reconciliation of philosophy and the Law, for this is precisely what it *appears* to be. But if the esoteric truth is that philosophy and the Law are incommensurable, then why attempt to hide this? Joseph already feels perplexed at the apparent incommensurability of philosophy and the Law (see Maimonides' introduction, p. 41). If, as Strauss must hold, *this* perplexity is grounded in the *truth* about the (actual) incommensurability of philosophy and the Law, what does Maimonides gain by 'misleading' Joseph into thinking that there is a *philosophical* content to Scripture? For Strauss, Joseph is *rightly* perplexed, he is 'on to something.' Why, then, disabuse him of this? For Strauss, the answer is that Joseph's perplexity, if followed to its conclusion, would lead him right out of the community of believers. Given this, such a defense of Judaism as Maimonides wished to provide for Joseph required a hiding of the truth of the incommensurability of the Law and philosophy. What we have, then, for Strauss is a defense of Judaism (a Jewish *kalām*) grounded in deceit, a defense in which membership in the community takes precedence over disclosure of the truth—a political rather than a philosophical solution. Perplexity gives way to delusion.

Unlike Strauss, Guttmann tended to be unimpressed by the exoteric-esoteric distinction which so appealed to Strauss. Guttmann believed that making such a distinction the hermeneutical foundation for the *Guide* ". . . frequently resulted in *arbitrary* reinterpretations of his [Maimonides'] system" (p. 206; my emphasis). For those, myself included, disposed to read Maimonides in a 'naive' sort of way, "straight," and impressed by the rigor and brilliance of his *explicit* philosophical argumentation, the Guttmann-Rabin edition will be refreshing. I would merely reiterate that, when reading an anti-Aristotelian critique in the *Guide,* such as one finds in the chapters devoted to the eternity or createdness of the world (2.13–25, pp. 94–117), one should not assume that Maimonides is adopting thereby an anti*philosophical* position. For Maimonides, Aristotle is not the only representative of a philosophical position. Consequently, an anti-Aristotelian position need not be construed as antiphilosophical; indeed, arguments on behalf of the createdness of the world order are both Platonic (philosophical) *and* biblical. In this way, then, "the philosophical content of the Bible" may be revealed.

In this introduction I have focused on a few points where it seems that Guttmann's views stand in need of clarification or modification. Scholarship proceeds apace. But it must be taken as a sign of the excellence of the initial effort that little more needs be said.

MAIMONIDES and his philosophy have been the subjects of much recent work. A full bibliography of books and articles in the major European languages is

1. D. R. Lachterman, "Maimonidean Studies 1950-86: A Bibliography." *Maimonidean Studies* 1 (1990): 197-216.

For the anglophone reader, the standard complete translation of the *Guide* is

2. S. Pines (tr.), *The Guide of the Perplexed*. Chicago: University of Chicago Press, 1963.

Selections from the *Guide* and/or other portions of the Maimonidean corpus may be found in

3. I. Twersky (ed.), *A Maimonides Reader*. New York: Behrman House, 1972.

4. R. L. Weiss and C. E. Butterworth (eds./trs.), *Ethical Writings of Maimonides*. New York: New York University Press, 1975.

5. D. H. Frank, O. Leaman, and C. H. Manekin (eds.), *Jewish Philosophy Reader*. London and New York: Routledge, 2000.

6. A. Halkin (tr.) and D. Hartman, *Crisis and Leadership: Epistles of Maimonides*. Philadelphia: Jewish Publication Society, 1985.

and in two medieval philosophy readers:

7. A. Hyman and J. J. Walsh (eds.), *Philosophy in the Middle Ages*, 2nd ed. Indianapolis: Hackett, 1973.

8. R. Lerner and M. Mahdi (eds.), *Medieval Political Philosophy: A Sourcebook*. Ithaca: Cornell University Press, 1963.

Among recent books in English devoted in whole or in part to Maimonides are

9. E. Benor, *Worship of the Heart: A Study of Maimonides' Philosophy of Religion*. Albany: State University of New York Press, 1995.

10. M. Fox, *Interpreting Maimonides: Studies in Methodology, Metaphysics, and Moral Philosophy*. Chicago: University of Chicago Press, 1990.

11. D. Hartman, *Maimonides: Torah and Philosophic Quest*. Philadelphia: Jewish Publication Society, 1976.

12. M. Kellner, *Dogma in Medieval Jewish Thought: From Maimonides to Abravanel*, pp. 10-65. Oxford: Oxford University Press, 1986.

13. _____, *Maimonides on Human Perfection*. Atlanta: Scholars Press, 1990.

14. _____, *Maimonides on Judaism and the Jewish People*. Albany: State University of New York Press, 1991.

15. H. Kreisel, *Maimonides' Political Thought: Studies in Ethics, Law, and the Human Ideal*. Albany: State University of New York Press, 1999.

16. O. Leaman, *Moses Maimonides*. London: Routledge, 1990.

17. Y. Leibowitz, *The Faith of Maimonides*. New York: Adama Books, 1987.

18. K. Seeskin, *Maimonides: A Guide for Today's Perplexed*. West Orange, N.J.: Behrman House, 1991.

19. J. Stern, *Problems and Parables of Law: Maimonides and Nahmanides on Reasons for the Commandments*. Albany: State University of New York Press, 1998.

20. I. Twersky, *Introduction to the Code of Maimonides (Mishneh Torah)*. New Haven: Yale Univeristy Press, 1980.

21. R. L. Weiss, *Maimonides' Ethics: The Encounter of Philosophic and Religious Morality*. Chicago: University of Chicago Press, 1991.

Recent anthologies devoted to aspects of Maimonides' philosophy are

22. J. A. Buijs (ed.), *Maimonides: A Collection of Critical Essays*. Notre Dame: University of Notre Dame Press, 1988.

23. J. L. Kraemer (ed.), *Perspectives on Maimonides: Philosophical and Historical Studies*. Oxford: Oxford University Press, 1991.

24. E. L. Ormsby (ed.), *Moses Maimonides and His Time.* Washington, D.C.: Catholic University of America Press, 1989.

25. S. Pines and Y. Yovel (eds.), *Maimonides and Philosophy.* Dordrecht: Martinus Nijhoff, 1986.

26. I. Robinson, L. Kaplan, and J. Bauer (eds.), *The Thought of Moses Maimonides: Philosophical and Legal Studies.* Lewiston, N.Y.: Edwin Mellen Press, 1990.

27. I. Twersky (ed.), *Studies in Maimonides.* Cambridge, Mass.: Harvard University Press, 1991.

Six recent books of a less historical, more systematic nature, which are grounded in large measure on Maimonidean principles, are

28. L. E. Goodman, *On Justice: An Essay in Jewish Philosophy.* New Haven: Yale University Press, 1991.

29. _____, *God of Abraham.* New York: Oxford University Press, 1996.

30. M. Halbertal and A. Margalit, *Idolatry.* Cambridge, Mass.: Harvard University Press, 1992.

31. D. Hartman, *A Living Covenant: The Innovative Spirit in Traditional Judaism.* New York: Free Press, 1985.

32. K. Seeskin, *Jewish Philosophy in a Secular Age.* Albany: State University of New York Press, 1990.

33. _____, *Searching for a Distant God: The Legacy of Maimonides.* New York: Oxford University Press, 1999.

For those wishing to follow out the Guttmann-Strauss debate concerning the nature of the *Guide* in particular and of Jewish philosophy in general, see:

34. J. Guttmann, *Philosophies of Judaism*, pp. 172-207, 503-4n125. New York: Schocken Books, 1973 [1933].

35. L. Strauss, *Philosophy and Law: Contributions to the Understanding of Maimonides and His Predecessors.* Albany: State University of New York Press, 1994 [1935].

36. J. Guttmann, "Philosophie der Religion oder Philosophie des Gesetzes?" *Proceedings of the Israel Academy of Sciences and Humanities* 5 (1974): 148–73 [response to Strauss [35] written 1940–45].

37. E. Schweid, "Religion and Philosophy: The Scholarly-Theological Debate between Julius Guttmann and Leo Strauss." *Maimonidean Studies* 1 (1990): 163–95.

38. K. H. Green, *Jew and Philosopher: The Return to Maimonides in the Jewish Thought of Leo Strauss.* Albany: State University of New York Press, 1993.

For general histories of medieval Jewish philosophy, see Guttmann [34] and:

39. I. Husik, *A History of Mediaeval Jewish Philosophy.* New York: Atheneum, 1976 [1916].

40. C. Sirat, *A History of Jewish Philosophy in the Middle Ages.* Cambridge: Cambridge University Press, 1985.

41. D. H. Frank and O. Leaman (eds.), *History of Jewish Philosophy*, pp. 83–573. London and New York: Routledge, 1997.

ACKNOWLEDGMENTS

As CHAIM RABIN in 1952 thanked Gibb, Walzer, Teicher, E. Rosenthal, and Plessner, great scholars all, so let me thank those who facilitated the republication of this edition: Betty and Chaim Rabin, Martin Seliger (on behalf of Julius Guttmann's literary estate), Don Howard, Yemima ben Menachem, Sarah Stroumsa, Paul Coppock, and, at Hackett, Jay Hullett.

In closing, let me say that it is an honor and a privilege to participate in Hackett's republication of the Guttmann-Rabin edition of the *Guide*. The end result of this venture, a story in itself, ties together scholars over a fifty-year period and a geographical dispersion of enormous magnitude. If ever one needed proof that the republic of letters knows no bounds, spatial or temporal, this volume constitutes such proof.

Daniel H. Frank
Lexington, Kentucky
April 1995
(revised August 1999)

INTRODUCTION

I

MOSES BEN MAIMON, commonly called Maimonides (1135–1204), is the leading Jewish thinker of the Middle Ages. His *Guide of the Perplexed* was published in the year 1190; thus even in point of time it forms the approximate central point of the mediaeval Jewish movement of thought. The importance of its contents makes it the pivot of mediaeval Jewish philosophy. It completely overshadows the previous attempts to interpret and justify Judaism with the methods of philosophy. Apart from the Kuzari of Judah Halevi – a work which follows a basically different line – the philosophical literature which preceded the *Guide* exercised hardly any influence on the further development of philosophical thought. This has a purely formal reason: the form of philosophy from which those works started was outmoded. Maimonides was almost the first to base his philosophical interpretation of Judaism on the system of Aristotle, which had meanwhile gained a monopoly even in Jewish circles and was to maintain its unrivalled position until the end of the Middle Ages. However, more than this, it was Maimonides' vastly superior achievement which pushed the works of his predecessors into the background. The clearest proof for this lies in the fact that until the end of the Middle Ages and even into the beginnings of modern times it retained its authoritative character. All later thinkers either enlarged upon its ideas, or where they proceed upon different lines find it necessary at every step to define their attitude to its point of view.

There is something extraordinary in the speed with which Maimonides' *Guide* came to be generally accepted as authoritative. Shortly after its appearance this work, written in Arabic, had reached all parts and groups of Arabic-speaking Jewry. A few years later it was done into Hebrew, first by Samuel b. Tibbon, then by Judah al-Harizi. Particularly in Ibn Tibbon's translation, and under the name of *Moreh Nebukhim*, which he gave to his Hebrew version, it soon occupied an important place in Hebrew literature. This Hebrew version exercised a much greater influence on Jewry than the Arabic original, for among the Jews of Arabic speech the creative energy in the field of philosophy was rapidly waning. The Christian countries of Southern Europe – Southern France and Northern Spain, and to some extent also Italy – were now taking the place of the Moslem countries as centres of Jewish spiritual life. It was in those regions that the *Guide* found enthusiastic adherents soon after its first appearance, and here it became the point of departure of that philosophical movement which continued into the beginning of modern times, and again and again centred its discussions upon the work of Maimonides.

The influence of this book, however, was not limited to the Jewish world or to the Middle Ages. It has been rightly said to form part of world literature. It was the only work of Jewish religious philosophy to attract the attention of the Moslem world, though only to a limited extent. For Christianity it had considerably greater importance. Having been translated into Latin as early as the first half of the 13th century, it exercised a profound influence upon the great scholastic writers of that century, and even more so upon those thinkers who brought about the predominance of Aristotelian philosophy in Christian scholasticism. Those writers contributed largely to the creation of that form of Christian thought which has maintained itself within the Roman Catholic church almost into our own days, in spite of constant struggles with other tendencies. Neither did the direct influence of the book diminish during the later Middle Ages. It can still be traced in some post-mediaeval thinkers who stand outside the scholastic tradition and belong to the beginnings of modern philosophy. A new translation into Latin at the beginning of the 17th century again drew attention to it. It cannot be said to have exercised any influence on the development of the philosophy of that time and was read more as a theological than as a philosophical work; yet a philosopher of the rank of Leibniz was fully conversant with its philosophical contents, and adopted some of its ideas.

Incomparably greater is the importance of Maimonides for modern Jewish philosophy. This applies not only to the last exponents of mediaeval thought in the 16th and 17th centuries. The most impressive proof that its ideas were still fully alive at that time is the case of Spinoza, who grew up under their spell. In spite of all methodical, metaphysical, and religious differences, Spinoza's own system has taken from Maimonides some essential features. Even after the middle of the 18th century, when the Jews entered the orbit of European culture and participated in its philosophical development, the connection of Jewish thought with Maimonides was not broken. A number of leading Jewish philosophers, from Moses Mendelsohn to Hermann Cohen, not only had to thank the *Guide* for their first training in philosophical reasoning, but continued to consider it their guide even after they had come to feel at home in the thought of their own time. This is as true of Mendelsohn, a follower of pre-Kantian metaphysics, as of men of the stature of Solomon Maimon or Hermann Cohen, who represented the critical philosophy initiated by Kant, or of Nachman Krochmal, a disciple of German speculative idealism. All of them considered Maimonides their model. While Solomon Maimon was guided by him in his whole philosophical attitude, the others followed him at least in their philosophical conception of Judaism.

Throughout all phases of this history – of which we have here given the merest outline – Maimonides' position has been that of the classical exponent of rationalism in Jewish religious philosophy. This rationalism believes in the power of human thought to grasp metaphysical truth. The truth of metaphysical discovery and that of divine revelation are for it essentially one and the same; the deep and innermost meaning of divine revelation can only be apprehended by philosophical interpretation of that revelation. Starting from these convictions, Maimonides attempted to show the identity of religious and metaphysical truth and to interpret the teachings of Judaism metaphysically. This attempt met with such success because it was able to preserve the basic character of the Jewish religion, and above all its conception of God, and to uphold them against more extreme philosophical tendencies. While in general adhering to the form of Aristotelian scholasticism current among Moslem thinkers. Maimonides transformed this in such a way that it could absorb the Jewish conception of God. On this basis he then undertook a thoroughgoing rationalization of the religious ideas and commandments of the Bible.

All facets of this approach have been equally important and influential in the Jewish Middle Ages. Elsewhere his influence was based on certain features of detail. Those Christian schoolmen like Albertus Magnus and Thomas Aquinas, who sought to create a Christian Aristotelian philosophy, borrowed from him the ideas which made it possible to build the Biblical conception of God into the system of Aristotle. Their strict adherence to church dogma, on the other hand, allowed them only a limited and cautious acceptance of his rationalization of the religious teachings of the Bible. At the beginning of modern times, when the domination of Aristotle's system was broken and philosophy began to go other ways, it was only natural that those of Maimonides' ideas which were taken from Aristotle, as well as the headings under which he sought to harmonize that system with Biblical religion, should lose much of their importance. For those interested in philosophy, only certain ideas kept their value which were independent of the particular form of Aristotelian thinking, such as those dealing with the relation of religious and metaphysical truth, of natural law and divine will, etc. His rationalization of Biblical teachings, on the other hand, found much sympathy in the 17th century. One thinker of the Platonizing school of Cambridge adopted Maimonides' explanation of prophecy, with only such small alterations as the outlook of his school demanded. The famous theologian John Spencer followed Maimonides in pointing out that a considerable part of Biblical ritual laws was to serve as a means to drive out heathen rites, and thereby laid the foundation of the historical interpretation of Biblical law. The Jewish thinkers of the 18th and 19th centuries who saw their model in Maimonides, were not so much attracted by the contents of his teaching as by the general tendency of his thinking. They did indeed borrow some of the contents of his thought, but this was of secondary importance as against the impulse they received from him. For them, the mediaeval thinker was not an exponent of narrow dogmaticism, but one who set the pattern of free philosophical interpretation of Judaism. The decisive point for the various forms of religious rationalism as embodied in the above-mentioned writers was not the particular pattern of Maimonides' rationalism, but the fact that he was a rationalist. They intended to do with the methods of modern rationalism the same for the exposition of Judaism as he had done with the methods of mediaeval rationalism. In his authority they found the justification of a rationalist interpretation of Judaism.

As his partisans saw Maimonides, so did his opponents. The frequently bitter and passionate criticism levelled against him was directed partly against his rationalist interpretation of Judaism and for the other part against his attempt to give to the Jewish teaching of God and His relation to the world its due place within the philosophical conception of the world. The extreme partisans of the Aristotelian system in Jewish philosophy during the 13th and 14th centuries considered this attempt a betrayal of philosophical truth to inherited religious ideas. For them the Biblical concept of God was nothing but an exoteric presentation, calculated to appeal to the ignorant masses, of the philosophical view of God and His relation to the world, which they maintained to its fullest extent. This criticism was continued in an even sharper form by Spinoza. In his *Tractatus Theologico-Philosophicus* the latter rejects as a baseless compromise every attempt at harmonizing philosophy and revelation, and it is precisely Maimonides whom he attacks as the chief exponent of that view. From the other side the champions of the unbroken rabbinical tradition opposed the philosophical interpretation of the Bible. They saw in every deviation from the literal sense a downright betrayal of the very faith of the Bible. This opposition to the philosophical interpretation of the Bible, which had been latent for a long time, came violently into the open after the publication of the *Guide*, and particularly after its translation into Hebrew. In the thirties of the 13th century a vehement struggle raged in the communities of Southern France and Northern Spain between the orthodox adherents of rabbinical tradition and the champions of philosophical enlightenment. In the main this struggle turned around the efforts to rationalize Judaism. When this struggle was renewed at the beginning of the 14th century, the opponents of philosophy did not indeed direct their attacks against Maimonides as much as against the more extremist tendencies that had appeared after him; however, Maimonides remained the one who had first taken this dangerous path. Until the very end of the Middle Ages there were not a few who considered his moderate rationalism more dangerous than the more extremist views, since no one would fail to perceive the contradiction between the latter and Judaism. Still, the strict traditional faith was not the only one to reject Maimonides' rationalism. It also met with hostility from a certain basically distinct attitude to religion, which sought the highest religious values not in the realm of thought, but in that of emotion and will. This contrast was expressed in its most pointed and clearest form in the Middle Ages by Hasdai Crescas at the turn of the 14th century. It recurs with a different emphasis in the writings of Samuel David Luzzatto in the 19th. With his religion, which was entirely rooted in emotion, he saw in Maimonides' intellectualism the opposite of the moral and religious attitude of the Bible. Maimonides' interpretation of the Bible was, therefore, for him a falsification of its real meaning. However, the very bitterness with which he polemicizes against Maimonides shows that he was as actual and alive for him as for his adherents. The dispute between Luzzatto and Krochmal with regard to the comparative evaluation of Maimonides and Ibn Ezra was not so much concerned with the historical conception of those two mediaeval thinkers as with Luzzatto's own attitude to the spiritual outlook they represented. The struggle about them, and particularly about Maimonides, was for both men a struggle about the justification of religious rationalism within the Jewish faith. As the representative of that religious rationalism, Maimonides stands, so to say, above history. All changes in the intellectual and religious life of Jewry are reflected in the changes of attitude with regard to Maimonides.

II

As in all provinces of philosophy, so in the philosophy of religion, many diverse manifestations are included under the concept of 'rationalism'. These differ not only in the degree of authority they ascribe to reason, but also in their conception of reason. Unless we are satisfied with using Rationalism as a mere catchword, we must in each individual case try to comprehend its character, range, and depth. This is certainly true for Maimonides. Only after the completion of our survey can we hope to gain a clear picture of the distinctive features of his rationalism. For the moment it must suffice to point out a few characteristic traits which are of importance in preparing us for his teaching.

Faith in the power of human reason is in Maimonides' mind combined with a profound consciousness of the limits of human understanding. On the very first pages of the *Guide* he draws a picture of human understanding which seems utterly to contradict any form of rationalism. The secrets of the world of metaphysics are completely closed to our mind. We live in a deep night, which is only broken by a sudden illumination, but this light disappears as quickly as it comes. It is impossible for us to retain the things revealed by these illuminations in the same way as we retain our perceptions in other fields. In any event this grade of perception is given to none but prophets. The perception of the philosophers is not like this lightning, only like the light which emanates from a luminous body; but it comes and goes as suddenly as that of the prophets. It is necessary for the speculative results of philosophical science to be complemented by intuitive apprehension of the truth before it can lead us up into the world beyond the senses. This view of the limitations of human perception recurs frequently in the work of Maimonides, though in other places different aspects are stressed and it is phrased in a more sober and factual form. Its most precise expression is the passage where he asserts that our thinking is fit only for the apprehension of the world which surrounds us but is unable to go beyond its boundaries (p. 56).

There is no contradiction between this conviction that human perception is limited and Maimonides' faith in reason. Only some rather extravagant and isolated expressions of his suggest such a contradiction, but they do not really fit in with his teaching as a whole. Even where he contrasts the sudden illumination of metaphysics with the steady progress of knowledge by means of discussion in other sciences, it is still – with prophets as well as philosophers – reason which receives this illumination. Above all, it is reason which enables us to realize the limitations of reason. Using close logical argumentation, he recognizes that the reality of our senses is dependent on a world beyond our senses. At the same time he sees that that world is in complete contrast to our reality and is therefore not to be apprehended by means of our thought-processes. This situation becomes most palpable when we come to the problem whether God can be apprehended. It is possible to demonstrate with the utmost metaphysical certainty that the world has its origin in a First Cause, in a being of necessary existence, and it can be concluded that this being must possess the highest degree of simplicity. But this knowledge carries within itself the consequence that we have no way of comprehending the nature of this World-Cause, since the perfectly simple cannot be comprehended by our thought-processes. The God of metaphysics is as such a Secret and Hidden God. The combination of those two features was the great attraction in Maimonides' theology for a mystic of the type of Meister Eckhart. The same is true for the entire field of metaphysical knowledge. It cannot know the world beyond the senses, whose existence it proves, except in its connection with our world. Of its nature it cannot say more than that it is different from that of the world of the senses. However, this knowledge is of positive value, in so far as it excludes every transfer of sensory notions and imagery into the metaphysical reality. This knowledge is the highest perfection attainable by man. With all its limitations, it discloses to him his connection with the metaphysical world. At the same time it provides a standard for the interpretation of the teachings of the Bible.

As Maimonides understands it, the philosophical interpretation of the Bible does not import any extraneous ideas into the Bible, but reveals its true and real meaning. The Bible contains the philosophical truth; however, the Bible is not written for the philosophers alone, but for the whole people, and its presentation is adapted to the understanding of the people. It is the task of philosophical exegesis to uncover the meaning hidden behind this method of presentation and to free it from its metaphorical and sensory trappings. Such an exegesis is the only means of reaching the ultimate aim of divine revelation. The peculiarity of Maimonides' rationalism can only be fully grasped if we realize that the ultimate aim of divine revelation is for him in the realm of theory. The knowledge of God, to which revelation intends to lead us, is a theoretical knowledge. Only by way of conceptual comprehension is it possible to attain true knowledge of God, and thereby true communion with God. It is, therefore, not sufficient to say that philosophy is in agreement with divine teaching: it is a central element of divine teaching as such. For this reason Maimonides does not see his task in creating a harmony between philosophy on the one hand and the Bible on the other, but in demonstrating the philosophical content of the Bible itself. We shall see later how he tried to get beyond the intellectualist one-sidedness of this approach. However, that attempt to give their due to other aspects of religious life does not affect his principle that philosophical knowledge constitutes the centre-piece of Jewish teaching in the Bible, as also in the talmudic interpretation of the latter.

Maimonides' view on these matters explains why he incorporated into his legal and talmudic works philosophical expositions of the basic teachings of Judaism. Those philosophical parts are not meant as digressions, secondary to the main content of those works, but are intended to convey the ultimate premises of Jewish teaching as contained in the Talmud and the final aims of the Jewish laws. In the introduction to his commentary on the Mishnah he passes from purely talmudic topics to the discussion of the problem of the final destiny of man. To his commentary on the *Pirke Aboth*, the tractate of the Mishnah which contains its ethical teachings, he prefixes a brief exposition of ethical philosophy. In connection with the passage in *Mishnah Sanhedrin* which states that all Israel has a share in the World-to-Come, with the exception of those who held certain heretical views, Maimonides first discusses the idea of the World-to-Come in detail from a philosophical point of view, and then goes on to enumerate the basic teachings of Judaism, the acceptance of which is incumbent on every Jew. In each case he means to bring out by systematic exposition the dogmas and ethical principles of the Mishnah itself.

The same attitude finds an even more pronounced expression in the fact that he prefaced his great *Code* with a section on 'The Fundamentals of the Law'. In it he interprets the teachings of the Law in conformity with his metaphysical system. He even gives a brief sketch of the cosmological and physical theories with which that system is bound up. He also expounds the ethical requirements of Judaism from the viewpoint of the Aristotelian system of virtues, though he uses the latter in a somewhat amended form. For him there was only one way to understand the Biblical and talmudic laws: in their dependence on the ultimate religious premises of Judaism. He did this by placing the exposition of the basic philosophical truths, which for him were identical with the teachings of the Torah, at the head of his work.

One might find a contradiction in the fact that Maimonides set himself in his *Guide* the task of reconciling the teachings of the Torah with those of philosophy. As is implied in the title of the book, he intends to help those whom the differences between the two lead to doubt either religion or philosophy, to free themselves from their confusion. The contradiction is, however, only on the surface, for the differences exist only as long as one insists on understanding the Torah in its literal sense and overlooking its deeper meaning. The philosophical exegesis of the Bible, which removes these differences, shows above all that the Torah contains within itself the highest form of philosophical truth.

True, it is also necessary to make certain changes in the generally accepted system of philosophy in order to realize its fundamental agreement with the Torah. Maimonides was convinced of its basic identity with the Torah, but he also saw clearly that some of its teachings contradicted the Torah. Nothing was farther from his mind than to gloss over these contradictions. However, he believed that those teachings were not necessary adjuncts of the basic axioms of that philosophy. They could be got out of the way without touching the fundamental teachings. With all his criticism of such teachings he believed to remain firmly on the soil of Aristotelian philosophy. It is this philosophy, Aristotelian philosophy correctly understood, which he found expressed in the Torah. There is little doubt that he underestimated the importance of the changes he introduced into the Aristotelian system. His criticism does not merely affect matters of detail bearing only on the periphery, but some opinions which are closely connected with the central ideas of the system. His philosophical originality lies above all in the penetrating acumen of his criticism and in his ability to reshape the Aristotelian system in conformity with it.

In the following chapters I shall deal with a few topics of special importance, mostly from those parts of the *Guide* which have been included in this selection. I hope to show by deduction from these what was the philosophical position which Maimonides had reached in this way, and how Jewish teachings appeared to him from his point of view.

III

The conviction of Maimonides and his followers that divine revelation and philosophy agree in their ultimate nature was founded above all on their view that philosophy provided a confirmation and scientific proof of the monotheism of the Bible. Aristotle had demonstrated that all happenings in the world derived from a supreme divine principle. All movement and change of things had its cause in an Unmoved Mover, free from all corporeality, whose nature lay in His thought. True, this Aristotelian God was only the cause of happenings in the world, while the world itself possessed existence independently of Him. In contrast to this, the Neoplatonic school derived also the existence of the world from God. It taught that the plurality of the world necessarily presupposes an ultimate cause and must have taken its origin in a primary divine Unity. The Arab Aristotelians incorporated this Neoplatonic conception into the Aristotelian system. They identified Aristotle's Unmoved Mover with the Neoplatonic One from which all Being of real things goes forth. The accidental and changing Being of real things must, so they argued, have its source in a principle possessed of necessary existence, a supreme world-cause whose nature includes existence and which is therefore above all change and transformation. Thus the Biblical belief in one God, to whom the Being of all things reverts, had been given its philosophical foundation.

However, the relationship of God to the world is here quite different from that in the Bible. This is true not only for the original system of Aristotle, which sees in God only the prime mover of things; it is equally true for the Neoplatonic teaching and the mediaeval Aristotelianism which stems from it. God is for these the supreme world-cause, but not the originator of the world. While according to the teaching of the Bible the world has been brought into being by a free act of creation on the part of God, these systems view it as the necessary result of the ultimate divine Unity, from which the plurality of things stems in a continuous process. The contrast of the two attitudes is expressed in that difference, that according to the Biblical belief in creation the world has a beginning in time, while in the Neoplatonic-Aristotelian theory eternal causation must correspond to the eternal Cause. This is the point at which Maimonides applies his critique of current philosophy and decisively transforms Aristotelian philosophy. The contradiction between the Biblical creation in time and the philosophers' eternal world had occupied the mind of the Middle Ages long before Maimonides, and was repeatedly recognized in its fundamental importance. Nevertheless the way in which Maimonides treats the problem constitutes an entirely new departure. His originality appears in the very formulation of the question. To maintain the idea of creation in time is for him not a thing important in itself; he would be prepared to accept the theory of an eternal world and to interpret the Biblical account of creation in accordance with it, if this theory could be harmonized with the belief in the free and spontaneous character of God's activity. This belief, with its corollary that God directs and rules according to His decree the world He has created, is a fundamental conviction of Judaism. Nothing can bridge the contradiction between it and the philosophical attitude which holds that the world comes forth from God of necessity and therefore denies God free disposition over the world. Only for this one reason, that it excludes the freedom of God's activity and implies a necessary origination of the world, is the theory of an eternal world incompatible with the teaching of the Bible.

Maimonides' originality and penetration reveals itself above all in the manner he solves this problem, and in his critique of the theory of his opponents. Before proceeding to follow up his line of thought we shall make two general observations. He does not attempt to prove that the world was created in time. He is content to demonstrate that no proof for the eternity of the world exists. The problem cannot be decided by philosophy, and decision rests therefore with religious belief. Secondly, in his philosophical argumentation he starts from the philosophical conception of nature. The Moslem dialecticians, who had before Maimonides criticized the philosophers' teaching of the eternity of the world, believed that for this purpose they had to renounce the assumption of a world governed by laws. Maimonides preserves the assumption of laws governing the course of nature in its Aristotelian form, but endeavours to show that it does not lead us to the deduction that the world is eternal and its origin a matter of necessity. Also with regard to the conception of God he places himself on common ground with the Neoplatonists and the Arab Aristotelians. He demonstrates that this conception of God, too, does not lead to the deduction that the world must of necessity come forth from God. For this reason he is convinced that he does not deviate in principle from Aristotelian philosophy, but only frees it from certain deductions which have no necessary connection with its basic character.

Aristotle himself had deduced from the character of natural laws that it was impossible for the world to have come into being, and that it must therefore be eternal. It is sufficient to make this clear to ourselves from one of his arguments. According to him all things in nature are composed of two factors, matter and form. By this one must not understand the modern concept of matter. The 'matter' of Aristotle is a substrate completely indefinite in itself, which contains within it only the possibility of accepting the forms of things, in the first instance of the four elements from which other things are compounded. Such a substrate is necessary for things to come into being. They become and perish owing to matter divesting itself of one form and accepting another. From this it results as a matter of course that matter itself cannot have come into being, since otherwise it should have been preceded by other matter, out of which it came into being. In a similar manner he demonstrates that movement cannot have had a first beginning, since every movement must have as its cause another movement. Each individual movement has come into being, but movement as such must be eternal.

Maimonides fully acknowledges this view as far as happenings within the world are concerned. Within the world no thing can come into being out of nothing, but can only take shape from an already existing matter. Similarly each movement has its cause in a movement preceding it in time. But these laws apply only within the existing world. They express the nature of things as they are arranged, but nothing entitles us to ascribe to these laws of nature an absolute validity and to extend their application beyond the limits of the world. True, the Biblical account of creation speaks of matter as having come into being, but it does not intend with this any natural manner of coming into being. It considers nature, including the laws governing it, a decree of divine will. This does not affect in any way the empirical validity of the laws of nature; all that is denied is the validity of these laws outside the limits of nature as we know it, regarding which no proof is possible. Maimonides' critique of the attempt to ascribe absolute validity to the laws of nature starts, of course, from the conception of nature current in his time. It applies, however, not only to that particular conception of nature, but would apply with equal force to the ideas of law in nature as held to-day. Here, too, we must differentiate between its validity within nature and absolute validity. If we ascribe to this conception absolute validity, then it is obviously impossible to speak of a creation of the world or its dependence on divine will. The question is whether it does in fact possess such absolute validity. To start from this assumption is nothing but a *petitio principii*. All modern attempts to combine recognition of the laws of nature with belief in the dependence of the world on a divine creator follow in the main this line of thought originated by Maimonides, however much they may vary it in detail.

As has been mentioned before, the Neoplatonists and following them the Arab Aristotelians endeavoured to prove that the assumption of creation in time contradicts also the true conception of the nature of God. If any being, they said, begins an activity which it did not carry on previously, then a change takes place within that being, which must be due to some cause. God, the being possessed of absolute necessity, is above all change, and His activity cannot be conceived of as dependent on any external cause. His activity can only be conditioned by His own nature, and for this reason must be as perpetual as is nature itself. Maimonides fully accepted the conception of God as a being of necessary existence and independent of any exterior cause, but he disagrees with the conclusion which was drawn from this. The proposition that the start of any activity presupposes a change in the agent which in turn requires an exterior cause, is in his view valid only for those finite and conditioned beings which we know from our own experience. We have no right to apply it also to the absolute cause of all being. Just because God is the being possessed of absolute necessity and incomparable with any other being, we must not apply to His activity the laws valid for all other beings. As His Being is absolute, so His activity is free and spontaneous. In this way Maimonides succeeded in combining the metaphysical idea of God held by the philosophers with the religious belief in the spontaneous and free character of divine creation.

Maimonides was not content with having disproved the philosophical objections to the idea of creation. To some extent following up the thought of Moslem theologians, he throws into relief the difficulties inherent in the philosophical teaching of the world proceeding from God by necessity; though he does not pretend that by stating these difficulties that theory has been strictly disproved. According to the philosophers, the world proceeds from God in a continuous process. Those beings which proceed immediately from God are incorporeal and closely approach God's simplicity and perfection. As the distance of beings from God increases, so their simplicity and perfection become less. At the extreme end of this process appears the corporeal world in its multiplicity, divergency, and crudeness. Maimonides demonstrates that this theory is unable to account even for the transition from unity to multiplicity, leave alone from spiritual to corporeal existence, which latter differs from the former not only in degree but in essence. However, he sees the strongest objection against it in the fact that the phenomena of nature do not exhibit the logical arrangement which according to it they ought to possess. If the world had proceeded from God by logical necessity, then it should be possible to apprehend by logic alone why its structure is just so and not otherwise and why things follow upon each other in just that order. In reality, such logical consistency is absent even in the heavens, which according to that teaching arise directly from the spiritual world. The uppermost sphere, which is completely devoid of stars, is followed by a sphere bearing the entire mass of fixed stars; this in turn by the planetary spheres, each bearing only one star. The same lack of system and order is also evident in the movement of the celestial spheres, both with regard to their speeds and directions. If, therefore, the world has its origin in God, it cannot have arisen from Him with logical necessity, but must be the work of a divine act of will, which arranged the phenomena of nature in a manner not deducible by logic, in order to realize thereby certain aims. This argument strikes at the decisive weakness of any theory of emanation that attempts to apprehend reality as the necessary unfolding of a supreme principle. It is therefore interesting to see that in the 19th century, when Hegel resuscitated the system of emanation in a different form, the same objection was raised: that it could not be squared with the accidental and irrational nature of the facts of reality. In our case, too, the irrational character of reality gives rise to the conclusion that the rise of the world from God cannot be understood as a logical process, but only as an act of will. In his critique of the idea of emanation, Maimonides again attacks directly only the Aristotelian-Neoplatonic formulation of the emanation theory with which he was familiar, but the basic notion of his critique reaches beyond this formulation. The penetrating rigour with which he defines the contradiction between belief in creation and the theory of emanation, lends his treatment of the problem of creation an importance far beyond the confines of the Middle Ages.

IV

The justification of the Jewish idea of creation provides the basis for the conception of God which expresses itself in the teaching concerning the attributes of God. This is probably the best known part of Maimonides' teaching altogether. At first glance we seem here to find ourselves in quite a different world. The point of departure of this teaching is the notion of God as a being possessed of necessary existence, containing within itself the consequence that God is absolutely simple. A being of absolute necessity conditioned by nothing is above all multiplicity and compositeness; for in a compound being, the elements which compose the whole are conditions for it. No positive assertion can be made regarding the nature of absolutely simple existence. Every statement which asserts a predicate of a subject contains thereby alone a multiplicity of elements. This elementary consideration is sufficient to exclude the possibility of any positive attributes meant to define the essence of God. It is not even permissible to ascribe to God in any positive sense the formal attributes of existence and unity, since they are not, as with other things, superadded to His essence, but identical with it. Equally inadmissible are any attributes that ascribe to God any relation to any other existence. It is not possible for an absolute being to be in any relation whatsoever to a being possessed of conditioned existence. Only two classes of attributes are admissible with regard to Him: those that describe Him as originator of some effects, and those that exclude from Him some imperfection or other. Every positive attribute is thus an attribute of effect, every attribute of essence must be negative.

This conception requires a far-reaching re-interpretation of the Biblical statements regarding God. The Bible contains almost on every page statements whose wording makes them appear as positive definitions of God's character. It ascribes to Him knowledge, power, mercy, lovingkindness, wrath, and jealousy. All these statements must either be understood negatively – i.e. as denying some shortcoming in God – or they describe God's actions, not His essence. In this latter manner, for instance, are to be taken the thirteen divine attributes revealed to Moses when he desired to know God. If God is said in that passage to be merciful and compassionate, this does not mean that we ought to attribute to Him the qualities of mercy and compassion – which as affections of the emotions can in any case not be applied to Him – but that He does good to His creatures even when they are not deserving of it.

Thus the place of the Biblical conception of God is taken by the Neoplatonic idea of God as the supreme One which eludes all knowledge: in one place Maimonides says expressly that we only know of God that He is, not what He is. He considers it as the highest degree of our knowledge of God that we comprehend that we cannot comprehend Him. God is the most perfect existence, but we cannot describe His perfection in any other way than by denying of Him every imperfection associated with created things.

However much this notion of God formally resembles that of the Neoplatonists, yet in its content it is completely different from the latter, and clearly exhibits the features of the Creator God of the Bible. The attributes of action do not merely denote some indefinite activity of God's, but an activity directed towards definite aims. When the Biblical attributes of mercy and compassion are interpreted as attributes of action, they still describe an activity directed towards definite ethical purposes. The same is true of the negative attributes: these exclude with regard to God those imperfections which are incompatible with His work as Creator. While Greek Neoplatonism in its strictest form considered God above knowledge, Maimonides denies of Him ignorance of things, since this would make it impossible for Him to create and direct them. True, he too agrees that one must not attribute to God knowledge in any positive sense as an independent quality distinguishable from other facets of God's essence. Both in the negative attributes and in the attributes of action, there remains the figure of the Creator who brings the world into existence by a free act of will and rules it by His decree.

This must not be taken to mean that through the back-door of negative attributes and attributes of action the traditional conception of God reappears unchanged. As before, the essence of God remains beyond our ken. All we are able to know is that this essence, at once perfectly simple and infinitely perfect, contains within itself also that perfection which provides the basis for the creation of the world. For Maimonides the idea of God's incomprehensibility is not merely of philosophical but also of religious importance. God is the God of Mystery even for religious consciousness. Our religious relationship to Him rests on the fact that this Mysterious and Hidden God is at the same time the Lord of the Universe, the commanding God, the God of justice and mercy.

v

Maimonides held belief in creation to be of such particular importance because it is indispensable for maintaining the belief in God's unfettered rule over the world. This he formulated by saying that only on the assumption of creation is there any possibility of miracles. On the supposition that the world rises from God by necessity, the world would be ruled entirely by the laws of nature, and every interference of God's into the course of events be excluded. Thus the miracle has a central importance for Maimonides. God's activity must stand above the inherent regularity of things, so as to realize His purposes in the world and to rule it according to His will.

However, Maimonides' conception of miracles is far from identical with that of naïve faith. First of all it must be supposed, if one is to believe in the eternal wisdom of God, that the miracles, as much as the regular happenings of nature, are contained in the divine plan of creation. When God created the world He determined all happenings until the ultimate future. He bestowed upon the world systematic orderliness, but in His plan of creation He included His unfettered interference with the happenings of the world. Maimonides departs even farther than that from the traditional view by divesting a large part of the miracles reported by the Bible of their supernatural character or by denying their reality. What urges him to do this is not the desire to restrict the number of miracles. He was fully aware that in principle it made no difference whether God interferes with the course of nature once or often. He objects not to the number, but to the character of certain Biblical miracles. He accepted the miracle as the means by which God realizes His purposes in the world. He denied the type of miracle in which God, or His messengers, the angels, talk to men as equals, in which, as in the story of Balaam, animals break into speech, or in which, to please a pious man, the order of things is violated for some trifling cause – in a word, those miracles where the atmosphere of the Bible closely touches that of legend.

Some of these miracles he treats as natural events. He points out that the Bible often describes an event as the work of God even when it does not derive from God directly but has been caused by Him through the concatenation of natural events. As an example he cites the 104th Psalm, where the winds are described as the messengers of God and the flaming fire as His minister. A large number of apparent miracles loses its miraculous character if one is acquainted with the Biblical use of language and interprets them accordingly – a thought which Spinoza took over in his *Tractatus Theologico-Politicus* with all the examples adduced by Maimonides. Numerous other miracles of the type defined above Maimonides divests of their external reality, seeing in them nothing but experiences of prophetic vision, which according to his theory of prophecy (to be discussed later) constitutes an essential element of revelation to the prophets. In dreams or waking, the prophet perceives the divine revelation as a vision of the senses. A good deal of apparent miracles belongs to this class. This applies above all to those Biblical stories in which angels appear in bodily form. Maimonides accepts the existence of angels, but he identifies the angels of the Bible – as far as they are not mere metaphors, as in Psalm 104 just cited – with the Intelligences which according to Aristotle produce the movement of the spheres. These beings can as little appear in bodily form as God himself. Wherever in the Bible angels appear bodily, only prophetic vision can be intended. It is obvious to what extent the stories of the Bible are rationalized by all this. The Bible is dissociated both from the naïve idea of miracles and the naïve form of belief in angels.

It is self-evident, with this attitude, that Maimonides also rejects belief in demons. It deserves special mention, however, that in contrast to many other Arab and Jewish philosophers he sharply disparages astrology. Neither is mentioned in the *Guide* except in passing, but his attitude to these problems is clear from his talmudic writings and his correspondence. He does not see in any of the views just mentioned a concession of religious faith to science: they are consequences of the conception of God which he views as the ultimate truth of the Bible. Neither is it possible that God, supreme over the world, should have commerce with men as with His equals, nor is there any room beside Him for the inferior powers of popular belief.

VI

We have seen that Maimonides rejects the view that the world proceeded from God by way of emanation. In a different sense, however, he incorporates the idea of emanation into his own system. The spiritual beings on whom the movement of the celestial spheres depends, have no importance for the origin of the world and like all other parts of the world are creatures of God, but God employs them to exercise His influence upon the lower parts of the world. Their influence flows upon the lower world. Of special prominence in this connection is the last in the series of those spiritual beings, the Intelligence which is connected not with one of the celestial spheres but with the terrestrial sphere. Among other things it is its task to bring the human faculty of thought into actuality. According to Aristotle every faculty can only unfold itself – or as the scholastics put it, emerge from potentiality into actuality – when its unfolding is brought about by a cause which already possesses in actuality that which is going to develop from this faculty. This is true for human thought, which can only become actual thinking if the faculty of thought in man is brought to its unfolding by a thinking which is already actual. Aristotle himself left the identity of this factor, which affects human thought, extremely vague. His Moslem followers interpreted him as meaning that this function is exercised by a superhuman Intelligence, namely that spiritual being which is attached to the world as a whole. For this reason that Intelligence is also called the Active Intelligence. This interpretation of Aristotle's ideas places human thinking, so to say, into a cosmic context. All human individuals receive their insight from a common source containing within itself all knowledge. Every act of cognition becomes thus a kind of illumination of the human mind by a superior mind – though this illumination takes place in full conformity with natural law.

This theory is of general importance because it makes it possible to account for the connection of man with God in a natural manner. Maimonides, in accepting the theory, also takes over this account up to a certain point. In the first instance he explains divine providence in this manner. Aristotelian scholasticism, for which every breach in the regularity of causal connections was out of the question, recognized providence only to the extent that it is possible to fit it into the law and arrangement of the world. In fact providence was for them only another name for the purposeful order of things due to God. Maimonides, too, seeks to define providence in such a manner as to avoid making it a perpetual disturbance of the natural sequence of events and turning daily life into a chain of miracles. God does not constantly interfere with the happenings of nature round about in order to protect His saints. He protects them from dangers by warning them in time. The medium through which the warning reaches them is the contact of man's mind with the Active Intelligence. Since this contact becomes firmer as the spiritual development of man progresses, the protection accorded to a man by providence is in proportion to his spiritual and intellectual level. It is evident, however, that Maimonides himself was not satisfied by this solution. He supplies a different one in the chapter of the *Guide* where he discusses the opinions of Job and his friends and finds in them the various philosophical and theosophical theories of providence. He interprets the opinion which Job reaches in the end, and by which he overcomes his doubts in divine justice, as meaning that the true happiness of man lies not in his external prosperity but in the bliss of his communion with God. Thus divine providence means that He bestows this bliss upon such men as are worthy of it and thereby raises them above all outward sufferings.

From the Moslem philosophers Maimonides also takes over a natural explanation of prophecy. As has been mentioned, however, he restricts this explanation to some extent. Both facts are equally significant for his philosophical and religious attitude. Since all human cognition is based upon contact of the human mind with a superior spirit and can be taken as an illumination of the human mind, it is an obvious conclusion to interpret prophecy as a heightened form of this illumination. The Moslem philosophers did this, probably following some Greek precedent, and thus turned prophecy into a natural phenomenon. Being the highest form of cognition, prophecy must needs contain within itself all lower forms; it is self-evident that all truth of philosophy is contained in prophecy. The prophet is indeed more than the philosopher, but this superiority finds its natural explanation in superior natural predisposition.

His superiority over the philosopher is in one respect one of degree. While the philosopher only reaches truth stage by stage in gradual logical progress, the superior intellectual powers of the prophet achieve such close contact with the Intelligence that illuminates him, that truth comes to him by intuitive perception. Moreover, his perception penetrates into depths which mere conceptual thinking could never reach. To this, however, must be added a difference in kind. The prophet announces the truth, which he shares with the philosopher, not in abstract expressions, but in imaginative similes and symbols. He teaches not only general truths, but announces definite events in the future. Finally, he is not only a teacher of truth, but a legislator. All this he is able to do because he possesses, apart from the highest faculty of thinking, also a perfect imagination. With him the influence of the Active Intelligence does not, as with the philosopher, stop at the intellect, but extends also over the imagination. It becomes the source of the prophetic visions discussed before; and owing to it the prophet is able to present abstract truth in concrete images, foresee certain events of the future which are not within the grasp of common conceptual thought, and as lawgiver to regulate concrete reality.

This theory accounts for all manifestations of prophetic activity which we can find in Biblical religion or in Islam, but in its ultimate meaning its conception of the relation of the prophet to God differs basically from that of the monotheistic religions. The prophet has ceased to be the messenger of God, who owes both his message and the powers needed for it to divine election; he receives his illumination in a natural way and has his prophetic vocation only in that sense in which every man of exceptional gifts has a vocation to certain corresponding achievements. In order to uphold the Biblical idea of the prophet as sent by God, Maimonides teaches that the illumination of a prophet can only take place if God wills it. He clothes this thought into the somewhat paradoxical form that God can deny prophetic illumination to those who are fit for it, if He does not wish to elect them. The purport of this idea is however clear: the will of God, just as it rules over every happening in nature, also determines the contact of man with the higher world of the spirit. The forces which affect this contact are also for Him nothing but a means of realizing His aims.

One consequence of the philosophical theory of prophecy is that the prophetic office is not restricted to any one people. As the prophet is also considered a religious legislator, it further follows that there may be several religions of prophetic origin. According to the rank of the prophet some of these may be more perfect than others. In fact the Moslem adherents of this theory teach that Mohammed was the greatest among prophets, and therefore his religion the most perfect; but this is merely a difference of degree. No basic difference exists any more between revealed and other religions. Maimonides avoids this conclusion by claiming for the prophecy of Moses that it was a phenomenon *sui generis*, not explicable through nature, and differing from all other phenomena of prophecy not in degree but in principle. This is, in his view, the kind of prophecy to which alone prophetic lawgiving is reserved. We find no prophetic lawgiver in the Bible except Moses. The patriarchs, particularly Abraham, did indeed communicate to others the truths given to them, but they gave no law. The later prophets did no more than admonish Israel to remain faithful to the laws given by Moses. The same applies to all other nations. Among them, too, we find prophets, such as Job and his friends, but no prophetic lawgivers. The Torah is not the highest among several prophetic legislations: it is the divine law *par excellence*, and as such valid for all times.

VII

Maimonides follows his Moslem predecessors in treating the religion revealed by God as a divine law. The same use of the term is found in Christian theology. For both Islam and Judaism this view corresponds to the facts of history, since both religions contain a divine system of law. This view is also correct in taking that law as political law, as is evident if one considers especially the laws of the Torah. It was easy to apply Plato's teaching of the philosopher as creator of the ideal state to the prophet. Maimonides, too, is influenced by this teaching in his analysis of the legislation of the Torah.

He saw clearly, however, that the divine law was distinguished by being more than a mere political law. In the penetrating way he followed up the implications of this, he made an essential step beyond the Moslem philosophers. While the sole aim of political law is to regulate the relations of men with men, and thereby to further their external well-being, divine law strives to perfect also the soul of man by communicating to him the supreme truth in a form in which he can understand it. This is the ultimate aim of the Torah; the regulation of social life is only a means to this end. Man must live in a well-regulated society; he needs security for his physical well-being, so that his spirit may be free for the acquisition of truth. However, all individual and social prosperity is only a means for the happiness and perfection of the mind. The ultimate meaning of divine revelation lies in this view not merely out-

side the sphere of political life, but outside the sphere of law itself. The Torah is a law which in the last instance aims not at
action but at the knowledge of God. It is a 'divine law', not
only because it was given by God, but because it leads man
to God.

Taking this general conception of divine law as his starting
point, Maimonides proceeds to interpret the individual prescriptions of the Torah. Two points are here of particular
importance: his view of the ethical prescriptions and of those
statutes that he calls ceremonial laws. He looks upon the ethical
prescriptions as a means to improve the social life of mankind.
For the preservation of peace and harmony among men it is
not sufficient that the compulsion of the law prevents them
from harming each other. They must acknowledge the rights
of others of their own free will and seek to live in peace with
them. It is the ethical virtues of the individual which make it
possible for society to be well-ordered. A well-ordered social
life is a condition of external well-being. Thus ethical conduct
and the laws of the Torah designed to bring it about serve this
lower purpose of divine legislation. The connection with the
ultimate purpose of the Torah appears only when Maimonides
considers ethics not from its social but from its individual aspect.
To be able to achieve true knowledge, man needs freedom, i.e.
full control of his instincts. Ethical self-discipline is the condition for the liberation of the spirit which is needed for the
achievement of knowledge. Even thus ethics remains a means
for a purpose beyond it. In a later context we shall see how it
rises above this.

Maimonides gives an elaborate justification for his attempt to
find a purpose also for those prescriptions of the Torah which
are concerned with worship and ceremonial. It would be in
contradiction with the wisdom of God if the law He gave did
not in all its parts serve some purpose. Of course, these sections
of the divine law must be understood from their ultimate
purpose. Maimonides had been preceded in this line of thought
not only by some of the earlier philosophers of religion, but
even some of the teachers of the Talmud recognized the justice

of inquiring into the 'reasons of the commandments', thus implying that they are to serve the ultimate purpose of divine law. Of course, the Torah itself indicates the purpose of some commandments, such as the Sabbath and the Fringes. Thus Maimonides expresses old and familiar thoughts in a new theoretical form, when he ascribes to those commandments the purpose of impressing certain religious truths on the people or to guide them to obedience to God and moral self-discipline. New in principle is only his method of explaining those laws which stand in no visible connection with the ultimate purpose of the Torah. He attributes to these the object of counteracting heathen practices of worship and magical practices current in the surroundings of ancient Israel, and of thus guarding against a relapse of the people into polytheism. E.g., he supposes the law which forbids to plant a vineyard with different species to be aimed against a rite with which the pagans hoped to increase the fertility of the vineyard; the prohibition of 'eating upon the blood' was to prevent the holding of sacrificial meals for fraternization with demons, in the way that the celebrants ate the meat and libated the blood to the demons, whose food it was held to be. Even farther he went in his explanation of the sacrifices. He did not take these as a counter to heathen practices, but as a concession to the psychology of the ancient Israelites, who under the influence of their milieu could not conceive of divine worship without sacrificial offerings. They were commanded to offer sacrifices to God so as to prevent them from offering them to other gods.

To trace the connection of Biblical prescriptions with pagan usages and ideas, Maimonides makes use of the 'Sabian' writings, in which he saw Arabic translations of works dating from the time before Moses. Although in reality these writings were composed in Islamic times, with some use of older sources, Maimonides did give a perfectly correct explanation of a number of Biblical prescriptions, as for instance the above-mentioned prohibition of eating upon the blood. The principle of his approach is, however, of greater importance than the truth or otherwise of any individual explanations based upon it. By ascribing to Biblical laws the purpose of combating heathen ideas and practices, and by referring for this to sources which for him were documents of ancient paganism, he was the first to attempt an explanation of at any rate part of Biblical legislation by means of the comparative study of religion. An English writer of the 17th century, John Spencer, developed this approach under constant reference to the authority of Maimonides, and through his agency it gained decisive influence on the comparative study of Biblical religion in modern times. We must remember, however, that for Maimonides this method was of no interest in itself, but designed to prove the wisdom of divine law in those laws which have no visible purpose. With the same consistency and decision as in his treatment of the miracles of the Bible he carried through his rationalist approach in his explanation of its laws and refused to see in the laws of cult and ceremonial arbitrary commands or practices with magical ends. For this gain he had to pay with the admission that that part of Biblical law which was directed against paganism had now no actuality, serving as it did the eternal purpose of the Torah, education to the belief in One God, only in certain time-bound circumstances.

VIII

In stating his view of the ultimate purpose of divine legislation Maimonides states at the same time his view of the purpose of human life. The ultimate object of the Torah is to perfect our soul through true knowledge, especially through knowledge of God. All other perfections which we are to obtain from the Torah, including moral perfection, serve in the last instance only that final purpose. The belief in knowledge as the supreme ideal of human life runs like a red thread through the entire *Guide*. In its very first chapter the Biblical statement of the creation of man in God's image is interpreted as meaning that through his gift of knowledge man becomes the image of God. The notion that man's spiritual being, not his corporeal structure, makes him an image of God, is further refined by adding that spiritual personality, the true essence of man, is identical with his power of rational thinking. The second chapter draws from this the conclusion that the first man judged originally things only from the theoretical point of view as true or false; only when the power of sensuality began to stir within him, and his reason had to withstand it somehow, he was forced to distinguish also between good and evil. The concluding chapters of the book revert in a somewhat altered formulation to its opening. Maimonides enumerates the various forms of human perfection and demonstrates that not only are property, strength, and bodily beauty possessions which do not belong to the essence of man, but that the same is true, in spite of their higher rank, also of his moral virtues, since the latter have no importance for man himself, only for his environment. They serve the interests of the society in which man lives and lose their meaning when we visualize man isolated from that society. What then remains, and thus proves to belong to his essence, is nothing but the virtues of his rational mind.

This, of course, is wholly Aristotelian. For Aristotle, too, the faculty of theoretical knowledge is the highest faculty of man. Since the supreme happiness of every being lies in the realization of its potential powers, so man's true happiness and perfection is to be sought in the unfolding of his rational faculty, i.e. in the knowledge of truth. Just as God is the highest mind, enjoying eternal beatitude in the apprehension of itself, so the happiness of knowing is the supreme good also for man. Maimonides goes even to some extent beyond Aristotle, declaring the supreme good to be the only true good, for which all others are mere means, while Aristotle thinks of the inferior goods as subordinate to the highest, but still as retaining their value in the whole scheme of human existence. At the same time Maimonides, just like his Moslem predecessors, gives Aristotle's life-ideal a religious interpretation, which in all probability can be traced back to Neoplatonic influence. He repeats in the sphere of knowledge the same process which we have just observed in his treatment of human purpose as a whole. Just as there knowledge, from being the highest purpose of life, had become the only true one, compared with which all other human purposes were mere means and preparations, so within the sphere of knowledge Maimonides recognizes only the knowledge of the world beyond the senses, particularly the knowledge of God, as a purpose in itself. The knowledge of empirical reality, which for Aristotle possessed a value of its own, serves for Maimonides only to give us access to the supernatural and in the last instance to God. Knowledge of God is the only true good. The only meaning of human life, with all its activities and possessions, is in nothing else but this; all powers of man must be directed towards this one aim. Thus the teaching that knowledge is the supreme good of mankind becomes an expression of the religious conviction that communion with God is the only true good.

The religious meaning of this ideal of knowledge is even more evident in the idea that the knowledge of God leads to a real connection with Him. As we have seen earlier on, all rational knowledge is based on the contact of the human mind with the superhuman Active Intelligence, a contact which becomes closer to the extent that knowledge increases in a man. Since this Active Intelligence in its turn is in contact with God, it becomes a medium through which contact between man and God is established. Hence reason is the link which unites us with God. It originates in God and at the same time raises us to Him. Human reason achieves independence of the body, and is enabled to survive its death, only by the transition of the mind from potentiality to actuality and in particular by metaphysical knowledge; eternal life is therefore attainable through knowledge of God. The picture is completed by drawing the emotional side of the process into the field of our considerations. Aristotle said that the highest happiness of man lies in knowledge. The conception of knowledge which we have just elaborated, however, defines the happiness of knowledge as the bliss of communion with God. Through knowledge man attains true contact with God: that contact provides for him supreme beatitude and fills him with the true love of God. Love of God in its turn urges man ever anew to seek the communion with God through knowledge and to hold on to it permanently. For this reason it is a vacillation of terminology rather than an inner contradiction when Maimonides designates as the highest purpose of man sometimes the knowledge of God and at other times the love of God which springs from it. The two are not discrete facts, but different facets of one and the same situation.

In his description of this communion with God the whole religious spirituality of Maimonides unfolds itself. In those last few chapters of the *Guide* which deal with it, the otherwise sober and matter-of-fact style of the work rises to a passionate ardour. This is all the more effective as it is still restrained by dispassionate logical thought. Indeed, logical thought becomes here itself expression of religious emotion. Yet we find here a religious attitude utterly different from that of biblical or talmudic Judaism. The contrast with the religious concepts of Bible and Talmud is evident in the position Maimonides assigns to morality. For the Bible the moral precept is the essential expression of the will of God and obedience to it the true service of God. For Maimonides, morality has become an expedient partly for the welfare of society and partly for the discipline of personality, whose ultimate perfection lies not in the moral but in the intellectual sphere. In accordance with this the relation to God has in the two systems an essentially different character. Humble submission to the will of God, confidence in, and surrender to, divine guidance take second place where knowledge is the link which unites us with God. Also love for our Father in Heaven, to the God of mercy and of compassion, is quite a different thing from a love for God which grows out of communion by knowledge. The religion of Maimonides, as we have seen it hitherto, is a religion of contemplation, intent absorption in God is the way by which man rises to Him. The contrast with the moral religion of the Bible becomes all the more obvious since contemplation is linked with the scientific knowledge of the philosophers, which at its highest point attains the immediacy of true intuition. Historically this type of religion springs not from Jewish but from

Greek soil. Its logical outcome is Spinoza's love of God through knowledge. While Maimonides had in his metaphysical treatment thrown into relief the difference between the Creator of the Bible and the Supreme Cause of Aristotle and the Neoplatonists, and had employed all the power of his mind to prove the justice of the Biblical idea of God, he was not conscious of the difference between the Biblical and the philosophical idea of the highest ideal of human life and of the path which leads man to communion with God. He followed philosophy and believed that it could be identified with the Bible.

In doing this, however, the Biblical conception infiltrates into the philosophical and imperceptibly transforms it. The cause of this is not simply that Maimonides could not escape the influence of Biblical tradition. The true reason lies in the necessary difference between the relationship to the Supreme Cause of philosophy and that to the God who spontaneously created and governs the world. The God of the Bible is not merely the object of our knowledge: He in turn knows man, knows him to the utmost recesses of his heart. Therefore the communion with God by knowledge, as Maimonides demonstrates, leads man to the conscious realization that God's eye permanently rests upon him and thus fills him with humility and awe. The fear of God, in a form in which it is only possible *vis-à-vis* a personal God, turns out to be an essential factor of the relationship of man to God. It seems to be in some contradiction to this if we read immediately afterwards that the actions commanded by the Torah are designed to produce in man the fear of God, the knowledge of God, and the love of God. The meaning of this passage, however, is evidently that the belief in the God of commandment and demand includes awe of God. Even the love of God now takes a new character, being as it were directed towards a God who on His part turns towards man. Its basis is no more solely the beatitude of knowledge, but a feeling of security and trust in God. The relation to God still remains linked with theoretical knowledge, because divine providence is in proportion to the level of knowledge of each individual. On this intellectual foundation, however, there arises a communion with God which wholly partakes of the character of personal contact.

Under the influence of the Biblical conception of God, morality finally regains the position which it had lost at an earlier stage. Having demonstrated in the final chapter of the *Guide* that the true perfection of man consists not in possessions or physical or even moral virtues, but only in his theoretical knowledge, particularly the knowledge of God, Maimonides quotes in support of his opinion the words of Jeremiah: 'Thus saith the Lord, Let not the wise man glory in his wisdom, neither let the mighty man glory in his might, let not the rich man glory in his riches; but let him that glorieth glory in this, that he understandeth and knoweth me, that I am the Lord which exercise lovingkindness, justice, and righteousness in the earth; for in these I delight, saith the Lord' (9, 22-3). Knowledge of God is here raised above all other human perfections – by wisdom Maimonides understands practical wisdom, i.e. moral perfection – but its subject is not the metaphysical existence of God but His moral government. At the same time it teaches that God demands from man a similar moral conduct. From this Maimonides draws the conclusion that knowledge of God only reaches its full perfection in the endeavour to resemble God by the exercise of justice and love, as far as this is within human power. In his teaching concerning divine attributes, Maimonides had already achieved a similar transposition of the idea of knowledge of God from the metaphysical into the moral sphere. In proof of his theory that we are unable to recognize God's essence, only His actions, and that all divine attributes, as far as they have a positive meaning, are to be taken as attributes of action, he had quoted the passage where Moses had asked to see the glory of God and had received the reply that he was unable to look upon the face of God. Only his other request, to know the ways of God, had been fulfilled. The 'ways of God' revealed to Moses, were the 'thirteen qualities of God' which express the moral government of God. In discussing that passage, too, Maimonides had said that the highest perfection of man is to resemble God in his actions and that the purpose of the knowledge of God was to lead him to such an imitation of God.

In neither case was it the contents of the Biblical passages alone which caused Maimonides to understand the idea of knowledge of God in a moral sense. The notion of God as the Creator and Governor of the world must needs lead to a corresponding notion with regard to the knowledge of God. No contemplative religious attitude can be united with such a conception of God. There is only an apparent contradiction between the claim that the highest perfection of man is to walk in the ways of God and the previously maintained subordination of moral to intellectual perfection. Maimonides evidently distinguishes between a form of morality which rests merely on the exercise of practical insight and one which stems from the knowledge of God. The former serves only the welfare of society and does not form part of the true essence of man, the latter is rooted in the highest stage of human knowledge and is the expression of man's communion with God. Its importance is therefore quite independent of its social consequences. This distinction is in Maimonides' treatment implied rather than clearly indicated. Altogether the moral concept of the relation of man to God is not discussed independently, but only expressed in the transformation of an originally contemplative religious ideal.

The two sides of Maimonides' religious attitude derive not alone from outside, from philosophy on the one hand and Jewish tradition on the other. Both find their place in his own religious life. His most intense religious need was for immediate communion with God, in which the connection with the world disappears completely. It is this side of his religiosity which finds its expression in the idea of communion by knowledge. He realized, however, that this communion with God requires some test in moral action. Thus he incorporates, through inner necessity, the idea of moral relationship between man and God. True, the moral religiosity of Judaism does not receive full justice in this way, and no complete harmony is achieved between it and the other religious motifs of Maimonides' teaching. This, however, is a tension of religious motifs which constantly recurs in the history of religion, particularly in that of Judaism, and which to overcome is the task of each age anew.

Jerusalem   JULIUS GUTTMANN

The Guide of the Perplexed *was intended for the educated public, not for the specialist. The Arabic original is, therefore, in a style no more technical than that of a thoughtful essayist would be in our own time. The direct apostrophe of the reader in many passages is here not an empty literary device, but the warm, sincere talk of one man to another. It has been my endeavour to preserve this atmosphere as far as possible while remaining faithful to the original text. However, the educated reader of the author's time was as familiar with the terminology of Aristotelian thought as we are with the terms of elementary science or psychology, and words like* essence, accident, emanation, *and* uncorporeality *formed part of his mental equipment in the same way as* chain-reaction *and* the ego *belong to ours. Moreover, the words for the ideas just mentioned are in the original ordinary Arabic nouns, with other, non-technical, uses and everyday associations which cannot be evoked by any rendering. The Latin technical terms, a heritage of the Aristotelian age of our own Western civilization, had therefore to be retained.*

The Bible-quotations, which form not only part of the argument, but an essential element of Maimonides' style, have been as far as feasible kept in the wording of the Authorised Version, though even those phrases are hardly likely to be as familiar to the English reader of to-day as were the stately cadences of the Hebrew to the mediaeval Jew. We have no way of knowing how Maimonides, or his oriental readers, understood every single phrase. Changes have been made only where the A.V. differs in essentials from the interpretation accepted among Jews, where the meaning of a word is altogether uncertain, or where Maimonides' use of a passage or his Arabic rendering of it provides us with clues to his interpretation. Beside Saadiah, Kimchi, and the lexicographers, I have derived much inspiration from the translation of I. Leeser and the 'American Jewish Version'.

The translation has been made from the Arabic text of Munk as edited by I. Joel in the Sifriyah Philosophit *of Junovitch (Jerusalem, 1931), with occasional use of the variant readings. Tibbon's version and the mediaeval commentators have been consulted in the edition*

*of Warsaw, 1930 (I. Breisblat), and the version of al-Harizi in the
edition of A. L. Schlossberg.*

*It is an agreeable duty for me to express my thanks to Professor
H. A. R. Gibb, Dr R. Walzer, and Dr J. L. Teicher, whom I
consulted on points of translation, and to Dr Erwin Rosenthal, who
facilitated my labours by lending me his copy of Munk's* Guide des
Égarés. *I am particularly grateful to Dr M. Plessner, who spared
neither time nor labour in going over my manuscript, drew my attention to slips and oversights, standardized the philosophical terminology, and made many helpful suggestions. I also wish to thank my
mother for typing out for me the larger part of this work; and last but
not least I thank the publisher, who by the publication of this series
has made himself so deserved of Jewish scholarship, for his helpfulness
and great patience during the preparation of this volume, which took
very much longer than originally planned.*

*The untimely loss to Jewish learning of Professor Julius Guttmann
– may his memory be for a blessing – deprived this edition of the
benefit of a revision by his hand. For its faults the translator alone is
responsible.*

C. RABIN

Oxford

SELECTIONS
FROM THE
GUIDE OF THE PERPLEXED

ABBREVIATIONS AND NAMES USED IN THE NOTES

A.V. The Authorised Version (King James Version) of the Bible in English.

Crescas Asher (Bonan) b. Abraham Crescas, commentator, wrote before 1438 (often called Ibn Crescas).

Duran Isaac (Profiat) b. Moses Duran, commentator of the fifteenth century (often called Ephodi).

Harizi Judah b. Solomon al-Harizi (d. 1218), translator.

Kimchi R. David Kimchi (R'DaK), Bible commentator (1160–1235).

MSS. Manuscripts.

Peshitta The canonical Syriac translation of the Bible.

Saadiah Saadiah b. Joseph al-Fayyumi (d. 940), philosopher and translator of the Bible into Arabic.

Septuagint The oldest Greek translation of the Bible (third-second century B.C.E.).

Siphre A commentary on several books of the Pentateuch (second century C.E.).

Shemtob Shemtob b. Joseph Ibn Shemtob, commentator of the fifteenth century.

Targum The Aramaic translations to the Bible. ('Targum' in the case of the Pentateuch refers to Targum Onkelos.)

Tibbon Samuel b. Judah Ibn Tibbon, translator (1150–1230).

vs. verse.

The Editor's Notes, which are denoted by numbers in the text,
will be found on pp. 205 ff. below.

THIS treatise has as its principal object to clarify the meaning of certain terms in the Bible. Of these, some are words bearing several meanings (homonymous), and ignorant people persist in taking them always in one of those meanings. Others are used in a metaphorical sense: these same people take them in their primary sense. Others again are of an ambiguous (amphibological) character, making sometimes the impression of being employed in their conventional sense, and sometimes of possessing several meanings.[1]

The aim of our treatise is, however, not to explain all these terms to the vulgar crowd or to mere beginners in philosophy, or even to those who study nothing but the Law – i.e. the legal and the ritual aspects of our religion (since the whole purpose of this and similar treatises is the true understanding of the Law). Its aim is rather to stimulate the mind of the religious man who has arrived at deep-set belief in the truth of our faith and who is perfect in the religious and moral sense. If such a man has also made a study of the philosophical sciences and grasped their meaning, and feels attracted to rationalism and at home with it, he may be worried about the literal meaning of some scriptural passages as well as the sense of those homonymous, metaphorical, or ambiguous expressions, as he has always understood them, or as they are explained to him. He will thus fall into confusion and be faced by a dilemma: either he follows his reason and rejects those expressions as he understands them: then he will think that he is rejecting the dogmas of our religion. Or else he continues to accept them in the way he has been taught and refuses to be guided by his reason. He thus brusquely turns his back on his own reason, and yet he cannot help feeling that his faith has been gravely impaired. He will continue to hold those fanciful beliefs although they inspire him with uneasiness and disgust, and be continuously sick at heart and utterly bewildered in his mind.

This treatise has a second purpose, namely, to throw light on some exceedingly recondite similes which appear in the prophetic books without it being made clear that they are similes. It therefore seems to the ignorant and unwary that these are to be taken in their literal sense without any hidden implication. When a person acquainted with the Truth considers such similes, taking them at their face value, he again experiences utter bewilderment. Only when one explains them to him, or at least points out that they are similes, can he find the right way and be relieved of his perplexity. This is the reason why I have called this treatise *Guide* * *of the Perplexed.* [2]

I make no claim that this treatise will solve all difficulties its readers might have, but I do feel sure that it resolves most of their difficulties, and the most important ones at that. Let the enlightened reader not demand or expect, however, that we shall deal exhaustively with all the subjects we take up, or discuss to the fullest extent the import of any simile on which we shed some light. No sensible person would do such a thing even in intimate conversation, how much less set such matters out in a book, where they would become a target for any conceited fool, upon which to let loose the arrows of his foolishness. In our legal works we have endeavoured to explain some of these matters and have drawn attention to many details. We have stated there** that the Story of Creation is an account of natural science and the Description of the Heavenly Chariot an account of the teachings of metaphysics. We commented upon the saying of the Sages: 'The Description of the Chariot*** must not be taught even to one student at a time, except that in the case of a learned man who can think for himself one may outline to him the subject in general terms' (Hagigah 11b, 13a). [3] Do not ask me, therefore, to give you here more than such outlines. Even so, these outlines will not appear in our treatise in their proper order or set out continuously, but scattered and mixed with other subjects which we desire to expound. For I want the Truths to flash forth for a moment and then to disappear, lest we contravene the will of God – which no one can

*Literally: Guidance.
**Mishneh Torah, Madda', ii. 12; iv. 10.
***Ezekiel ch. 1.

contravene – who caused the Truth relating to the perception of Him to be hidden from the vulgar crowd, as it is written: *The secret of the Lord is with them that fear Him* (Psalm 25, 14).

Even with regard to the natural sciences it is not always possible to teach their principles openly just as they are, as is expressed in the well-known dictum of our Sages: 'The Story of Creation must not be taught to two students at once' (Hagigah, *ibid.*). If one would fully explain those matters in a book, it would mean teaching them to thousands. For this reason they are mentioned in Scripture only by way of simile. The Sages also speak of them in riddles and similes, following the example of Scripture; for these are things closely interwoven with metaphysics, and they themselves are metaphysical secrets.

Do not imagine that these great mysteries are completely and thoroughly known to any of us. By no means: sometimes Truth flashes up before us with daylight brightness, but soon it is obscured by the limitations of our material nature and social habits, and we fall back into a darkness almost as black as that in which we were before. We are thus like a person whose surroundings are from time to time lit up by lightning, while in the intervals he is plunged into pitch-dark night. Some of us experience such flashes of illumination frequently, until they are in almost perpetual brightness, so that the night turns for them into daylight. That was the prerogative of the greatest of all prophets (Moses), to whom God said: *But as for thee, stand thou here by Me* (Deuteronomy 5, 31*), and concerning whom Scripture said: *the skin of his face sent forth beams* (Exodus 34, 29). Some see a single flash of light in the entire night of their lives. That was the state of those concerning whom it is said: *they prophesied that time and never again* (Numbers 11, 25).** With others again there are long or short intermissions between the flashes of illumination and lastly there are those who are not granted that their darkness be illuminated by a flash of lightning, but only, as it were, by the gleam of some polished object

*In Hebrew vs. 28.
**Thus Siphre; A.V., with Targum: 'and did not cease'.

or the like of it, such as the stones and suchlike (phosphores-
cent) substances which shine in the dark night; and even that
sparse light which illuminates us is not continuous but flashes
and disappears as if it were *the gleam of the ever-turning sword*
(Genesis 3, 24). The degrees of perfection in men vary according to these distinctions. Those who have never for a moment
seen the light but grope about in their night are those concerning whom it is said: *They know not, neither will they understand;
they walk on in darkness* (Psalm 82, 5). The Truth is completely
hidden from them in spite of its powerful brightness, as is also
said of them: *And now men see not the light which is bright in the
skies* (Job 37, 21). These are the great mass of mankind; and
there is no reason to take them into account when dealing with
the subject of our treatise.

It must be clearly understood that when one of those who
have attained to any of the aforementioned degrees of perfection wishes to tell, by word of mouth or in writing, anything
of the mysteries which he has grasped, it is not possible for him
to expound clearly and systematically whatever he has comprehended, as he would have done in any other science which
has an established method of instruction. When he tries to
teach others, he has to contend with the same difficulty which
faced him in his own study, namely, that matters become clear
for a moment and then recede into obscurity. It appears that
this is the nature of this subject, be one's share of it large or
small. For this reason when any metaphysician and theologian,
in possession of some Truth, intends to impart of his science, he
will not do so except in similes and riddles. The writers on
this subject have used many different similes, varying not only
in details but in their essential character. In most cases they
placed the point which they wanted to be understood at the
beginning of the simile, in its middle, or at its end, as they
could find no simile to fit the subject in its full extent. Moreover, they would distribute the illustration of one subject they
wanted to explain over several mutually incompatible metaphors. Even more difficult than this are cases where one single
simile serves for several distinct subjects, its beginning fitting

the one and its end the other, or even all of it may be a metaphor to illustrate two related subjects within the field of that discipline. [4] Yet if anyone wants to teach it without the help of similes and riddles, his exposition of it will be so obscure and oracular that he will become even less intelligible than if he had used metaphors and riddles.

One might say that the learned and the thinkers are led into this course by Divine Will as much as by the limitations of their own nature. When the Almighty God wished to lead us to perfection and to order the affairs of our community* by means of his practical commandments, He knew that this was only possible after inculcating some rational beliefs, chiefest among them the knowledge of His divine nature to the extent of our ability. But this presupposes a knowledge of metaphysics, which again must be preceded by some acquaintance with natural science, since natural science borders on metaphysics and must be studied before it, as will be clear to anyone. God therefore let His Holy Writ begin with the Story of Creation – which as we have explained is equivalent to an account of natural science. But that is a great and lofty subject, and our minds are too imperfect to comprehend this most momentous of all subjects just as it is. Since the needs of the exposition of metaphysical truths necessitates, as in this case, the introduction of profound and obscure detail, it was done in vague similes and riddles. This has been indicated by our Sages in the dictum: To tell the power of the work of Creation to flesh and blood would have been impossible: therefore Scripture expresses itself without much detail, 'In the beginning God created the heavens and the earth' (Midrash Hagadol on Genesis 1, 1). Thereby they draw your attention to the fact that these matters are esoteric. As Solomon puts it: *Far off and exceedingly deep, who can find it out?* (Ecclesiastes 7, 24). The exposition of all these things is therefore clothed in words with several meanings, so that the vulgar can take them, according to their lights, in one sense, while the perfect and educated man will take them in quite a different sense.

*So the Hebrew versions. Arabic MSS.: communities.

INJUNCTIONS TO THE READER OF THIS TREATISE

If you want to get the greatest benefit from reading this book and not to miss any of its points, bring the various chapters of it to bear on the interpretation of each other. Nor should you be satisfied, in reading any particular chapter, with merely understanding its general argument, but try to get at the full import of each word employed in the course of exposition, even if it has nothing to do with the subject of that chapter. For the expressions used in this treatise have not been chosen at random, but are carefully thought out and meticulously marshalled, so as not to fall short of the full explanation of any difficulty. Anything in it which seems out of place in fact contributes to the elucidation of some subject discussed in another place. Therefore do not treat such passages with suspicion, which would only be an insult to the author and depriving yourself of benefit. Rather study carefully every point that demands it and go on pondering over it; for just these will resolve for you the greatest difficulties of the Law which disturb the minds of most intelligent people.

I implore every reader of this treatise in the name of God Almighty not to interpret even a single word of it to anyone else unless it clearly agrees with the opinions expressed by former authoritative writers on our Law. If he understands any of it in such a way as not to agree with the views of my illustrious predecessors, let him not so interpret it to others, nor rush into disproving me, for it may well be that he has misunderstood my words. He would thus harm me in return for the good I wanted to do him and would be one *that renders evil for good* (cf. Psalm 38, 21). Nay, I ask every one into whose hand my treatise falls to study it carefully; if it relieves any of his difficulties, even a single problem that is in his mind, let him be grateful to God and satisfied with what he has understood. If he finds in it nothing of use to himself, let him forget that it was ever written. Should anything in it appear to him detrimental, I would ask him to try and find a more favourable explanation for it, even, though it might seem a little far-fetched, and to give me the benefit of the doubt,* as is our duty towards every man (cf. Aboth 1, 6), how much more so when it comes to our religious teachers, the bearers of our Law, who endeavour to communicate** the Truth to us according to their ability.

I am certain that even a mere tyro, who has no experience of philosophical reasoning, will benefit from some chapters of this book. Men of perfection who are deeply religious but perplexed in their minds – as I mentioned before – will benefit from all its parts, and will derive the utmost satisfaction and pleasure from it. As for those whose minds are confused and tainted with unsound ideas and fallacious methods of thought, which they believe to be sound knowledge, considering themselves thinkers though they know nothing whatsoever that deserves the name of knowledge – those people will be shocked by many parts of this book. Our arguments will be all the more difficult for them to stomach, not only because they will not see any sense in them, but also because they demonstrate the falsehood of the trash they call their own, which is their stored-up wealth for the hour of need.

God knows that I have hesitated for a very long time to commit to writing the things which form the subject of this treatise, for they are mysteries, and during all the long years of our exile – of which alone we possess the literary heritage*** – no book on these has been composed in our religion. How then should I take such a revolutionary step as to write about them? However, I based my decision on two maxims: one is the principle to apply to such situations the verse: *it is time to act for the Lord; they have made void Thy Law*§ (Psalm 119, 126), the second the adage of the sages 'let all thy acts be for the sake of Heaven' (Aboth 2, 17). I have taken these two maxims as my

---

*Literally: 'to judge me in the scale of righteousness'.

**Perhaps: endeavour by their exercise of independent thought (*ijtihâd*) to communicate . . . (Plessner).

***i.e., we cannot know what works may have existed before the exile.

§ By the Rabbis (Berakhoth 63a) interpreted as 'when it is time to act for the Lord, one may violate Thy commandments'. It is doubtful whether Maimonides takes it here in this sense.

guide in what I have written in some parts of this treatise. Altogether it is my nature that when I cannot help expressing my true conviction except in such a way that it pleases one man of worth and displeases ten thousand fools, I would rather speak to that one man and pay no attention to the murmurs of all that multitude. I claim the right to save that man of worth from his embarrassment and to lead him out of his perplexities so that he attains perfection and peace of mind.

PREFATORY REMARKS

Contradictions or inconsistencies may be found in a book through any one of seven causes. . . .

The fifth cause is the exigencies of method in teaching and explaining. It may happen that an involved and abstruse point has to be mentioned by way of introduction to the treatment of an easily understood subject which is quite properly discussed before that other one, because one should always proceed from the easier to the more difficult. The teacher must then rely on some superficial and crude method of explaining the point in question, without trying to expound it in full, and leave it to the imagination of his audience to understand of it what must be understood for the present. In the proper place he can then treat that more involved matter in full and bring out its true meaning.

The seventh cause is the difficulty experienced in discussing very profound matters, some details of which must be kept hidden while others can be revealed. In the course of dealing with a subject it may be necessary to mention (such) a matter and to base it on one premise, while in another place the circumstances may call for basing it on a contradictory premise. The vulgar must however not be allowed under any circumstances to become aware of the contradiction of these premises, and the author will therefore at times adopt every possible means to camouflage it. [5]

After these prefatory remarks I shall now proceed to deal with the terms that require elucidation of their proper meaning in the various passages according to the sense required there. They will serve as a key to places which are at present guarded by locked gates. Once we have unlocked those gates and entered the realm beyond them, our souls will find rest there, our eyes will find delight and our weary bodies will recover from their toil.

BOOK I

Open ye the gates, that the righteous nation which keepeth the truth may enter in
(Isaiah 26, 2)

CHAPTER I

IMAGE AND LIKENESS

PEOPLE think that the word *tzelem* (IMAGE) in Hebrew refers to the outward shape and contours of a thing. This has been a cause of crass anthropomorphism because of the verse: *Let us make man in Our image after Our likeness* (Genesis 1, 26). They think that God is of the IMAGE of man, i.e. his shape and outline, and thus fall into unalloyed anthropomorphism, in which they firmly believe. It appears to them that by abandoning this belief they would deny Scripture, nay, the very existence of God would be called in question unless they imagine Him as a body with face and hands like themselves in shape and design, only – as they deem – bigger and brighter, and its substance not of flesh and blood. That is the highest degree of incorporeality* they are prepared to grant to God.

You will find in the course of this treatise the complete demonstration of the falsity of anthropomorphism and the arguments for the true unity of God, which makes no sense without rejection of anthropomorphism. In this chapter we intend to explain only the terms IMAGE and LIKENESS. I maintain that 'image', as it is used in current speech to denote the shape and outline of a thing, is in Hebrew *to'ar* (FORM) as used in the phrases: *beautiful of form and beautiful of appearance* (Genesis 39, 6), *what form is he of?* (1 Samuel 28, 14), *like the form of princes* (Judges 8, 18). This word is also applied to the image or form which the craftsman produces, as in *he formeth it (yetha'arehu) with red chalk*** . . . *he formeth it with a compass* (Isaiah 44, 13). That is a term which cannot, God forbid, under any circumstances whatsoever be applied to the Almighty Lord.

*Literally: remoteness (from human conditions).
**Thus Kimchi, presumably following Saadiah. The exact meaning is unknown.

51

The word IMAGE, on the other hand, is applied to physical form, i.e. the essential feature of a thing by which it becomes what it is, which constitutes its true character in so far as it is that particular thing. In man this feature is the one from which springs human perception. It is because of this intellectual perception that the words *in the* IMAGE *of God He created him* (Genesis 1, 27) are used. [6] For the same reason Scripture writes: *thou wilt despise their* IMAGE (Psalm 73, 20), because 'contempt' attaches to the soul, i.e. the generic form, not to the shapes and outlines of the limbs. I suggest further that the idols are called IMAGES because what is intended by them is their supposed function, not their shape and outline. I maintain the same with regard to the IMAGES *of your hemorrhoids* (1 Samuel 6, 5), because what was intended by those was their function of dispelling the disease of hemorrhoids, not the shape of hemorrhoids. If however you do not accept my explanation of these two phrases, and take IMAGE in both in the sense of shape and outline, then IMAGE is a term of several meanings or one of amphibological signification, which can be applied to generic form as well as to the form of an artifice and shapes and outlines of natural bodies. In the phrase 'we shall make man in our IMAGE' the generic form is intended, that is intellectual perception, and not the shape and outline.

Thus we explain the difference between IMAGE and FORM and the meaning of IMAGE. As for *demuth* (LIKENESS) it is a noun derived from *damah* 'to be like', which again is applied to function or character. The phrase *I am* LIKE *a pelican of the wilderness* (Psalm 102, 6*) does not imply that he had wings and feathers like the pelican, but that he was sad like the pelican. Similarly, *nor any tree in the garden of God was* LIKE *unto him in his beauty* (Ezekiel 31, 8) refers solely to the feature of beauty. So too, *they have venom in the* LIKENESS *of the venom of a serpent* (Psalm 58, 5), and *his* LIKENESS (*dimyono*) *is as a lion greedy of his prey* (Psalm 17, 12), all imply resemblance in function, not in shape and outline. Similarly *the* LIKENESS *of the throne* (Ezekiel 1, 26) only implies resemblance with regard to

*In Hebrew vs. 7.

the function of being elevated and exalted, not that of being square or thick or having long legs, as some poor spirits think. The same applies to *the* LIKENESS *of the living creatures* (Ezekiel 1, 13).

Since man is distinguished by a very remarkable function, which does not exist in anything else beneath the sphere of the moon, namely intellectual perception, which is not exercised by any of the senses or outer limbs or inner organs, this is compared with divine perception, which needs no tool – though this is not a true comparison, but a superficial first impression. Because of this function, the divine intellect bestowed upon him, it is said of man that he is in the image and likeness of God, not because God is a body and therefore possesses a shape.

CHAPTER II

SOME years ago a certain man well versed in the sciences set me a strange problem. It is worth while here to study both the question and the answer I gave in solving it. Before I mention the problem and its solution I want to state the fact well-known to every Hebrew scholar, that the noun *Elohim* has the meanings of God, angels, and judges who govern states. Onkelos the proselyte – on whom be peace – has rightly seen that in the verse *and ye shall be as* GODS *knowing good and evil* (Genesis 3, 5), the last meaning is intended, since he says 'ye shall be like lords'. Having thus agreed that the term is homonymous, let us begin with relating the problem.

My enquirer said that from the simple meaning of Scripture it appeared that at first it had been intended for man to be like the other animals without intellect and thought and without any ability to distinguish between good and evil. When he had rebelled, that very fact of his rebellion brought him that immense perfection which makes man so unique, that he should possess this discernment which we have. It is the noblest function found within us and it constitutes our human character. This, my correspondent said, was the astonishing thing,

that his punishment for rebellion should be to give him a perfection which he did not possess before, namely the intellect.
What else is this than the story we are told of a man who was
rebellious and exceedingly wicked, and in the end was transformed into a star and placed into the sky?

This was the general sense of the question, though not the
exact words. Listen now to the arguments of my reply. I said:
You go in for philosophy with your half-baked ideas and
brainwaves, and you think you can understand a book, which
has guided ancients and moderns, in passing, in a few moments
snatched from drinking and lovemaking, just as you would
glance at a book of histories or of poetry? Stay and think, for
the matter is not as it appears to you at first blush, but as will
emerge when we give our full consideration to the passage. The
intellect which God bestowed on man as his ultimate perfection was the one which was given to Adam *before* his dis-
obedience. It is that one which is meant by saying that Adam
was made *in the image and likeness of God.* Owing to it he could
be addressed (by God) and receive commands, as is said *and the
Lord God commanded the man* (Genesis 2, 16). Such instructions
cannot be given to animals or beings not gifted with intellect.
By his intellect man distinguishes between truth and falsehood.
This faculty existed in him to its full extent. The distinction
between good and bad, however, is a matter of general agreement, not of intellectual activity. One does not say 'it is good
that the sky is spherical' or 'it is bad that the earth is flat', but
one applies to such statements the terms true and false. In our
tongue one expresses true and false by *emeth* (TRUTH) and
sheqer (FALSEHOOD), while good and bad are expressed by
tobh (GOOD) and *ra'* (EVIL). By his intellect man knows
TRUTH from FALSEHOOD, a distinction which applies in all
intellectual activities. With regard to this, man had reached the
highest stage of development with nothing but his natural
sense and his innate intellectual concepts, so that because of
these it was said of him: *Thou hast made him lack but little of being
God* (Psalm 8, 6). At the same time he possessed no faculty for
dealing with the generally agreed in any manner, and had no

no need for intellect

sense for it. Not even the most obviously bad thing from the point of view of the generally agreed, that is the uncovering of one's private parts, was bad in his eyes, nor would he have grasped that it was bad. [7]

When, however, he became disobedient and turned towards the lusts of his imagination and the pleasures of his physical senses, as is indicated by the verse *that the tree was good for food and was a lust for the eyes* (Genesis 3, 6) – then only he was punished by being deprived of intellectual perception. This was the reason why he disobeyed the command of God which had been given to him by virtue of his intellect. He thus acquired the sense for the generally agreed, and became absorbed in judging things as to their being good and bad. [8] Now he realized what he had lost, and into what state he had fallen. For this reason Scripture says: 'Ye shall be as *Elohim* knowing GOOD and EVIL', not 'knowing TRUTH and FALSEHOOD', or rather 'perceiving TRUTH and FALSEHOOD', GOOD and EVIL are not logically necessary at all, but TRUTH and FALSEHOOD are. Just consider the passage: *And the eyes of them both were opened and they* knew *that they were naked.* It does not say the eyes of them both were opened and they *saw* that they were naked, because what he *saw* then was the same that he had seen before. There was no covering on his eyes that was removed, but his state of mind changed so that he considered bad what he had not considered bad before.

It may be remarked that the word *paqah* 'to open' always refers to the bestowal of mental awareness, never to a bodily act of seeing, as in the verses: *God opened her eyes* (Genesis 21, 19), *then shall the eyes of the blind be opened* (Isaiah 35, 5), *opening the ears, he heareth not* (Isaiah 42, 20), in which last passage the sense is as in *that have eyes to see, and see not* (Ezekiel 12, 2).

CHAPTER XXXI

THERE are some objects which the human intellect is by its nature enabled to perceive. Other things and relations exist, though the nature of our intellect precludes us from perceiving them in any way or by any means whatsoever,* as if the gates of perception were locked between it and them. Again there exist some things of which it perceives one aspect and remains unaware of others. The faculty of perception does not imply that it perceives everything, just as the senses have perception but do not perceive beyond a certain distance. The same limitations apply to other bodily powers. If a man can lift two hundredweight, he is still not able to lift ten. Everyone knows that there are differences with regard to powers of perception and other physical faculties between individuals of the same species, but there is also a limit to these which cannot be extended indefinitely. The same is true with regard to intellectual perception in man. Different individuals vary greatly in this respect, as is well known to those who occupy themselves with the sciences. This goes so far that one person may understand a matter by turning it over in his mind while another one never understands it; even if it is explained to him in every possible manner and with every possible illustration for any length of time, his mind does not grasp it at all, but is too dull to understand it. Even these differences are not limitless: there can be no doubt that the human intellect has a limit at which it stops. Of the things that lie beyond it man realizes that they cannot be perceived. He feels no desire within him to know these, because he is fully aware that this is not possible and that there are no means to achieve it. Thus we do not know the number of the stars in the sky or whether this number is odd or even; we are ignorant of how many kinds of animals, minerals, and plants there are, and the like. Beyond these things there are others which man greatly longs to apprehend. We find that eager striving of the mind to seek out the truth about them and to investigate them in every thinking group of people and in every period. Concerning those matters there are many different views, thinkers debate fiercely and misunderstandings constantly arise, all because our mind is so firmly attached to the search for the perception of these things – or rather the longing for them – and everyone believes that he has discovered a

*i.e., according to the commentaries: directly or indirectly.

method to know the truth regarding them. Yet the human intellect is powerless to produce any evidence about them, for there can be no difference of opinion about a thing whose nature is known by evidence. Any contention and opposition in such a matter comes from a fool who practises what is called 'contradiction of evidence'. One finds indeed people who contradict statements such as that the earth is a sphere or that the firmament revolves,* and the like, but they have nothing to do with our investigation.

Such matters to which this kind of confusion applies are very common in metaphysics, few in natural science, and do not exist in the mathematical sciences. According to Alexander of Aphrodisias the causes of differences of opinion are three. One is the lust for authority and power that turns man from perceiving the truth as it is; the second is the subtlety and profundity of the subject to be apprehended and the difficulty in apprehending it; the third is the ignorance of the apprehender and his inability to apprehend things that are given to perception. So far Alexander. In our own times there is a fourth cause which he fails to mention because it did not exist with his contemporaries, namely, habit and education. [9] Men have an ingrained love for the things to which they are accustomed and are so fond of them that the bedouins for instance, in spite of their disordered life with its lack of pleasures and shortage of food, dislike the cities and take no delight in their pleasures. They prefer the evil circumstances to which they are accustomed to the pleasant circumstances to which they are not used. They derive no enjoyment from living in palaces, wearing silk, or the luxuries of baths, ointments and perfumes. The same happens to a man with regard to the opinions to which he is accustomed and in which he has been brought up: he is fond of them and defends them zealously and abhors other opinions. For this reason, too, man is blind to the truth and prefers the views with which he is familiar. Thus the mass of men clings to anthropomorphism and many other errors in metaphysics, as we shall explain later, because of habit and because of having

*Or: is circular.

been brought up upon texts traditionally held in esteem and belief. True, the apparent sense of these texts leads to anthropomorphism and unsound fancies; but they are meant to be read as similes and riddles, for reasons I shall mention later on.

Do not imagine that our statement about the imperfection of human intellect and its restriction to certain limits is merely an assertion derived from Scripture (Exodus 33, 20, 23): it is a point which the philosophers have made, having fully realized its truth without reference to any established school or opinion. It is a fact to be doubted only by one ignorant of the available evidence.

FROM CHAPTER XXXII

On the other hand it was not the intention of those sayings of the Prophets and Sages to lock the gate of speculation altogether and to restrain the intelligence from apprehending what can be apprehended, as is claimed by some foolish weaklings who would like to turn their inability and silliness into virtue and wisdom, and the perfection and learning of others into a disability and transgression of the Law, *that put darkness for light and light for darkness* (Isaiah 5, 20). The intention of those sayings is to tell you that human intelligence has a limit at which it stops. There is no need to pick at the words used in this or other chapters with reference to intelligence, since their purpose is to guide towards the conclusion intended in those chapters, not the investigation of the nature of intelligence. That will be dealt with at length in other chapters.

CHAPTER XXXIV

For five reasons one should not begin instruction with metaphysics, nor even direct attention to any matters requiring attention, leave alone divulge such matters to the vulgar crowd.*

The first reason is the inherent difficulty of the subject, its

*Thus Duran and Shemtob.

subtlety and profundity. This is indicated by Scripture, where it is said: *That which is far off and exceeding deep, who can find it out?* (Ecclesiastes 7, 24), and *Whence then cometh wisdom?* (Job 28, 20). It is hardly correct to start instruction with the most difficult, profound, and unintelligible subject. One of the best known similes in our religion is the comparison of wisdom with water, in which our Sages have discovered so many meanings. One of them is that he who can swim brings up pearls from the bottom of the sea, while he who cannot swim drowns; for this reason only the well-trained swimmer should attempt to swim.

(2) The second reason is that all beginners' minds are lacking in capability. Man is not granted his full perfection right from the start, but that perfection exists only potentially, so that at first he is in actuality devoid of it: *Man is born like a wild ass's colt* (Job 11, 12). Nor if a man possess some potential gifts, these will necessarily become realised. He may stop short of his full development either because of some causes which prevent him from reaching it, or because of lack of such training as would bring out the potential abilities. This is clearly put in the verse: *not many become wise** (Job 32, 9); our Sages say 'I see that men of virtue are few' (Succah 45b), because the causes which prevent one from reaching perfection are many indeed and distractions abound. When can one, therefore, achieve full preparation and sufficient leisure for training so as to bring out one's potentialities?

(3) The third reason is the need for a long period of preparatory studies. Men by nature long to get on to the ultimate truths, and will often be impatient with elementary studies or fight shy of them. If it were possible to reach the ultimate truths without the elementary studies usually prefixed to them, these would not be preparatory studies but superfluous diversions. If you would suddenly stir up even the dullest of men as though you were waking one slumbering, and ask him: Don't

---

*A.V.: 'Great men are not always wise'. The rendering demanded by the context here has so far been traced only in the *Yalqut* (13th century) and *Metzudath David* (17th century), but must be old.

you long to know right now what is the number of the heavens and their shape and what they contain, what the angels are, how the world was created and what is its purpose with regard to the inter-relation of its constituent parts, what is the soul, how it came into the body, whether the soul of man leaves the body, and if so, how, and by what means, and for what destination, and similar problems – he will reply: 'Certainly', and will naturally long to know the true answer to all these things. He will, however, expect this longing to be assuaged and all this knowledge imparted to him by a word or two from you. Were you to suggest to him that he should neglect his business for a week, so as to understand all these things, he would not do it, but would remain satisfied with the preposterous ideas with which he is familiar. He would certainly be shocked if you told him that there is something which needs many preparatory studies and long investigation. You realize, of course, that these subjects are closely interwoven, since nothing exists but God Almighty and all His works, and His works are the only things in existence apart from Him, and there is no way to apprehend Him except through His works. It is they that indicate His existence and the nature of the beliefs we ought to hold concerning Him, i.e. what we should assert or deny of Him. We must, therefore, examine the nature of all existing things so that we can from every science derive true and reliable data to assist us in our metaphysical speculations. How many data derived from the properties of numbers and geometrical figures do we not employ to indicate to us certain things which we have to deny of Him, which denial then brings us so many other insights? I suppose you will easily perceive the importance of astronomy and natural science for recognizing in what relation the world stands to Divine government, if you want to know the truth, not old wives' tales. There are other theoretical sciences which, though no data for metaphysics may be derived from them, yet serve to train the mind and to strengthen its powers of deduction and of ascertaining the true nature of things that are essential to argument, and remove the confusion which reigns in the minds of most thinkers owing to confusion of essential and accidental points and the consequent errors. To all this must be added the benefit these sciences confer, by teaching us to define correctly the concepts connected with metaphysics.* In fine, though these disciplines are not indispensable for the study of metaphysics, yet they definitely are useful in matters connected with that science.

One who strives for human perfection must therefore train himself first in logic, then in the mathematical disciplines in their proper order, then in the natural sciences, and finally in metaphysics.[10] Many, of course, stop at one of these stages. Even if their minds are fit, they are cut off by death while still in the propaedeutic stage. Now just suppose we would not accept under any circumstances any opinion based on tradition, nor submit to any guidance given by means of allegories, but would insist on complete description by essential definitions and on demonstrative proof for whatever we are to believe – a thing which could be done only after the long preparation described. Surely the result would be that all men would die before they knew whether there was any God in the world or not, leave alone that omnipotence must be attributed to Him or any defects denied of Him. No one would escape that ignominious death except *one of a city or two of a family* (Jeremiah 3, 14).[11]

(4) The fourth reason lies in the diversity of natural disposition. It is clear, and proved by evidence, that moral virtues are a prerequisite of intellectual virtues. The attainment of true intellectual values, that is perfect intellectual ideas, is impossible except for a man whose moral character is properly trained and who possesses dignity and balance. There are many people whose native character and temper is wholly unsuitable for the attainment of perfection. A person whose heart is hot by nature and who is strong, will always be excitable, however much he trains himself. One whose testicles have a hot and humid temperament and are strongly built, and whose spermglands produce much sperm, will find it difficult to be chaste even with the hardest training. Others are lightheaded and rash,

*Thus Duran. Or: quite apart from seeing those subjects as they really are.

with irregular, sudden movements. This indicates some fault of constitution and unsoundness of temper difficult to define. Such people never can achieve perfection. To labour with them in this discipline is utter foolishness on the part of him who tries to instruct them; for this science – as you well know – is not like medicine or geometry, and not everyone is fit for it for the reasons we have just mentioned.

Moral preparation is necessary for a man to be thoroughly upright and perfect, *for the froward is an abomination to the Lord: but his secret is with the righteous* (Proverbs 3, 32). For this reason alone one should not teach this subject to the young. In any case they would not be able to acquire it because of their seething nature and the preoccupation of their minds with the burning flame of adolescence. Only when that perturbing flame dies down and they achieve some dignity and balance and their hearts are at rest and their temper gentle, they are able to arouse their souls to that degree of apprehending God, i.e. metaphysics or the 'Description of the Chariot'. As Scripture says, *the Lord is nigh unto them that are of a broken heart* (Psalm 34, 19) and *I dwell in the high and holy place, also with him that is of a contrite and humble spirit*, etc. (Isaiah 57, 15).

⑤ The fifth reason is the occupation with the needs of the body, which are the first stage of perfection, especially if the care of wife and children is added to it, and more so if to this is joined the search after the luxuries of life, a feature which tends to increase in importance according to one's manner of life and the corrupt customs of one's milieu. A man may be well-nigh perfect in all the respects we have described, but when his energy is taken up with his essential requirements – not to speak of the unnecessary – and his interest in them increases, interest in theoretical studies diminishes correspondingly and becomes flooded out. His study will be carried on distractedly and vaguely, without any real attention to the subject, and he will not apprehend what he is able to apprehend or he will apprehend it in a confused and vague manner, half understanding it and half failing to understand.

For all these reasons these studies are fit only for very select individuals, not for the vulgar crowd. That is why they should be kept out of reach of the beginner and he be prevented from any acquaintance with them, just as a child is prevented from eating heavy foods and lifting big weights.

CHAPTER XXXV

THOUGH in these last chapters we have stressed the fact that metaphysics is a dangerous and subtle subject, which few can understand and which must not be divulged to the mass of the people, it must on no account be imagined that these strictures apply to our denial of anthropomorphism and divine affections. On the contrary, just as children and the masses must be taught that God is One and none but He must be worshipped, so they must be authoritatively instructed that God is not a body, that there is no resemblance between Him and His creatures in any way whatsoever, that His existence does not resemble theirs and His life is not of the same kind as theirs, that His knowledge has no similarity with knowledge possessed by any creature, and that the difference between Him and them is not one of degree but one of kind. All must clearly realize that our knowledge and His knowledge, or our power and His power, are not different merely in quantity or intensity, since the stronger and the weaker are necessarily within the same species and the same definition embraces both, and likewise any proportion can only be between two things within one species, as has been proved in the natural sciences. Everything that is attributed to God Almighty, however, is so completely different from any of our own attributes that no common definition can ever be found for the two. In the same way one applies to His existence and the existence of other things the term 'existence' by way of homonymy, as I shall explain later. So much is enough for children and common people to fix in their minds the notion that there is a Perfect Being which is neither a body nor a force within a body, that He is God, that no manner of imperfection attaches to Him, and that therefore He is not subject to affections.[12]

The discussion of His attributes, however, how their inadmissibility is established, and the meaning of the attributes ascribed to Him; likewise the discussion of His creation, of whatever He created, of His manner of directing the universe and His providence for what exists apart from Him, of the meaning of the terms 'His Will', 'His Perception', and 'His Knowledge' with regard to all He knows; the meaning of prophecy, its degrees, the meaning of its several names that all refer to the same thing – all these are profound matters, the true 'secrets of the Law'. They are the Mysteries constantly referred to in Scripture and in the writings of our Sages. These are the matters that must not be taught except in outline, as we have indicated, and only to the type of person described above. The rejection of anthropomorphism, however, and the denial of resemblance and affections, these are matters that must be publicly declared and explained to everyone according to his power of comprehension, and authoritatively taught to children, women, illiterates, and halfwits, just as they must be taught parrotwise that He is One and eternal and no one must be worshipped beside Him. Acknowledgement of the unity of God is not possible without denying that He has a body, because a body is not One, but composed of matter and form – that is two in one – and is divisible and consists of parts. [13]

If they have been educated in this manner and then grow up and find difficulty in the expressions used by Scripture, their meaning must be made clear to them. One must encourage them to understand these passages as allegories and draw their attention to the existence of words with several meanings and metaphorical uses, as explained in this treatise, so that their belief in the Unity of God and the truth of the Holy Writ is not impaired in any way. If there is one whose intelligence is not sufficient to understand the allegorical interpretation of a passage, or to grasp that the same words may have different meanings, then tell him: 'The learned know how to interpret this verse aright, but you just get it into your head that God Almighty is not a body and has no affections because affections mean change, and God is not affected by any change; nor does

He resemble any thing that is apart from Him nor does any definition embrace Him and anything else at the same time in any way. This utterance of the Bible is truth and there is a correct interpretation for it.' At this one should stop; but on no account must anyone be allowed to hold a belief in anthropomorphism or to believe that any of the things that affect bodies affect God, as little as he would be allowed to believe that there was no God or that there were several Gods or that worship was due to any other being.

CHAPTER L

" faith" - facts -not theological virtue

THE reader of this work must be quite clear in his mind that belief does not mean any formula of faith one utters but the notions one has in one's mind, and the conviction that reality corresponds to those particular notions.* If you accept true or presumedly true opinions you can utter them without forming a notion* of their import and really believing in them, leave alone seeking certainty about them. That is easy enough. Many illiterates learn by heart formulas of faith without attaching any notion to them at all.[14]

If, however, you are one of those high-minded people who strive to reach a higher stage, that of speculation, and to believe with absolute certainty that God is truly One, His Unity being true Unity without any trace of compositeness or divisibility in any manner whatsoever, you must know that God has no essential attribute whatever in any form or any manner. As we cannot admit that He is a body so we cannot admit that He has any essential attribute.

If one believes Him to be One and to possess a number of attributes, one in fact *says* that he is One and *thinks* that He is many. This is the same as what the Christians say: He is one, but He is three, and the three are One. There is no difference between this and saying: He is One but has many attributes, and He and His attributes are One, though such a person may

*Literally: having a picture in their mind. The term refers to an intuitive intellectual perception or rational activity of the imagination.

believe in incorporeality and in immateriality* to the fullest extent.[15] This kind of belief reduces all our effort and search to an attempt to discover what we should say, not what we should believe. For belief presupposes a notion in one's mind, belief being the conviction that the situation in the external world corresponds to the notion one holds in one's mind. If furthermore such a belief, once arrived at, cannot be doubted in one's mind in any way whatsoever, and the mind cannot discover any method of rejecting such belief, or even envisage the possibility of doubting it, then the belief becomes a certainty.

If you succeed in freeing yourself from emotions and habits, and are intelligent, and consider carefully what I say in the following chapters with regard to the denial of attributes, you cannot help it becoming a certainty with you. Then you will be one who forms a notion of the 'Unity of God', not merely one who pronounces the words with his lips without a notion of their meaning. The latter person belongs to those of whom it is said: *Thou art near in their mouth and far from their conscience* (Jeremiah 12, 2). No, a man should belong to those who have a notion of, and apprehend the truth, even when they do not utter it, as is recommended to the pious: *Commune with your own heart upon your bed and be still perpetually* (Psalm 4, 5).

CHAPTER LI

MANY things obviously and manifestly exist. Some of these are primary intellectual concepts and sensory impressions, others, things close to these in character. Even if left to his own devices, a man would not need anyone to point these out to him. Such are the existence of movement and man's freedom to act, the phenomena of generation and corruption, and the nature of things apparent to the senses, such as the heat of fire and coolness of water, and many suchlike things.

Since some strange views have been put forward, by error or with some ulterior motive, views which contradict the nature of existing things by denying what is perceived by the senses or implying the existence of the non-existent, philo-

*Literally: simplicity.

sophers have been compelled to assert the truth of the manifest or to deny the existence of things wrongly imagined. Thus we find Aristotle asserting the existence of movement because it had been denied, or producing evidence against the existence of atoms because it had been asserted.[16]

Our denial of essential attributes in God belongs to this type of argument. It is really a primary intellectual concept, namely, that the attribute is something different from the essence of that to which it is attributed; that it is a state of the essence and therefore an accident. If the attribute is itself the essence of the thing to which it is attributed, then the attribute is either a mere verbal repetition, as would be saying 'man is man', or an explanation of a term, as saying 'man is a reasoning animal'. For 'reasoning animal' is the essence and nature of 'man'. The proposition does not contain a third term except 'animal' and 'reasoning', i.e. 'man', who is completely described only by the combination of the two terms.* The function of this description** is to explain the term, no more, as if one said 'the thing which is called man is the thing which is compounded of life and reason'.

It is thus evident that an attribute must be one of two things. Either it is the essence of the thing to which it is attributed, and thus an explanation of a term. This kind of attribute we reject with reference to God, not for this reason but for another one, which we shall explain later on. Or the attribute is different from the thing to which it is attributed, and thus an idea added to that thing. Consequently that attribute is an accident of that essence. By protesting that the attributes of God are not accidents, we cannot alter the fact that they are. Every new idea added to the essence is accessory to it, not completing its inherent character; that is exactly what 'accident' means.

Furthermore, if the attributes are many, then many things must have existed eternally. Belief in Unity cannot mean essentially anything but the belief in one single homogeneous

*Or: no third term is available for the definition of man, except 'animal' and 'reasoning'.

**Arabic has the same word for 'attribute' and 'description'.

uncompounded essence; not in a plurality of ideas but in a single idea. Whichever way you look at it, and however you examine it, you must find it to be one, not dividing itself in any manner or for any reason into two ideas. No plurality must be discoverable in it either in fact or in thought, as will be proved in the course of this treatise.[17]

CHAPTER LII

WHENEVER anything has an attribute affirmed of it, and we say of it: it is so-and-so, that attribute must fall under one of five headings:

Firstly, the thing may be described by its definition; thus man can be described as a reasoning animal. An attribute of this type indicates what the thing is (its quiddity). We have proved that this is nothing but an explanation of the name. This type of attribute is generally agreed to be inadmissible in the case of God, since there are no pre-existing causes that could be causes of His existence so that He might be defined by means of them. For this reason all thinkers who use their terms precisely are entirely agreed that God cannot be defined.

Secondly, something may be described by a part of its definition. Thus man may be described as 'animal' or as 'reasoning'. The point about such attributes is their inherent mutual connection with the things to which they are attributed. If we say 'every man has reason' that can mean nothing else but that every being that proves to be human will also prove to be gifted with reason. This type of attribute is universally regarded as inadmissible with regard to God, for if there were such a thing as a part of His quiddity, His quiddity would be compound. This is just as absurd with reference to God as the assertion disposed of in the last paragraph.[18]

Thirdly, something may be described by means of a thing outside its nature and essence, something not required for the complete establishment of its essence. That thing would therefore be a quality adherent to it. Quality, i.e. the category, is an accident. If an attribute of this type were to be ascribed to God,

He would be subject to accidents. Merely to mention this is enough to show how far removed from His nature and essence it is to consider him as possessing qualities.

Well may one wonder that those who ascribe attributes to God find it possible to deny that He can be compared or has qualities. They say 'God cannot be qualified'. What can that mean except that He has no qualities? Yet whenever one asserts the essential attachment of any attribute to an essence, it must either constitute that essence, and thus be the essence itself, or, be a quality of that essence.

These three classes of attributes, viz. those describing what the thing is, those describing part of what it is, and those describing a quality of what it is, have thus been demonstrated to be inadmissible with reference to God, because they all imply compositeness. This, as we shall prove later, cannot be admitted with reference to God.

The fourth class of attributes is that which describes a thing in its relation to something else, such as a time, place or other individual. Thus you may describe Zayd as the father of someone, or as the partner of someone, or as living in a certain place, or as one who lived at a certain point in time. This type of attribute does not imply plurality or change in the substance of the thing described, because it is all the same Zayd who is the father of Bakr, the partner of Umar, the employer of Khalid, or who lives in a certain house, or was born in a certain year. These relations are not his substance or have anything to do with his substance, as would have been the case with qualities.

At first glance it seems as if this type of attribute could be applied to God. On closer consideration, however, they prove to be inadmissible. It is obvious that God cannot stand in any relation to time and place. Time is an accident pursuant to motion, namely when the latter is considered from the point of view of sequence and thus becomes measurable, as is explained in works devoted to this subject. Motion is a thing that attaches to bodies. God is not a body, and therefore there can be no relation between Him and time.[19] Similarly no relation is possible between Him and space. The question to be discussed is whether there is any relation, in the proper sense, between Him and any thing created by Him, so that this might be applied as an attribute.

It is obvious at the first glance that there is no correlation between Him and any of His creatures, since an essential feature of correlation is the mutuality through equality of the two related terms. God, however, _must_ exist, and everything else _may_ exist, as we shall explain later, and therefore correlation is unthinkable. One might think that some other type of relation is possible between the two, but this is not so.[20] One cannot imagine any relation between intellect and a colour, though both have the same kind of existence according to our system. How then can we imagine a relation between a thing and Him who shares no common trait with anything outside Him at all, for the term 'existence' is only applied to Him as well as to creatures by way of homonymy and in no other way. There is, therefore, no possible true relation between Him and anything He has created, because relation can at any time be only between two things of the same immediate species, but if they are merely of the same class no relation can exist between them. We cannot say 'this red colour is stronger, or weaker, than, or equal to, that green colour', though both of them belong to the same class, that of colours. If the two terms belong to different classes, no relation at all is possible between them, even according to the primitive standards of popular thinking. It makes no difference if the two classes are under the same category. For instance, there is no thinkable relation between a hundred cubits and the pungency of pepper; the first is a quantity and the second is a quality. There is also no thinkable relation between knowledge and sweetness, or kindness and bitter taste, though all these are in the category of quality. How then could there be any relation between God and any creature, when there is that immense difference in the nature of existence, greater than which no difference can ever be.

If any relation could be imagined, then it would follow that the accident of relation could attach to God. Though it is not an accident attaching to His essence, it is still an accident of sorts. In that case we should be forced to admit that God has attributes, though we should narrow these down to relations. Still, these are the kind of attributes that could most easily be granted in reference to God, since they would not imply a plurality of pre-existent things nor any change in His substance consequent on change of the things with which He would stand in relation.

The fifth class of positive attributes is to describe a thing by its action. By 'its action' I do not mean the capacity of habitual professional activity, as in the terms 'carpenter' or 'blacksmith'; these are of the category of quality, as we have mentioned before. By 'action' I mean the action that the thing has carried out, as when one says: Zayd is the one who has made this door, or built a certain wall, or woven this garment. This kind of attribute is far from contact with the essence of the thing to which it relates. It is therefore quite permissible to apply this type of attribute to God, especially as we know (as will be explained later on) that these different actions do not emanate from different elements within the essence of the agent, but all the different actions of God are from His essence, not from anything added to it, as we have explained before.

To resume the argument of this chapter: God is One in every respect without plurality and without additions to His essence. The many different attributes found in the books as indicating Him are due to the manifold character of His actions, not to a plurality in His essence. Some of them have the purpose of indicating His perfection, according to what we consider perfection, as we have explained before.

CHAPTER LIV

THAT first and greatest of all thinkers, our teacher Moses, of blessed memory, made two requests and both his requests were granted. His first request was when he asked God to let him know His essence and nature; the second, which was the first in point of time, was when he asked Him to let him know

His attributes. God's reply to the two requests was to promise that He would let him know all His attributes, telling him at the same time that they were His actions. Thereby He told him that His essence could not be apprehended in itself, but also pointed out to him a starting point from which he could set out to apprehend as much of Him as man can apprehend. And indeed, Moses apprehended more than anyone ever did before him or after him.

His request to know the attributes of the Lord is contained in the passage: *Shew me now thy ways and I shall know thee, to the end that I may find grace in they sight* (Exodus 33, 13). Consider carefully the wonderful expressions contained in this passage. The phrasing 'Shew me now thy ways and I shall know thee' indicates that God is known by His attributes: if one knows the WAYS one knows Him. The clause 'that I may find grace in thy sight' indicates that he who knows God is he that finds grace in His sight, not he who merely fasts and prays. Everyone who knows Him is well beloved and drawn near; but he who does not know Him is in disfavour and rejected. The degree of favour or disfavour, drawing near or rejecting, is in proportion to the degree of knowledge.

But we are straying from the subject of this chapter; let us return to it. After having requested to know the attributes of God, he asked for forgiveness for the people, and was granted forgiveness for them. Then he requested to apprehend God's essence, in the words: *shew me now thy glory* (ibid. 18). Then only he was granted his first request, namely, 'shew me now thy ways', it being said to him: *I will make all my goodness pass before thee* (ibid. 19). The answer to the second request, however, was: *Thou canst not see my face: for there shall no man see me and live* (ibid. 20).

The expression 'all my goodness' is meant to indicate that all existing things would be shown to him, concerning which it was said: *And God saw every thing that He had made, and behold, it was very good* (Genesis 1, 31). By their being shown to him I mean that he was allowed to apprehend their nature and their connection, and thus would know how God governs them, both in general and in particular. This meaning is indicated by the verse: *in all my house he is well-established** (Numbers 12, 7). This means that he understood all that exists in my world with true and well-founded comprehension, since wrong opinions are not well-founded. When God shows you these actions, then they are** His attributes. That the thing which Moses was promised to be given to apprehend was His actions is proved by the fact that he was afterwards given to know purely actional attributes: *merciful and gracious, longsuffering and abundant in goodness and truth*, etc. (Exodus 34, 6–7). Thus it is proven that the WAYS which he requested to know and which he was given to know, were the actions emanating from God. The Sages call these *middoth*, 'dispositions',*** and speak of 'thirteen dispositions of God' (Rosh Hashanah f. 17b). The same word is used by them also to denote moral qualities, as in the 'four dispositions in almsgivers, four dispositions in those who go to the house of study' (Aboth 5, 16–17), and other cases. What is meant here is not that God possesses moral qualities but that He produces actions similar to the ones emanating from ourselves by virtue of such moral qualities, or rather states of the soul. Of course there is no suggestion that God is subject to such states of the soul. [21]

Scripture does not mention more than those thirteen qualities, in spite of the fact that Moses had apprehended 'all His goodness', that is all God's actions. The reason is that these actions of God refer to the creation and government of mankind. This is what Moses ultimately intended by his request, as is shown by the end of the verse: . . . *and I shall know thee, that I may find grace in thy sight: and consider that this nation is thy people*, for the leadership of whom I require actions upon the pattern of Thy actions in leading them.

It is thus clear that WAYS and DISPOSITIONS are one and

*A play on the two meanings of *ne'eman*, 'established' and 'trusted'; the latter meaning appears in all versions and commentaries.

**Reading *idhâ adrâka*. Emend perhaps: wrong opinions are not properly founded in perception. Thus Moses, as we see, perceived those actions, which were . . . (cf. Harizi).

***Literally: measures.

the same thing, namely, the actions emanating from God in the world. Whenever we apprehend one of God's actions, we apply to God the attribute from which this action proceeds, i.e. call Him by a name derived from that action. For instance, we apprehend the tenderness with which He provides for the formation of the embryos of animals and bestows both on the young creature and on those that will bring it up after its birth, powers designed to guard it from death or damage and to further its natural functions. Such action on our part would presuppose affection and tender feeling. That is what we mean by mercy, and we therefore use of God the term Merciful, just as it is said: *Like as a father is merciful to his children* (Psalm 103, 13) or *And I shall be merciful unto them as a man is merciful unto his son* (Malachi 3, 17). Of course God is not experiencing the feeling of affection or tenderness but such actions as a father will do for his child through pure love, compassion, and affection, do emanate from God with regard to His favourites, though they are not caused by affection or change. If we give a thing to someone to whom we are not obliged to give it, that action is called in our language grace or favour (*haninah*), as in *give them unto us as a favour* (Judges 21, 22); *with which God hath favoured me* (Genesis 33, 5); *because God has favoured me* (ibid. 11), and many similar cases. God brings into existence and provides for, those towards whom He has no obligation to do so; for this reason He is called Gracious.

Again we find among the actions emanating from God and affecting mankind some terrible misfortunes which befall individuals so as to destroy them, or disasters affecting whole tribes, nay whole regions, and wiping out children and children's children and sparing neither the land nor its produce, * such as land being swallowed up by the sea, earthquakes, and deadly thunderbolts, or the attack of one people against another in order to destroy them with the sword and efface their last traces, and many other things like these. Such actions would not be committed by any of us towards his fellow men except

---

*An Arabic idiom which may mean here: neither women nor children (cf. ḥarth 'wife').

in violent rage or deep hatred or revenge. Because of such actions God is called Jealous, Taking Vengeance, Reserving Wrath, and Furious. This means that such actions as with us would spring from psychological states like jealousy, revenge, hatred, or anger, emanate from God because those that are punished thereby have deserved them, not in consequence of any affection – far be it from us to impute to Him such lack of perfection. In the same manner all Divine acts are actions that resemble human actions springing from certain affections and psychological states, but with God they do not spring from anything that is in any way superadded to His essence.

A ruler – if he is a prophet – must model his conduct on these attributes. Acts of this kind should with him spring from mature reflection and be commensurate with the crime, rather than from mere affection. He should never give rein to his anger or allow his affections to get the better of him, for all affection is evil, but he must keep aloof from them as far as that is possible for man. If he does so, he will on some occasions be 'gracious and merciful' to some men, not out of tenderness and sympathy, but because such a course is indicated. To others he will be 'jealous, revengeful, and angry' because they deserve it, not out of mere annoyance. This will go as far that he may give orders to burn a man alive without being annoyed or angry or ill-disposed towards him, only because he considers that he has deserved such treatment and realizes the great benefit that is likely to accrue from such an action to many others.

This is illustrated by the Biblical passage commanding the extermination of the seven nations. It is said there: *thou shalt save alive nothing that breatheth* (Deuteronomy 20, 16), and immediately afterwards: *that they teach you not to do after all their abominations, which they have done unto their gods; so should ye sin against the Lord your God* (ibid. 18). That is to say, do not imagine that this is cruelty or revenge, but it is an act commended by human reason, viz. the removal of all those that cause others to stray from the path of Truth, and generally of impediments in the way to perfection, which is the perception of God. Nevertheless it is right that acts of mercy, forgiveness, kindness, and compassion should be done by a ruler much more frequently than acts of retaliation; for the thirteen dispositions are all of them dispositions of mercy, save one: *visiting the iniquity of the fathers upon the children* (Exodus 34, 7). (The words usually translated 'that will by no means clear (*naqqeh lo yenaqqeh*) the guilty' mean really 'that will not bring about utter desolation', as is proved by the verse: *and she being desolate (niqqathah) shall sit upon the ground* (Isaiah 3, 26).) It must, however, be clearly understood that the phrase 'visiting the iniquity of the fathers upon the children' refers only and alone to idolatry, not to any other transgression. The evidence is in the ten commandments, where it is said: *visiting the iniquity of the fathers upon the children unto the third and fourth generation of them that hate me* (Exodus 20, 5). No one can be called 'one who hates God' except he who commits idolatry, as is said: *every abomination to the Lord, which he hateth, have they done unto their gods* (Deuteronomy 12, 31). Only the fourth generation is mentioned, because the fourth generation is the utmost any man can see of his own progeny. When the population of an idolatrous country is killed off, the ancestor who committed idolatry is killed, and the children of his children's children, i.e. the fourth generation. The passage thus indicates that one of the commands of God – and thus no doubt one of His acts – is that the progeny of idolaters should be killed, though immature, in a body with* their fathers and grandfathers. This same commandment we find continually everywhere in the Torah, as in the case of the Beguiled City, where it is said: *destroying it utterly and all that is therein* (Deuteronomy 13, 16). All this, as we have explained, is for the purpose of wiping out the very traces of them that might lead others to grave corruption.

We have strayed somewhat from the subject of this chapter, but it has become clear to us why of all His actions only these are enumerated, namely, that they are needed in the government of countries. The highest virtue to which man can aspire is to become similar to God as far as this is possible, that means

---

*Reading (with Tibbon) *ghumár*.

that we must imitate His actions by our own,[22] as has been indicated by our Rabbis in their comment on the words: *Ye shall be holy* (Leviticus 19, 2): 'As He is gracious, so be thou gracious; as He is merciful, so be thou merciful' (*Siphre* on Deuteronomy 10, 12). The outcome of our discussion is thus that the attributes which are applied to Him in Scripture are attributes of His acts, but He himself has no attributes.

CHAPTER LVII

MORE ADVANCED OBSERVATIONS ON THE SUBJECT OF ATTRIBUTES

IT is obvious that existence is an accident affecting that which exists. It is, therefore, a concept superadded to the essence of that which exists. This is an incontrovertible fact. Whenever the existence of a thing is due to a cause, its existence is a concept superadded to its essence. But whatever possesses an existence not due to any cause – and such is God alone, for this is what we mean when we say that God exists necessarily – the existence of such a thing is its essence and character and its essence is its existence. Such a thing is not subject to the accident of existing, so that its existence should be a concept superadded to its essence. He exists necessarily and perpetually, not because existence came to Him from without or affected Him as an accident. He therefore exists without existence, and similarly lives without life, is powerful without power, and knows without knowledge. All these derive from a single concept without any multiplicity, as we shall explain later on.[23]

It must also be clearly realized that unity and multiplicity are accidents affecting the thing which exists insofar as it is many or one. This is proved in the *Metaphysics* (v, 6; x, 2). As number is not the thing counted, so unity is not the thing which is one. All these are accidents of the class of discrete quantity which affect the numerable things in existence, because they are subject to such accidents. As for that which exists necessarily and is truly simple without being in any way liable to compositeness, as it is absurd to think of it as affected by the accident of plurality, so it is absurd to think of it as affected by the accident of unity. I mean to say by this that His unity is not a concept superadded to His essence, but He is one without unity.

These subtle concepts, which almost pass the comprehension of our minds, are not readily expressed by words. Words are altogether one of the main causes of error, because whatever language we employ, we find the restrictions it imposes on our expression extremely disturbing. We cannot even picture this concept except by using imprecise language. When we desire to indicate that the Divinity is not plural, all we are able to say is that He is one, although both, 'one' as well as 'many', are terms of quantity. We must therefore compress our meaning and guide the mind to the proper understanding of our intention by saying 'one, but not by unity'. It is just the same when we use the word 'ancient'* to indicate that He did not come into being. The lack of precision in our use of 'ancient' is obvious, since one can only apply the term to something affected by time, which is an accident supervening to movement, which implies a body. Furthermore it belongs to the class of relative terms. When you use 'ancient' of the accident of time, it is like saying 'long' and 'short' with regard to the accident of one-dimensional extension. One cannot really employ the terms 'ancient' and 'come into being' of anything to which the accident of time does not apply, any more than one can say of sweetness that it is either crooked or straight, or of a sound that it is salty or unseasoned. Such things are evident to one who has some practice in assessing the true meaning of ideas and expresses them with full rational comprehension, if he isolates them properly and does not employ the vague sense suggested by the words in common usage.**

Wherever you find the words 'first' and 'last' employed in Scripture in speaking of God (e.g. Isaiah 44, 6), this is to be taken in the same way as the passages where He is described as

---

*Used in philosophical Arabic for 'uncreated'.

**Other reading: taking them in their absolute sense, not with the connotation of comprehensiveness suggested by the words.

having eyes or ears. The meaning of those terms is that God is not affected by change and in no way ever acquires new properties, not that He falls under the category of time, so that some analogy might result between Him and things subject to time, and it can be said of Him that He is FIRST and LAST. All these terms are 'according to the parlance of men' (Berakhoth 31b). So, too, when we say ONE we mean thereby that He has no peer, not that His essence is affected by the concept of unity.

CHAPTER LVIII

MORE DIFFICULT THAN THE PRECEDING ONES

YOU must understand that the description of God by means of negative terms is the only sound description which contains no element of loose terminology, and implies altogether in no circumstances a lack of perfection in God. His description by positive terms, on the other hand, comports polytheism and a lack of perfection in God in the way we have demonstrated.

First I must explain how negative terms can in a manner be attributes, and in what way they differ from positive attributes. Then I shall show how it is that we have no way of describing Him except by negative terms and no others. An attribute is not something specifying the thing described in such a way that it cannot share the attribute with anything else. On the contrary, an attribute may describe something even if it shares that attribute with other things and is not peculiar to it. For instance, if you see a man from a distance and ask: what is that which is visible? the reply may be: some living being. This is without any doubt a correct description of the thing seen, though it does not set it aside as a peculiar thing from all others. Some specification does, however, result, namely, that the thing seen is not an object of the vegetable or mineral class. In the same manner also, if there is a man in a certain house, and you know that there is some object in it, but not what it is, you may ask: what is in this house? and may receive the reply:

there isn't a vegetable or mineral object in it. Then you obtain some specification and know that a living being is in the house, though you do not know what kind of living being it is. From this point of view the negative attributes have something in common with positive attributes, because they must necessarily produce some specification, even though this specification means merely the removal of the negated items from among those that we had before imagined un-negated. The difference between negative and positive attributes is in this, that positive attributes, even when they do not specify, indicate some part of the totality of the thing which we desire to know. This may be either a part of its substance or one of its accidents. The negative attributes do not in any manner tell us anything about the essence of the thing which we wish to know as it is, except incidentally, as in our example.[24]

After these prefatory remarks I state that it has been proved that God exists by necessity and that He is non-composite, as we shall prove, and we can apprehend only that He is, not what He is. It is therefore meaningless that He should have any positive attribute, since the fact that He is is not something outside of what He is, so that the attribute might indicate one of these two. Much less can what He is be of a composite character, so that the attribute could indicate one of the parts. Even less can He be substrate to accidents, so that the attribute could indicate these. Thus there is no scope for any positive attributes in any way whatsoever.

It is the negative attributes which we must employ to guide our mind to that which we ought to believe concerning God, because from them no plurality can result in any way. They can guide the mind to the utmost limit of what man can apprehend of God. For instance, it has been proved to us that something must exist apart from those objects which our senses apprehend and which our reason can encompass with its knowledge. We say about this thing that it exists, meaning that it is absurd to say that He does not exist.[25] Then we apprehend that its existence is not like the existence of, say, the elements, which are lifeless bodies, and consequently say that He lives, meaning that God is not subject to death. Then we apprehend that this being is also not like the existence of heaven, which is a living body, and consequently we say that He is not a body. Then we apprehend that this being is not like the existence of an Intelligence, which is neither a body nor subject to death, but is due to a cause, and consequently say that God is eternal, meaning that there is no cause which called Him into being. Then we apprehend that the existence of this Being, which is its essence, is not only sufficient for that Being itself to exist, but many existences emanate from it. It is, however, not like the emanation of heat from the fire or the automatic connection between light and the sun, but it is an emanation which He perpetually keeps going, giving it a constant flow arranged according to a wise plan, as we shall show. We shall say on account of these arrangements that He is omnipotent, omniscient, and possessed of will. By these attributes we mean to say that He is neither powerless nor ignorant nor distracted or disinterested. When we say He is not powerless, we mean that His existence is sufficient to bring into existence things other than Himself. When we say He is not ignorant, we mean that He apprehends, i.e. lives, for whatever apprehends lives. When we say He is not distracted or disinterested, we mean that all those existing things run along an ordered and planned course, not without supervision and coming into being just by chance, just like anything which a person possessed of will plans with purpose and will. [26] Then we apprehend that there is no other being like this one. When we, therefore, say He is One, we mean thereby to deny any plurality.

Thus it becomes clear that every attribute with which we describe Him is either an attribute of action or has the purport of negating its own absence* if our intention thereby is to apprehend His essence rather than His works. These negative terms are also not used absolutely of God, but only in the manner mentioned before, that one denies of a thing something that by the nature of things could not exist in it, as when we say of a wall that it does not see. [27]

*Read perhaps *salabu ṣifatin 'adimaha*, the negation of an attribute he does not have.

You know well, dear reader, that the heaven is a moving body, and that we have measured it in yards and feet and have complete data on the extent of its parts and of most of its movements, and yet our minds are completely unable to apprehend what it is, although we know that it must necessarily possess matter and form, but not matter of the kind that is with us. For this reason we can only describe it by indefinite nouns, * not by definite positive terms. We say that the heaven is not light and not heavy, does not suffer action and is therefore not receptive to impressions, it has no taste or smell, and similar negative terms. All this is because we are ignorant of that kind of matter. What will be the position then of our minds when they endeavour to apprehend that which is free from matter, non-composite to the utmost degree, of necessary existence, has no cause and is not attained by anything additional to its perfect essence – the meaning of its perfection being the denial of all shortcomings, as explained before? We can only apprehend that He is; that there exists a Being unlike any other being which He brought into existence, having nothing whatsoever in common with them, who has no plurality in Him, and is not powerless to bring into existence things other than He himself, and that His relation to the world is that of the captain to the ship. This also is not a true relation, and not even remotely resembles the real one, but it serves to guide the mind to the idea that God governs the universe, meaning that He supports it and keeps its order as it should be. This point will be explained in a more concrete manner.

Praise be to Him who is such that when our minds try to visualize His essence, their power of apprehending becomes imbecility; when they study the connection between His works and His will, their knowledge becomes ignorance; and when our tongues desire to declare His greatness by descriptive terms, all eloquence becomes impotence and imbecility.

*i.e. *nomina infinita*, nouns incorporating a negative.

CHAPTER LXIX

As is commonly known, the philosophers refer to God as the First Cause.* Those known as *Mutakallimun* anxiously avoid this nomenclature, and call Him the Doer. They think it makes a great difference whether we call Him Cause or call Him Doer. Their argument is: if we call Him a cause, there must necessarily be something caused. This leads us to admit that the world is uncreated and necessarily co-existent with God. If we call Him Doer, we need not envisage the co-existence of that which is affected by his doing, because the Doer may exist long before that which he does. What is more, they cannot picture the Doer being a Doer except by assuming that he exists before that which he does.

This argument shows that they do not realize the distinction between that which is potential and that which is actual. It must be clearly understood that there is no difference between the terms Cause and Doer in this respect. If you call a thing Cause when the act of causation is still a potentiality, it precedes the effect in time. When it is actually a cause its effect necessarily exists by virtue of its existence as a cause in actuality. Similarly, if you call the Doer so when the act of doing is actuality, then the thing done must necessarily co-exist with him. Before the builder builds the house he is not a builder in actuality, only potentially, just as the building materials are only potentially a house before the house is built. As soon as he starts building he becomes a builder in actuality, and the existence of a building becomes a necessary implication. Thus we have gained nothing by substituting the term Doer for the term Cause. What we intend to prove by this discussion is the equivalence of the two terms. We call Him Doer, though His handiwork may not exist, because there is nothing to restrain Him from doing whenever He wishes. We can also call Him Cause in exactly the same sense, although the effect may not exist. The reason why the philosophers do prefer the name Cause over the name Doer must not be sought in their well-known belief that the

*Arabic and Hebrew possess two synonyms for 'cause', which are often, as here, used side by side.

world is uncreated, but in certain other ideas, which I shall briefly set out here.

In the Physics (ii, 3 and ii, 7) it is proved that everything that has a cause is caused by some thing, and that causes fall into four classes: matter, form, maker, and purpose. Some are immediate causes, others indirect, but every one of these four is called cause. They hold the view – which I do not contradict – that God is Maker, Form, and Purpose. They refer to God as Cause in order to imply these three causes, meaning that He is the Maker of the world, its Form, and its Purpose.

In this chapter I intend to demonstrate what we mean by saying of God that He is the Maker, the Form of the world, and at the same time its Purpose. There is no need for you to worry at this stage about the question whether God brought the world into being or whether it is necessarily co-existent with Him, as the Philosophers maintain, because that matter will be discussed at length in a suitable manner. Here we are concerned only with God as efficient cause of the individual acts happening in the world, in the same way as He is the efficient cause of the world as a whole.[28]

It is explained in the Physics (ii, 3) that we must in each case seek a further cause to every cause belonging to one of the four kinds just enumerated. To any thing which comes into being one can find these four proximate causes, to these further causes, and to those again further causes, until one arrives at the ultimate causes. Thus something is caused and its efficient cause is such-and-such. This efficient cause in turn has an efficient cause and so on until one comes to a first mover, who is the true efficient cause of all these intervening items. E.g. A is moved by B, B is moved by C, C is moved by D, D is moved by E, and so on *ad infinitum*. But let us stop, for the sake of illustration, at E: there can be no doubt that it is E which moves A, B, C, and D. One would be correct in saying of the motion of A that it is due to E.

It is in this sense that every action in the existing world can be attributed to God, whichever more proximate agency be directly responsible for it. We shall deal with this later in more detail. He therefore is the ultimate cause in so far as He is an efficient cause.

In the same manner we find, when we follow up the natural forms which came into being and cease to exist, that each must necessarily have been preceded by another form which prepared that matter for receiving this form. The earlier form was again preceded by another form, until we come to the ultimate form which is prerequisite to the existence of the intervening forms, which in their turn are the cause of the latest form. That ultimate form in the whole of the existing world is God. It must not be thought that when we say of God that He is the ultimate form of all existing things, we are thereby referring to that Ultimate Form of which Aristotle says in his *Metaphysics* that it neither came into being nor ceased to be (vii, 8). The form which is mentioned there is physical, not a separate intellect. When we say of God that He is the ultimate form of the world we do not mean it in the way that the form bound up with matter is the form of that matter, as if God were the form of a physical body. This is not at all what we want to say, but as every existing thing possessing a form is what it is only by virtue of its form, and when that form ceases to exist the thing itself ceases to exist, so, exactly the same as this relation, is the relation of God to all the last principles of the existing world. By virtue of the existence of the Creator everything exists. God assists its continued existence by means of the function which, for want of a better name, is called* emanation, as we shall expound in later chapters of this treatise. If one could imagine the Creator not to exist, then the whole existing world would not exist, and the very essence of the last principles would cease to be, as well as the ultimate effects and all intervening links. It results that God is to the world in the same relation as form to a thing possessing form, whereby it is what it is. Through the form its true character and essence is established. That is the relation of God to the world. From this point of view it can be said that He is the ultimate form, and that He is the form of forms, i.e. that from which the existence

*Literally: is called by metonymy, *or* by a name other than its real name.

and permanence of every form in the world is ultimately derived. The subsistence of forms is due to Him, just as things possessing forms acquire permanence through their forms.[29] Because of this function He is called in our language *hey-ha-olamim*, which means 'Life of the World', as will be proved later on.

The same considerations apply to final causes, or purposes. If a thing has a purpose, you may seek a purpose for that purpose. Thus one can say, for example, that the material cause of a throne is wood, its effective cause the joiner, its formal cause squareness of a certain type, and its final cause that one should sit on it. Now you may ask what is the final cause or purpose of sitting on the throne, and you will be told: so that he who sits on it is raised above the ground. Then you may go on asking what is the purpose of being raised above the ground. You will then receive the reply: so that he who sits upon it gains in importance in the eye of the beholder. If you then asked further what is the purpose of his gaining importance in the eye of those who see him, you will be informed: so that he may be feared and respected. Ask then what is the purpose of his being feared, and the reply will be: so that his commands will be carried out efficiently. Ask further what is the purpose of his commands being carried out efficiently, and you will be told: so as to prevent men from harming each other. Then you want to know what is the purpose of that, and it will be answered: so that they continue in an orderly existence. In this way each purpose requires a further purpose, until the matter ends with the absolute will of God, according to the opinion of some – as will be explained later – so that the last answer would be: thus God wills it. According to another opinion, which will also be explained later, the matter will end with the decree of His wisdom, so that the last answer would be: thus His wisdom decrees. Thus the consistent investigation of every purpose will lead us to His will or His wisdom – according to which opinion we accept. Both of these have proved, according to our system, to be identical with His essence. Neither His will or intention nor His wisdom are things in any way separable from His essence, i.e. different from His essence. God is, therefore, the ultimate purpose of everything. Moreover, the purpose of all things is to resemble as far as possible His perfection, and that is what we mean by His will, i.e. His essence, as will be shown later. For this reason we say of Him that He is the Purpose of Purposes.[30]

I have now made clear why one says of God that He is Maker, Form, and Purpose, and that this is why the Philosophers call Him Cause, and not merely Maker. I must add, however, that one of those *Mutakallimun* thinkers was foolish and impertinent enough to maintain that, if one assumed the Creator to be non-existent, there would be no logical compulsion to assume also the non-existence of the thing which He had brought into being, namely the world, because there was no need for the work to perish if its maker went out of existence after having made it. This would be quite correct if God were nothing but a Maker, and the thing He made did not require His support for its continued existence. When the joiner dies, the chest he has made does not cease to exist, since he has no influence on its continued existence. Since God, however, is also the form of the world, as we have explained before, and supports its continued existence and permanence, it is absurd to believe that the supporter could disappear and yet the thing he supports continue to exist although it has no existence except by virtue of the support it receives. This is all that need be said concerning the errors of the theory that God is only Maker, and not also Purpose and Form.

BOOK II

[Maimonides adduces four proofs for the existence of God, which originated with Aristotle, or were developed in the Aristotelian School of antiquity and the middle ages along Aristotelian and Neoplatonic principles. These are followed by several proofs of the unity and incorporeality of God.

In twenty-six propositions prefaced to this chapter, Maimonides exhibits the principles on which these proofs, and particularly the proofs for the existence of God, are founded, and which for the greater part belong to the Aristotelian system of physics. In order to avoid the necessity of entering into the details of Aristotle's teaching of physics, we omit here the two first proofs for the existence of God and the last proof for God's Unity. We also quote here only those propositions which are necessary for the proper understanding of the remaining proofs.]

PROPOSITIONS

xviii. Everything that emerges from potentiality to actuality must do so because of something else which is outside the thing itself. If the cause of its emergence were within the thing itself, and there were no restraining cause, that thing would at no time be potential, but always actual.

xix. Everything for whose existence there is a cause is, as far as its essence is concerned, of possible existence; for if its causes are present it will exist, but if they are not present, or non-existent, or there has been a change in their relation to that thing by which they call it into existence, then the thing does not exist.

xx. If a thing is, as far as its essence is concerned, of necessary existence, then its existence can in no way and under no circumstances have a cause. [31]

xxi. If a thing is composed of two items, and that composition is the indispensable cause of its existence as it is, then it is not of necessary existence in its essence, since its existence depends upon the existence of its two parts and upon their being put together.

xxii. Every body is necessarily composed of two items and necessarily substrate to accidents. The two items that constitute it are its matter and its form. The accidents to which it is substrate are quantity, shape, and position.[32]

xxiii. Everything that is potential and has in its essence an element of possibility may at some time not exist in actuality.

xxiv. Everything that is something potentially must needs be possessed of matter, because possibility always applies to matter.

CHAPTER I

THE third philosophical argument in this connection is taken from the writings of Aristotle, though he propounded it in quite a different context. It runs as follows:

There is no doubt concerning the existence of some things, viz. those perceived by the senses. To these one of three cases must apply – there being no others possible: either nothing is subject to generation* and corruption, or everything is subject to them, or some things are permanent and others are transitory. The first alternative is obviously absurd, because we can constantly observe things coming into being and ceasing to be. The second alternative is also absurd, as will appear after some reflexion: if everything were subject to generation and corruption, then every single thing would be liable to cease. As you know, however, in a species that which is possible must necessarily come to pass. It is therefore unavoidable that existing things should perish. If all are destroyed, it is absurd that anything should exist, since no one would remain in existence so as to bring other things into existence. It would therefore necessarily follow that nothing at all exists. However, we can observe that things exist, and we ourselves exist. From this consideration it results that if there exist, as we are aware, things that come into being and perish, then there must also exist some being that neither comes into being nor perishes. That unborn and imperishable being cannot be thought of as liable to perish. It must exist by necessity, not by possibility.[33]

It has also been said that its existence by necessity may refer

*Literally: becoming.

either to itself or to its cause. If so, its existence or non-existence may be possible as far as its essence is concerned, but necessary as far as its cause is concerned. Thus its cause would be the one that exists by necessity, as has been shown in the nineteenth proposition. It is thus proven that there must of necessity be some being that exists by necessity with regard to its own self. If this being did not exist, no being at all would exist, neither one subject to generation and corruption nor one not subject to them – if, as Aristotle says, there were such a thing as the latter, not subject to generation and corruption because it is caused by a cause which exists by necessity. This is a proof which admits of no doubt, no rejection, and no counter-argument, except by those who have no idea of the technique of philosophical demonstration.

We add on our part that in the case of anything existing by necessity with regard to its own self it must necessarily be admitted that its existence has no cause, as has been said in the twentieth proposition. Nor can there be in it any plurality of notions in any respect, as has been said in the twenty-first proposition. It follows that it is neither a body nor a force in a body, cf. the twenty-second proposition. From this consideration it is proven that there is a being existing of necessity with regard to its own self, that it is the one whose existence has no cause, and which is not compound and therefore neither a body nor a force in a body. That is God – Whose Name is exalted. It is likewise easy to demonstrate that it is absurd to think that existence necessary with regard to their own selves can be found in two beings. In that case the generic quality of necessary existence would be a notion superadded to the essence of each one of the two, and neither of them would exist by necessity through its essence alone, but through that property, the generic quality of necessary existence, which is found both in that thing and in other things. It can be shown in a number of ways that duality is not possible in a thing that exists of necessity, neither through the existence of equals nor that of antagonists. The reason for all this is the absolute non-compositeness and absolute perfection which allows nothing of its own kind to exist apart from itself and the absence of cause from every point of view. Thus there is no possibility of a plurality (of things existing by necessity). [34]

A fourth argument, again philosophical. It is well known that we constantly witness things, which hitherto existed potentially, emerging into actual existence. Everything that passes from potentiality to actuality must have done so by virtue of a factor outside itself, as we have said in the eighteenth proposition. It is obvious that that factor was at first a potential cause for the emergence of that thing and then became an actual cause. The cause for its power remaining potential in the past may be sought either in some impediment within itself, or the fact that there was at first some connection missing between it and the thing it subsequently brought into actuality, and only when that connection became established it actually could cause the emergence of that thing. Each of these two cases necessarily requires a factor causing its emergence or removing the impediment. The same considerations apply concerning the second factor of emergence or the factor removing the impediment. But this chain cannot go on forever. We must necessarily arrive in the end at a factor of emergence which exists perpetually in one condition and in which nothing is potential. I mean that nothing in its essence must be potential, for if something in its essence existed only possibly it might cease to exist at times, as has been explained in the twenty-third proposition. It is absurd to think that such a thing could be material; it must be incorporeal, as has been shown in the twenty-fourth proposition. That incorporeal being which does not admit of any possibility, but is essentially existent, is God. It has been made clear above that He is not a body. He is therefore One, as has been shown in the sixteenth proposition. [35]

All these are methods of demonstrating the existence of One God who is neither a body nor a force in a body, without denying that the world is uncreated.

Here is another method to demonstrate the inadmissibility of belief in a bodily God and the necessity of belief in unity. If there were two Gods, there would necessarily be one property common to both, namely that property by which each of them would deserve the name God. There would also necessarily be one property in each by which they would be distinct from each other and be two. Either each of them may have a property not possessed by the other. Then each of them would be composed of two properties, so that neither would be a first cause and therefore exist by necessity with regard to his own self, but each of them would have causes, as has been shown in the nineteenth proposition. Or the differentiating property is found only in one of the two; then the one having the two properties would not exist by necessity with regard to his own self.

Another method of proving the unity of God. It has been definitely proved by demonstration that the whole universe of existing things is like one organism in which everything hangs together, and that the force of the sphere circulates within this lower matter and shapes it. * If this is accepted as true, it would be absurd to believe that one God is in charge of one part of this universe and the other in charge of another part, since these parts hang together. Therefore, if the universe were divided between them, they would either have to act at different times or would constantly act together, in such a way that no act would come about unless both participate in it.

The idea that the two Gods act at different times is absurd for a variety of reasons. Let us assume that during the time that the one acts it would be possible for the other to act. What is the cause then that the one acts and the other is inactive? If again we assume that during the time that one acts the other is restrained from acting, then there must be another cause which makes it possible for the one to act and impossible for the other – since time is not differentiated in any way and the field of action is one in which everything hangs together, as we have explained. Furthermore, both of them would be subject to time, since their activity is timebound. Also each of them would at the time of his activity emerge from potentiality to actuality; this would presuppose a factor causing their emergence into actual-

*Or: prepares it for receiving shape.

ity. More than that, the essence of both of them would include the element of possibility.

The alternative, that both of them act constantly on everything that exists, so that neither acts without the other, is also absurd, as I shall show. Wherever we have an entity of such a kind that an action can only come about through all of its parts, it is not possible for one of its constituents to be considered an effective cause in itself, nor can any of them be a first cause of that action, but the first cause is the junction of the parts of that entity. It has been proved that a thing which exists by necessity cannot possibly have a cause. Furthermore, the junction of the parts of an entity is an event, and thus in need of a cause in its turn, namely the cause that brings about the junction. If the cause effecting the junction of that entity, through which alone any act can come about, is one, then there can be no doubt that it is God. If the cause effecting the junction of this entity is again compound, then the same principles must be applied to that second entity as to the first. We shall necessarily arrive in the end at a single cause for the existence of the one universe, whichever view we take and whether we assume it to have been created after non-existence or consider its existence an eternal necessity. This argumentation has also shown that the fact that the whole universe is one points to the cause of its existence being one.[36]

CHAPTER XIII

THE views of people with regard to the problem whether the world is without beginning or created – having regard only to the opinion of those who believe that a God exists* – are of three kinds:

The first view, which is the one held by those who believe in the Law of Moses, is that the whole world – I mean everything that exists, apart from God Himself – was brought into existence by God after having been completely and absolutely

*Reading *ilâhan maujûdun.*

devoid of existence. They hold that only God alone existed and nothing beside Him, neither angel nor sphere nor anything that is within the sphere. Then He brought into existence all existing things, as they are, by His will and volition, and not from anything. Time itself, according to them, is one of the things created, since time is consequent upon movement and movement is an accident of that which moves; the thing that moves, and upon the movement of which time is consequent, was created and came into being, not having existed before.

When we say that God *was* before the world was created, where the word 'was' implies time; and likewise all the associations in our mind when we think of the infinite duration of His existence before the creation of the world – all this is assumed time or imagined time, not true time. There can be no doubt that time is an accident. In our system it is just one of the created accidents such as blackness and whiteness. It does not belong to the class of qualities, though, but is an inherent accident of movement, as will be clear to anyone who has understood what Aristotle said in explanation of the true nature of time.

We shall here discuss a subject which is not strictly part of the matter with which we are dealing, but has some bearing on it. The analysis of the concept of time has presented difficulties to most thinkers, so much so that they became bewildered as to whether it had any real existence or not, as happened to Galen and others. The reason for this is that it is an accident of an accident. Those accidents that have a primary existence in bodies, such as colours and tastes, can be understood without further ado, and their purport can easily be realized. Those accidents, however, that have accidents as their substrate, such as brilliancy in colours and curvedness and roundness in lines, are very hard to grasp. This is especially so when on top of this the substrate accident is not permanently in one state but changes from one state to another. Then the concept becomes even more difficult to grasp. With time the two things come together. It is an accident pursuant to motion, which itself is an accident of the thing that moves. Motion is not like blackness or whiteness which are permanent states, but it is the very nature and essence of motion that it does not persist in one state even for a single moment. This is one of the reasons why the nature of time is so difficult to investigate.

What I want to make clear is that time in our system is a created thing that has come into being like all other accidents as well as the substances which are the substrates of these accidents. Therefore the creation of the world by God cannot have taken place in a temporal beginning, as time itself was one of the things created. You must give very careful consideration to this matter, so as to be ready to deal with the objections which are impossible to avoid for anyone who is not aware of this point. If you admit the possibility of time having existed before the world, you will be led into accepting the belief that the world is uncreated, for time is an accident and must needs have a substrate. Thus something would of necessity have existed before this present world existed. That, however, is just the view from which we try to get away.[37]

This then, is the first view. It is, without any doubt, the one on which the Law of Moses is based. It comes in importance immediately after the dogma of the unity of God – make no mistake about that. It was our father Abraham himself who first proclaimed this view, having arrived at it by speculation. For this reason he would call upon *the name of the Lord the God of the World* (Genesis 21, 33),* after he had put this view clearly into words by speaking of *the Maker*** of heaven and earth* (Genesis 14, 22).

The second view is the one held by all the philosophers of whom we have heard or which we have read. They say that it is absurd to believe that God should bring forth something from nothing. In their opinion it is also not possible for a thing to pass away into nothing. This means it is not possible for a thing possessing matter and form to come into being after this matter had been completely devoid of existence. To describe God as having the power to accomplish this is in their opinion

---

*The rendering with 'world' (a meaning which *olam* never has in Biblical Hebrew) appears also in Targum and Talmud (Sotah 10b). A.V. 'the everlasting God'.
**A.V. (with all versions): 'possessor'.

the same as to describe him as having the power to unite two opposites* at the same time, or to create His own equal or to become a body or to create a rectangle with the diagonal equal to its side, and similar impossibilities. [38]

We can deduce from their arguments that they mean: just as there is no lack of power imputed to God in the fact that God does not create impossibilities – because the impossible has a permanent character which is not produced by anyone and can therefore not be changed – so there is no lack of power imputed to God if He is not thought to be able to bring forth something from nothing, since this belongs to the category of impossibilities. They therefore hold that there is some matter in existence, having no beginning just as God has no beginning, that God does not exist without it, nor it without God. They do not hold that its existence is of the same rank as the existence of God, but they think Him to be the cause of its existence. It would be to Him in the relation of, say, the clay to the potter or the iron to the ironworker. This is the matter from which He creates whatever He wills, forming it one time into heaven and earth and another time into something else. Those who follow this opinion believe that the heaven, too, has come into being and is liable to perish, but that it did not come into being from nothing and will not perish into nothing. As the individual living beings come into being and perish out of existing matter and into existing matter, so the heaven comes into being and perishes, and its coming into being and ceasing to be takes place in the same way as that of other existing things.

The people of this class are divided into various sects, the number and opinions of which it would be useless to mention in this treatise. The general and fundamental tenet of this sect, however, is as I have described it to you. It is also the belief of Plato. We find that Aristotle reports of him in the *Physics* (viii, 1; 251*a*17) that he, Plato, believed that the heaven had come into being and was liable to perish. You can find this opinion clearly expressed in the Timaeus (38 *bc*). However, Plato did not hold the same belief as we (Jews), as some people think who

*Tibbon adds: in one object.

cannot analyse opinions and do not think precisely, and therefore imagine that our view is the same as his. This is not so. We believe that the heaven came into being, not out of another thing, but out of absolute non-existence. He believes it to have been brought into existence* and being out of another thing. This, then, is the second view.

The third view is that of Aristotle, of his followers and commentators. He says the same as the followers of the sect just mentioned, namely that a thing composed of matter can never be brought forth out of no matter. He goes beyond this, however, and says that the heaven does not fall under the laws of generation and corruption in any way. To put his view briefly, he claims that this universe as a whole, such as it is, never ceased and never will cease to be as it is. The one permanent thing which is not subject to generation and corruption, namely heaven, will always be so. Time and motion are eternal and continuous, having neither come into being nor being liable to cease. Things that come into being and perish, namely those beneath the lunar sphere, will not cease to be so. That means that primary matter essentially neither comes into being nor perishes, but the forms follow each other in it: it divests itself of one form and clothes itself in another. This whole order both in the higher and the lower regions cannot be upset or stopped, or any innovation made in it other than those implied in its own nature, nor does anything ever happen within it that is in any way contrary to the laws of nature. He also says – though not in so many words, but it can be deduced from his opinions – that he considers it impossible that God should in any way change His will or exercise any fresh volition. True, all this universe as it is was brought into being by God's will, but not made out of non-existence. Just as it is impossible that God should cease to be or that His essence should change, so he thinks it impossible that He should change His will or exercise any new volition. The conclusion is thus forced upon us that this universe, just as it is now, has been so forever and will be so in the most distant future.

*Reading *mûjada*. Other reading: to have existed (potentially).

This is a brief but adequate presentation of the various views.*
They are the views of those who accept the existence of God in
this world as proven. Others know nothing of the existence of
God, but pretend that things come into being and perish by
purely accidental aggregation and separation, and that there is
no one to guide and arrange their existence. Such are, according to Alexander, Epicure and his school, among others. There
is no point for us in expounding the views of those sects since
the existence of God is definitely proven, and it is useless to
discuss the views of people who base themselves on a proposition the opposite of which is evident. It is also useless for us to
undertake an investigation into the truth of the views of the
second school of thought, who believe heaven to be created but
transitory, since they accept the idea of something uncreated.
In our opinion there is no difference between one who holds
that heaven must necessarily have originated out of something
else, or will perish and pass into something else, and the belief
of Aristotle that it neither came into being nor is liable to perish. [39] The aim of everyone who follows the Law of Moses and
Abraham, or any similar outlook, is to believe that there is
nothing whatsoever uncreated and co-existent with God, and
that the production of existent things from non-existence on
the part of God is not impossible, but – according to some
thinkers – even necessary. Now that we have established the
various views I shall proceed to explain and summarize the
arguments of Aristotle for his view and the reasons that led him
to it.

CHAPTER XIV

ARISTOTLE maintains that motion neither comes into being
nor ceases to be. He refers to motion in an absolute sense. He
argues that even if we assume motion to have come into being
we must admit that everything that comes into being is preceded by motion, namely its own emergence into reality and
its coming into being after it had not been. Motion must thus

*Other reading: an account of those views and their essential meaning.

have been pre-existent, namely the motion by which this latter motion came into being. That former motion must necessarily be uncreated, or the sequence would be continued indefinitely. [40] Following from this thesis he further maintains that time neither came into being nor is liable to cease, because time is pursuant to motion and inherent in it. There is no motion except in time, and time cannot be conceived except through motion, as has been shown. This is one of the methods by which he establishes the eternity of the world.

Another proof of his is by maintaining that the prime matter which is common to the four elements cannot have come into being or be liable to perish. Were we to assume that prime matter came into being at some time, we should have to admit that there was some matter from which it originated, and also that the matter which thus originated possessed form, since this is what constitutes 'coming into being'. Our axiom, however, is that prime matter is matter not possessing form. It must thus necessarily be considered not to have come into being out of another thing and therefore to be eternal and imperishable. This again implies that the world is uncreated. [41]

These are the essential methods used by Aristotle to establish the eternity of the world by basing his argument on the structure of the world itself. There are, however, other methods, mentioned by those who came after him. They deduced these proofs from his philosophical system so as to establish the eternity of the world while accepting the existence of God.

One of these is as follows: Assuming that God brought the world into existence out of non-existence, we would have to admit that God was before the creation of the world a Doer only potentially: after He had created it He became a Doer in actuality. Thus God would have emerged from potentiality into actuality, and there would be a factor of possibility within Him. He would then require some cause to cause Him to pass from potentiality into actuality. This is very difficult, and is an objection which demands from every intelligent person an effort of thought, so as to dispose of it and to demonstrate its hidden inconsistencies.

Another method starts from the fact that if an effective cause acts at one time and does not act at another, this is due to supervening causes restraining or furthering its action from without or within. Thus restraining factors would have obliged God to refrain from doing what He willed, and the conducive factors would have imposed upon Him to will what He did not will before. The Creator, may His name be glorified, is not affected by the appearance or cessation of factors that would make Him change His will, hinder Him, or restrain Him. There is thus no reason to think that He should have acted at one time and not acted at another time. His activity is perpetually actual, just as He perpetually exists in actuality.[42]

CHAPTER XVI

IN this chapter I shall explain what my own view on this problem is, leaving for later the arguments for what I am trying to prove. I should like to add that I am not satisfied with the arguments that have been produced by those *Mutakallimun* who claim to have proved that the world was created. I do not deceive myself by calling sophistic arguments proofs. If a man claims to have produced proof regarding some problem by means of sophistic arguments, this does not strengthen my faith in that thesis, but weakens it and provokes opposition to it, because when the inadequacy of the arguments becomes apparent, one's mind becomes unwilling to admit the truth of the statement for which these arguments are adduced. It would in such a case have been better had the matter for which no proof is available remained open, or had one of the two contradictory opinions concerning it been accepted by dint of tradition. I have expounded the methods the *Mutakallimun* employ to establish that the world is created, and have pointed out the weak spots in their arguments. Similarly I consider all the arguments of Aristotle and his school for the eternity of the world not as decisive proofs, but as assertions open to grave doubts, as you will learn later on.[43]

What I want to say is that there is no inherent improbability in the belief that the world was created, which belief I have shown to be the intent of our Law. All the philosophical arguments from which it appears that the matter is otherwise – as we have mentioned – can be shown to be invalid and without convincing force. Once this point is conceded to me, and thus the problem whether the world is created or not is completely open, I accept the traditional solution of it as it is given by prophecy. Prophecy provides an answer to problems which speculation is unable to solve. We shall later show that prophecy need not be rejected even according to the view of those who believe in an uncreated world.

When I have demonstrated the possibility of our proposed view, I shall proceed to show its superiority over other views by speculative argument, too – I mean the superiority of the view that the world is created over the view that it is eternal – and shall demonstrate that though we may not get rid of some discomfort in admitting that it is created, we experience much greater discomfort in admitting that it is eternal. I shall now proceed to develop the methods by which the arguments of all those who argue for the eternity of the world can be invalidated.

CHAPTER XVII

WHENEVER a created thing comes into being after it had not been – though its matter may have existed and only divested itself of one form and taken another – its nature after its creation, completion, and permanent establishment differs from its nature at the moment when it came into being and began to emerge from potentiality to actuality, and this again differs from its nature before it was set in motion to emerge into actuality.

For example, the nature of the female sperm, while it is still blood in the blood-vessels, differs from its nature at the moment of conception, when it meets with the male sperm and is set in motion. Again, its nature at that moment is different from that of the complete organism after birth. There is no justification whatsoever for arguing from the nature a thing possesses when it has come into being, is complete, and has become established in its most perfect state, about the nature the same thing had when it was moving towards coming into being. Neither can one argue from its circumstances at the moment of its being set in motion about its circumstances before it was set in motion. Whenever you err in this respect, and advance arguments derived from the nature of the actual thing about the nature of the same thing while in potentiality, grave doubts will arise in your mind, and things that necessarily exist will appear absurd to you, while absurd things will appear necessary. Taking our example, assume that a man of very perfect physical habitus had been born and his mother died after feeding him for a few months. Then the father charged himself* with the entire upbringing of that babe on a desert island, so that it grew up and reached the age of discretion without ever having seen a woman or the female of any other species of animal. One day he would ask one of the men about him: 'how do we exist and in what circumstances have we come into being'. Then the man he asked would reply: 'every one among us came into being in the abdomen of an individual of our own species and like to ourselves, but female, and of such-and-such appearance. Each one of us was small of body when in the abdomen, and would develop and be nourished and grow little by little, being alive, until he would reach a certain size. Then an outlet would be opened for him on the lower side of the body, through which he would pass outside. Then he continues growing until he becomes as you see us.' That orphan youth can hardly help asking: 'But when that individual among us was small in the womb, being alive, moving, and growing – did he then eat and drink and breathe through his mouth and nose, and relieve his bowels?' On receiving a negative reply to this he would no doubt rashly call his interlocutor a liar and prove that all these simple truths are impossible, deriving his arguments from observation of the perfect and established being. He would say: 'If you stop anyone of us breathing for a short while, he

*Harizi and Falaguera prefer the reading: Then some men charged themselves. ...

will die and his movements will cease. How can one imagine that one of us can be inside a thick-walled vessel enclosed within a body for months, and still go on living and moving? If one of us swallowed a bird, that bird would die immediately it came into his stomach, how much more so in the lower abdomen? If anyone of us would not eat food and drink water through his mouth for a few days, he would certainly die. How then can an individual remain alive for months without eating and drinking? If you pierced the abdomen of one of us he would die after some days. How can one maintain that the navel of that embryo was open? How is it possible that he did not open his eyes or stretch out his arms or straighten his legs, although all his limbs were sound and not affected in any way, as you say?' Thus the whole pattern of life would prove to him that it was not possible for man to come into being in that manner.

Now, dear reader, consider this parable carefully and try to understand it. You will see that this is precisely our situation with regard to Aristotle. We, the followers of Moses and Abraham, believe that the world came into being in a certain fashion, and that certain things arose from certain others, and certain things were created after certain others. Aristotle contradicts us, deriving his arguments from the nature of the established, completed, actual universe. We are assuring him that its state after its establishment and completion does not in the least resemble its state when it came into being, and that it was brought into existence after absolute non-existence. What arguments then need we bring against anything he says? Such arguments are necessary for those who claim that the nature of this universe, as established, points to it having been created. I have told you clearly enough that I make no such claims. [44]

I shall now mention Aristotle's essential arguments and show you that they do not affect our position at all, since we maintain that the entire world was created by God out of non-existence, and that He brought it into being in such a way that it emerged as perfect as you see it now.

Aristotle says that primary matter is eternal. He proceeds to bring arguments for this from things that come into being and perish, and to demonstrate that the primary matter cannot have come into being. This is perfectly correct. We, too, do not claim that primary matter came into being as man comes into being from sperm or perishes as man perishes by turning into dust. We claim that God brought it into existence from nothing in exactly the state in which it is now, namely that everything comes into being out of primary matter and that everything that came out of it perishes and turns back into it, and that it is never found devoid of form, that it is the ultimate background of generation and corruption and does not come into being as the things that come from it, or perish as the things that turn back into it. We say it is created *ex nihilo* and that if He who made it out of nothing wishes so, He can again make it vanish completely and absolutely.

We say the same about motion. He argues from the nature of motion that it can neither have come into being nor cease. This is correct. We assert that once motion had come into existence possessing the nature with which it is now established, it is unimaginable that it should as a whole come into being or cease totally, in the same way as individual movements come into being or cease. In an analogous manner we must treat all that is connected with the nature of motion.

The same applies to his statement concerning circular motion having no beginning (Physics viii, 9). This is correct once the spherical body performing a circular motion has come into existence: no beginning of this motion can be imagined.

You are well advised to get a firm hold of this argument. It is a high wall I have built round the Law, a wall that surrounds it on all sides and keeps away from it stones, whoever it may be that throws them. Should Aristotle, or rather those who adopt his views, attempt to argue with us, and say: 'If the existing universe gives us no clue, how do you know that it has come into being and that there was another nature which brought it into being?' – then we shall reply: 'This proof is not incumbent on us for our purposes. Our purpose at the moment is not to establish that the world is created, but to prove that it might be created, and that our assertion cannot be proved false by arguments drawn from the nature of the existing universe. About the latter we do not dispute.' Now that the possibility of our assertion is established, as we have shown, we shall return to demonstrate the greater probability of the view that the world is created.

At this stage our opponents have only one thing left, and that is to find some arguments proving it impossible that the world was created, not taken from the nature of the universe but from what our reason tells us about God. Such are indeed the three arguments I have mentioned before, in which they argue the eternity of the world by starting from God. I shall show you in the next chapter how the weakness of these arguments can be demonstrated, so much so that they lose any value as arguments.

CHAPTER XVIII

THE first argument they mention and with which we have to deal is their assertion that we are forced to admit God would have passed from potentiality to actuality, since He would have acted at one time and not acted at another. It is very easy to see how this objection can be refuted. This qualification only applies to something composed of matter, admitting of possibility, and form. There is no doubt that such a body, when it acts in its form after having been inactive, proves to have contained something potential which passed into actuality, and we must seek the factor which caused it to do so. This principle has been proved only with regard to material bodies. Anything that is not a body and contains no matter has no element of possibility inherent in its essence in any way. All its properties are perpetually actual, and our qualification does not apply to it. It is not precluded from acting at one time and not acting at another; this cannot be considered in the case of the incorporeal as change or as transition from potentiality to actuality.

As an instructive instance of this we may adduce the Active Intelligence, as described by Aristotle and his school. It is incorporeal and may be active at one time and inactive at another, as has been proved by Alfarabi in his treatise *De intellectu et intellectis*. He has there a passage which I shall quote here: 'it is obvious that the Active Intelligence is not always active, but is active at one time and inactive at another'. What he says is evidently true. While this is the case, no one would say that the Active Intelligence changes, nor that it was potentially active and has become actual when it acts at any given moment in a manner in which it has not acted before. The reason is that there is no relation or any similarity whatsoever between the corporeal and the incorporeal either at the time of activity or at the time of refraining from activity. The word 'action' is used of the material forms and of the incorporeal only by way of homonymy. Therefore, when the incorporeal does not at any given time act in the same way as it acts afterwards, there is no need to assume that it has passed from potentiality to actuality, as we find it to be the case with things consisting of forms combined with matter.

According to the second argument, the world must be considered as uncreated because no encouraging, supervening, or restraining factors can be admitted in the case of God. This objection is difficult to dispose of, and the answer is of a subtle nature. Follow therefore attentively. It must be fully realized that every agent gifted with will carries out his actions by reason of something. If he acts at one time and does not act at another, this must necessarily be by reason of restraining or supervening factors. For example, a man wants to have a house, but does not build it because of some restraining factors. Thus the materials may not be available, or they may be available but cannot be given the proper shape because of lack of tools. Sometimes both materials and tools may be available, and still he does not build because he does not want to do so, being able to manage without shelter. When, however, further factors supervene, such as heat or cold which force him to seek shelter, then he will want to build. It is thus clear that supervening factors may change the will and restraining factors may counter the will, with the result that he does not act according to it. All this is true where actions take place by reason of something outside the will itself. When, on the other hand, action has no other purpose in any way but to conform with an act of will, such will does not require any motives. Although there may be nothing to stop the person whose will it is, yet it is not necessary for that person to act perpetually, there being no external purpose by reason of which he should act, so that it should be necessary to act whenever there are no obstacles in the way of achieving that purpose. In our case action is dependent on nothing but will.

It might be objected: all this is true, but is not the fact that He wills at one time and does not will at another to be taken as a change? To this we can reply in the negative. The nature and essence of will is in the fact that one is free to will or not to will. If this will is exercised by a material being, which implies that that being seeks with it an exterior purpose, then the will is changed in accordance with restraining and supervening causes. The will of the incorporeal, however, which is in no way influenced by anything other than itself, does not change. The fact that He wills something now and something else tomorrow does not constitute a change in His essence and hence does not require an outside cause, just as the fact that He acts or does not act does not constitute a change, as we have just proved. It will be proved later on that our will and the will of the incorporeal are both called by that name only by way of homonymy, and there is no similarity between the two kinds of will. Thus this objection, too, has been disposed of. It is demonstrated that this argument does not prove us necessarily wrong, which is what we have set out to show. [45]

Aristotle also mentions certain things on which all nations in ancient times agreed, such as the idea that the angels are in heaven or that God is in heaven. Similar ideas are also expressed in Biblical passages, if we take these in their literal meaning. These are not arguments for the eternity of heaven, as he wants them to be. These things have been said to draw our attention to the fact that the existence of heaven indicates to us the existence of incorporeal intelligences, namely spiritual beings and angels, and they again indicate to us the existence of God, who moves and controls them, as we shall show later on. We also shall demonstrate that there is no argument that indicates, according to our system, the existence of the Maker as clearly as that provided by the heavens. These indicate also according to the view of the philosophers – as we have said before – the existence of Him who moves them as well as the fact that He is not a body nor a force in a body.

Having demonstrated to you that our assertion is at least possible and not an impossibility, as say those who proclaim that the world is uncreated, I shall retrace my steps and prove in the next chapters that our view is the more acceptable on speculative grounds, as well as showing up the inherent absurdity of Aristotle's view.

CHAPTER XIX

ENOUGH of the views of Aristotle and all those who hold that the world is uncreated, will be clear to you by now to enable you to realize that he considers that this universe proceeds from the Creator by way of necessity and that God is a cause and the universe something caused: their relation is thus automatic.*
As it cannot be said of God why or how He exists just so, I mean in Unity and incorporeality, so one cannot say of the world as a whole why and how it exists just so. All this inevitably exists as it is: the cause and the thing caused by it. There is no possibility of their not both existing or being any different from what they are. According to this view, therefore, it necessarily follows that everything should always have the same nature and no thing should ever change its nature in any way whatsoever. According to this view any change in the nature of any existing thing is an impossibility. All these things, therefore, cannot be due to the design of one who chose and willed that they be thus. Had they been due to the intention of

*Or: the world is therefore necessarily existent.

anyone they would not have existed thus before the act of intention had taken place.

According to our view, on the other hand, it is obvious that they are there by intention, not by necessity. It is possible that He who intended can change them and have another intention, though not just any intention, because there is a permanent category of the impossible which cannot be set aside, as we shall show. My purpose in this chapter is to demonstrate to you with arguments almost amounting to proof that this universe of ours indicates to us that it is necessarily due to intention.

CHAPTER XXII

THERE is a theorem on which Aristotle and everyone who calls himself a philosopher are agreed, that from a simple thing only one simple thing can result by necessity. If a thing is compound, then things will result from it in the same number as the simple elements from which it is composed. For example, in fire there is a compound of two qualities, heat and dryness; the result is that it heats through its heat and dries through its dryness. Similarly, when a thing is composed of matter and form, certain things result from it owing to its matter and certain other things owing to its form – assuming the thing to be of multiple composition. In accordance with this theorem Aristotle says that only one single simple intelligence derives directly from God, and nothing else. [46]

A second theorem is that not any chance thing can result from any other chance thing, but there must always be some relationship between the cause and its effect. Even in the case of accidents not just any accident can derive from any other chance accident, such as a quantity from a quality or vice versa. Similarly no form can result from matter, nor any matter from form.

A third theorem is that whenever a doer acts by intention and will, not by natural force, many different actions may emanate from him.

A fourth theorem states that if a whole is composed of different substances juxtaposed, it deserves the name of compound more truly than a whole composed of different substances in mixture. For example a bone or muscle or vein or nerve is simpler than the whole of the hand or foot, which are composed of nerves, muscles, veins, and bones. This is too obvious to waste any more words on it.

After these prefatory remarks I shall deal with Aristotle's assertion that the first intelligence is the cause of the second, and this the cause of the third. In this way, even if their number came to thousands, the last intelligence would still, without any doubt, be simple. Whence, then, does the composite character originate which is, on Aristotle's own assertion, found necessarily in the things existing around us? Let us concede to Aristotle his whole theory that the further the intelligences are removed from the first, the more compound their functions become, because of the greater number of intelligibles apprehended by them. Even if we concede to him this wild guess, we must still ask how the intelligences came to be a cause from which the spheres resulted, and what relationship is there between matter and the incorporeal which contains no matter whatsoever. But suppose even that we concede to him that each sphere has as its cause an intelligence in the manner described, that intelligence may be described as compound since it apprehends both itself and other things. Thus it is, so to say, composed of two things. From one of these two the next intelligence below it results, from the other the sphere. One must then ask: if the sphere is supposed to have resulted from that one simple idea, how can a sphere have resulted from it, since a sphere is composed of two kinds of matter and two kinds of form, viz. the matter and form of the sphere itself and the matter and form of the star fixed to it? If everything existed by mechanical necessity, we would definitely require for this compound a compound cause, from one part of which the body of the sphere and from the other part of which the body of the star would result. This would be true if the matter of all stars were one and the same. It is, however, likely that the substance of the bright stars differs from that of the non-luminous stars: as is well known, each body is composed of matter and form peculiar to itself.

It must be clear to you by now that these things cannot possibly be consistently viewed as having arisen from mechanical necessity, as he says. It is similar with the differences in the movements of the spheres: it does not correspond to the manner in which these are arranged underneath each other to such an extent as to justify the claim that there is any mechanical necessity in it. We have spoken about this before. [47]

There is, however, another point which upsets all that is established as natural law when applied to the condition of the spheres. Since the matter of all spheres is one and the same, why is the result not that the form of one sphere is transferred to the matter of another sphere, as happens beneath the lunar sphere as a consequence of the adaptability of matter? Why does this particular form remain permanently in that particular matter, when the same matter is common to all? My God, the next thing is that someone will make out a case that the matter of each sphere is different from that of the next. In that case the form of the motion would not be any indication of the matter (of which the moving body is composed).* This is contrary to all principles.

Furthermore, since the matter of all stars is one and the same, by what are they individually distinguished? Is it by their forms or by accidents? In either case it would be necessary for those forms or accidents to be transferable and to apply to each of them in turn, lest the adaptability of matter cease to operate. It thus becomes clear to you that when we speak of the matter of the spheres or of the stars, this does not imply the same meaning as the matter around us. It is mere homonymy. Every one of the heavenly bodies that exist has an existence of a distinctive kind which it does not share with anything else. If so, how comes it that there is some analogy, in so far as all spheres turn and all stars are permanent?

If, on the other hand, we believe all this to be due to the design of someone who made it and imparted to it its dis-

*Or: any proof of (the unity of) matter.

tinctive character as directed by His wisdom that passes comprehension, none of these problems affect us. They only affect
those who claim that all this exists by virtue of mechanical
necessity, not by a personal will. That latter view does not
conform with the order of the universe, and no convincing
reason or proof has ever been advanced for it. Withal some
very weighty contradictions attach to it. One is that God,
whom every sensible person acknowledges to be perfect from
every possible point of view, is thought of as merely existing by
the side of all existing things without any initiative. If He
wanted to do so much as to lengthen the wing of a fly or
shorten the leg of a caterpillar, He could not do it. Still,
Aristotle would say that God does not want such things, and
that it is absurd for Him to want things different from what
they are. This does not exactly mean emphasizing the perfection of God; rather it implies that He has some shortcomings. [48]

I know that many zealous partisans will accuse me on account
of these statements either of having imperfectly understood
what they say or of intentional distortion. Nonetheless I shall
not for this reason refrain from stating briefly what I have
grasped and understood, however insufficient it be. In brief,
therefore, I admit that all Aristotle says concerning the universe
between the sphere of the moon and the centre of the earth is
undoubtedly true. Only those will differ from him there who
either have not understood him, or who want to defend their
prejudices, or have been misguided by them into denying
observable facts. On the other hand all Aristotle's description
of the part of the universe situated beyond the sphere of the
moon is in the nature of guess and conjecture, with few excep-
tions, leave alone what he has to say on the order of the intelligences and some of the metaphysical theories he holds,
which contain the greatest improbabilities and most obvious
contradictions, evident to people of all faiths, as well as spreading wicked falsehoods for which he gives no proof.

Do not criticize me for having set out the doubts attaching to
Aristotle's view. You may ask whether we have any right to

reject a view and maintain the opposite because of mere doubts. The case is not like that at all. We are only treating this philosopher as his followers told us to treat him. Alexander makes it clear that in all cases where conclusive proof is not possible, the two extreme and incompatible solutions must be applied and after investigating what doubts attach to each of the two opposites, the solution must be adopted which carries less doubt with it. This is the method which Alexander says he employs with regard to all those views enunciated by Aristotle about metaphysical matters which are not proven. Indeed, all those who lived after Aristotle are constantly saying that Aristotle's views on this subject raise less doubts than any other possible views. This is what we did. Once we became convinced that this problem – whether the heavens have come into being or are eternal – allows of no proof for either of the contradictory solutions, and have set out the doubts attaching to both views, we have shown you that the assumption of eternity raises more doubts and is less compatible with the beliefs that ought to be held with regard to God. Quite apart from this, the view that the world was created is the one held by our father Abraham and our prophet Moses, peace be upon them.

CHAPTER XXV

IT should be clearly understood that our reason for rejecting the eternity of the world is not to be sought in any text of the Torah which says that the world is created. The passages which indicate that the world is created are no more numerous than those that indicate that God is a body. The method of allegorical interpretation is no less possible or permissible in the matter of the world being created than in any other. We would have been able to explain it allegorically just as we did when we denied corporeality. [49] Perhaps it would have been even much easier. We would in any case not have lacked the capacity to explain those texts allegorically and establish the eternity of the world just as we explained those other texts allegorically and denied that God was a body. If we have not done this and do

not believe in it, this is for two reasons: one is that it is conclusively proved that God is not a body. We must of necessity
explain allegorically all those passages the literal sense of which
is contradicted by evidential proof, so that we are conscious
that they must be allegorically interpreted. The eternity of the
world is not conclusively proved. It is therefore wrong to
reject the texts and interpret them allegorically because of pre-
ference for a view the opposite of which might be shown to be
preferable for a variety of reasons. This is one reason; the other
is that our belief that God is not a body does not destroy in
our eyes any of the ordinances of our Law or belie the statements of any prophet. There is nothing contrary to Scripture
in it, except that the ignorant think it is. As we have explained,
there is no contradiction, but this is the real intention of the
text. If, on the other hand, we believed in the eternity of the
world according to the principles laid down by Aristotle – that
the world exists by necessity, that the nature of no thing ever
changes and that nothing ever deviates from its customary behaviour – this would destroy the Law from its very foundation
and belie automatically every miracle, and make void all hopes
and fears the Law seeks to inspire, unless, of course, one
chooses to interpret the miracles as well allegorically, as did the
Batiniyya sect among the Moslems. In this way we would end
up in some kind of idle prattling.

Again if we believe in the eternity of the world according to
the second theory we have expounded, that of Plato, namely,
that the heavens themselves are transitory, such a view would
not upset the ordinances of the Law, nor would its consequence
be the belying of miracles, which, on the contrary, would be
possible. The various passages could be interpreted in accordance with it. One might even discover many equivocal
passages in the text of the Torah and elsewhere with which it
could be connected and which might even be considered to
argue for it. However, there is no cogent incentive for us to do
so unless that theory were proved. Since it is not proved, we
shall neither allow ourselves to be beguiled by this theory nor
pay the slightest attention to that other theory, but shall take

the texts in their literal meaning. We say, therefore, that the Law intimates to us a thing which we have no power fully to apprehend. The miracles bear witness that our claim is true.

It must be clearly understood that once we believe in the world being created, all miracles become possible and the Law itself becomes possible, and any question that might be asked in this connection is automatically void, even such questions as the following: why did God accord a revelation to this one and none to others? Why did God prescribe this Law to a certain nation and not to others? Why did He give the Law at the time He gave it and not before or after? Why did He ordain these positive and those negative commandments? Why did He distinguish any particular prophet by those miracles that are mentioned, and no others took place? What did God intend by this act of lawgiving, and why did He not implant these commandments and prohibitions in our nature, if that was His purpose? To all these questions answer can be made by saying: thus He wanted, or: thus His wisdom decreed it. Just as He brought the world into existence when He willed and in this form, without our being able to analyse His will in this connection or the principles by which His wisdom selected these particular forms or that time, so we do not know His will or the motives of His wisdom in determining all the things concerning which we have just asked. If one says that the world necessarily had to be as it is, all these questions must be asked, and cannot be disposed of except by reprehensible replies which both contradict, and make nonsense of, the literal sense of all those Scriptural passages concerning which no sensible person can doubt that they are to be taken in their literal sense.

This, then, is our reason for recoiling from that theory. This is why people of worth have spent their lives, and others will go on spending their lives, in speculating on this problem. For if it were proved that the world is created – even in the manner this is stated by Plato – all the objections of the philosophers to us would fall to the ground. If, on the other hand, they would succeed in providing a proof for its eternity according to Aristotle's view, the Law in its entirety would fall to the ground and other manners of thinking would take its place, for I have made clear to you that the whole of it hangs on this one point. Give it, therefore, your most earnest consideration. [50]

CHAPTER XXVII

I HOPE to have made it quite clear that the belief in a created world is fundamental to our entire Law. It is by no means fundamental to the Law, on the other hand, to accept the belief that it will perish after having been created and come into being. None of our beliefs will be disturbed if we believe it to be everlasting.

You may object that it has been proved that everything that has come into being is liable to perish. If, therefore, the world has been brought into being, it will perish. The answer to that is that this is not a necessary conclusion. We have not made any claim that the world was brought into being by the same process as physical objects which are subject to the laws of nature. That which has come into being by the course of nature must necessarily and automatically perish by the course of nature. Just as its nature decreed first that it should not exist thus and then it became thus, so its nature must necessarily decree that it should not forever exist thus, since it is recognized as true that by reason of its nature this existence does not perpetually attach to it.

Our claim, however, is based on Scripture, which says that things exist and disappear according to the will of God, not by blind necessity. According to this theory we are not driven to the conclusion that if God brings into existence a thing that did not exist before, that thing is inexorably doomed to perish again. Everything depends on His will: if He wills, He causes it to perish, and if He wills, He causes it to remain; or we may say it depends on the decree of His wisdom. It is possible for Him to cause the thing to remain for all eternity and to make it as everlasting as He Himself. You know no doubt that though the Sages state the Throne of Glory to be created they never say that it will cease to exist. No statement of any prophet or

Sage implies that the Throne of Glory will perish or cease to exist; on the contrary, the text of Scripture bears witness to its perpetual existence. Similarly the souls of the righteous are in our opinion created but will never cease to exist. According to the view of some, who follow the literal meaning of the Midrashim, their bodies, too, will have everlasting enjoyment; a belief resembling the well-known beliefs held by some concerning Paradise.

In short, on speculative grounds it is not necessary to assume the end of the world as inevitable. There remains thus only the method of reference to the utterances of the prophets and Sages as to whether there is any definite statement that this world will inevitably perish or not. Most of our common people believe that there exist such statements and that all this world will perish. I shall make it clear to you that this is not so. On the contrary, many Scriptural passages say that the world is everlasting, while in all those cases where the literal sense implies that the world will perish, it is absolutely clear that it is metaphorical, as I shall explain.

If one of the literalists refuses to accept these arguments and says he must believe that the world will perish, we shall not grudge it to him. He must be told, however, that the end of the world is not necessitated by its being created, but that he believes it – as he himself claims – because he accepts the contents of that metaphor which he interprets literally. This does not harm religion in any way.

CHAPTER XXIX

I T must be clearly understood that when one does not understand the language of a person whom one hears talk, one is indeed aware that he is talking but does not understand what he means. Even worse than that, one may hear in his speech words which according to the language of the speaker have a certain meaning and may happen in the language of the listener to have the opposite meaning to that which the speaker intended. The listener will in such cases assume that they mean the same for the speaker as for himself. Thus, if an Arab heard a Hebrew speaker utter the word *abâ*, the Arab would assume that he was speaking of a person who disliked something and did not want it. What the Hebrew intended to say was that he was pleased with that thing and wanted it.

The same happens to the vulgar crowd with regard to the words of the prophets. They do not understand some of them at all, but rather, as it is said: *and the vision of all this is become unto you as the words of a writing that is sealed* (Isaiah 29, 11). Some of them understand the opposite of, or something incompatible with, the real meaning, as it is said: *for ye have perverted the words of the living God* (Jeremiah 23, 36). It must be clearly understood that every prophet has a style of his own. It is as if it was the manner of speech peculiar to that person. In that manner the revelation peculiar to him makes him speak to those who understand him.

Having made these prefatory remarks I wish to point out the fact that it very frequently happens in Isaiah's utterances, though rarely in those of other prophets, that when* he tells of the breakdown of a government or the ruin of a great nation, he expresses this by saying that the stars have fallen and the heavens been rolled up, the sun darkened and the earth laid waste and shaken, and many suchlike metaphors. It is the same with the Arabs, who say, when someone has been affected by a major misfortune, that 'his heavens have collapsed upon his earth'. Likewise, when Isaiah describes the rise of a dynasty or the renewal of its fortunes, he uses such expressions as the increase of the light of the sun and moon, the emergence of a new heaven and a new earth, and the like of it, just as people,** when describing the ruin of a person, nation, or city, attribute to God fits of rage and violent hatred against these, while when speaking of the rise of a nation they attribute to God emotions of joy and gladness. They refer to the states of anger against them with terms like He went out (to war), He descended, He

---

*Crescas and Duran: that Isaiah often carries his metaphors through consistently while others do this but rarely. When . . .

**Other reading: other prophets.

roared, He thundered, He shouted, and many others. They also say He commanded, He said, He acted, He did, etc., as I shall enumerate in detail later on. Also when the prophet informs us of the ruin of the inhabitants of some place, he substitutes for that place the whole human race, as Isaiah says: *and the Lord will have removed mankind far away* (Isaiah 6, 12), meaning the destruction of Israel. Zephaniah says in the same connection: *and I will cut off mankind from off the face of the earth, saith the Lord: and I will stretch out mine hand upon Judah*, etc. (Zephaniah 1, 3-4). This point must never be lost from sight.

After giving you a general account of this phraseology, I now give detailed proof of the truth of my assertions. When God informed Isaiah of the collapse of the Babylonian empire and the destruction of Sennacherib and his successor Nebuchadnezzar and the end of his kingdom, he began to describe their misfortunes and defeats in the last days of their rule and the sufferings that would befall them, as they befall every defeated army fleeing from the power of the sword. He says: *For the stars of heaven and the constellations thereof shall not throw their light; the sun shall be darkened in his going forth and the moon shall not cause her light to shine* (Isaiah 13, 10). In the same description he further says: *therefore I will shake the heavens and the earth shall remove out of her place, in the wrath of the Lord of hosts and in the day of his fierce anger* (ibid. 13). I do not think that anyone can be so foolish and blind and clinging to the literal meaning of metaphors and rhetorical figures as to believe in earnest that the heavenly stars and the light of the sun and moon were affected when the empire of Babylon collapsed, or that the earth came off its hinges, as he says. No, all this is a description of the state of the defeated. To him indeed all light will appear dark and all sweetness bitter. In his imagination the earth has no room for him and the sky presses upon him. The same applies to Isaiah's description of the lowliness and depressed condition of Israel during the reign of the wicked Sennacherib, when he became master of *all the fortified cities of Judah* (Isaiah 36, 1), of their captivity, their defeat and the recurrent misfortunes which befell them through him, and the ruin of all the

Land of Israel by his hand. He says: *Fear and the pit and the snare are upon thee, o inhabitant of the earth. And it shall come to pass that he who fleeth from the noise of the fear shall fall into the pit, and he that cometh up out of the midst of the pit shall be taken in the snare: for the sluices from on high are open and the foundations of the earth do shake. The earth is utterly broken down, the earth is crumbled in pieces, the earth is moved exceedingly. The earth shall reel to and fro like a drunkard*, etc. (Isaiah 24, 17–20). And in the end of that same passage he sets about describing what God will do to Sennacherib, the annihilation of his arrogant domination over Jerusalem and the disgrace into which God would cast him for it. He says in metaphors: *then the moon shall be confounded and the sun ashamed, when the Lord of hosts shall reign*, etc. (ibid. 23). Jonathan ben Uzziel, peace upon him, interpreted this passage very well indeed. He says that when those things would happen to Sennacherib because of Jerusalem, the idolaters would realize that this was a divine act and would be frightened and confused. He says, in fact 'they that worship the moon will be confounded and they that bow to the sun will be dejected, for the sovereignity of God will be revealed, etc.'. Again, when he sets out to describe how Israel will be at rest after the death of Sennacherib and their land will be fertile and prosperous, and their affairs will prosper through the efforts of Hezekiah, he says by way of metaphor that the light of sun and moon will increase; for just as in speaking of the defeated he said that the light of sun and moon had gone and become darkness with regard to the defeated, so their light increases in the sight of the victorious.

Then, again, Isaiah sets out to give Israel the good news of the destruction of Sennacherib and all the nations and kings that were with him, as it turned out in the end, and their victory by the help of God alone. Speaking in metaphors, he says to them: look how those heavens are cut up and this earth is worn down and all who dwell on it are dead, while you are safe. It is as if he said that those who had embraced the whole earth and of whom it was thought – to express it by way of hyperbole – that they would last as long as the heavens, had swiftly perished and gone like smoke. Though their monuments were prominent and as established as the earth itself, those monuments disappeared like a worn-out garment. In the beginning of this passage he says: *For the Lord shall comfort Zion; He will comfort all her waste places*, etc. *Hearken unto me, my people*, etc. *My righteousness is near, my salvation is gone forth*, etc. *Lift up your eyes to the heavens and look upon the earth beneath: for the heavens shall vanish away like smoke and the earth shall be worn out like a garment, and they that dwell therein shall die in a like manner; but my salvation shall be forever and my righteousness shall not be abolished* (Isaiah 51, 3–6).

In speaking of the restoration of the kingdom of Israel and its future stability and perpetuity, he says that God will make a new heaven and earth. He does so because he consistently in his style represents the authority of a king as if it was a world peculiar to him, i.e. a heaven and an earth. Then having opened with tidings of consolation, and said: *I, even I, am he that comforteth you*, and so on (12), he then says: *I have put my words in thy mouth and I have covered thee in the shadow of mine hand, that I may plant the heavens and lay the foundations of the earth, and say unto Zion, Thou art my people* (16). Speaking of the permanence of power in Israel and the decadence of the famous great empires, he says: *for the mountains shall depart* (54, 10). In mentioning the permanent reign of the Messiah and stating that the kingdom of Israel will not be broken, he uses the words: *thy sun shall no more go down* (60, 20). Isaiah continues to speak in these consistent metaphors, obvious as such to all who understand the meaning of what he says. He describes the circumstances of the exile in all detail, then the return of independence and the wiping out of all that distress. In metaphorical language he says that God will create another heaven and another earth, while the present ones will be forgotten and their traces effaced. He immediately continues to explain this by stating in effect that by saying 'He would create', he meant that God would bestow upon them a condition of everlasting joy and gladness in place of that distress and hardship, so that the former distress would not be remembered any longer: *For behold, I create new heavens and a new earth, and the former shall not be remembered nor come into mind. But ye be glad and rejoice forever in that which I create, for behold, I create Jerusalem a rejoicing and her people a joy. And I will rejoice in Jerusalem,* etc. (65, 17–18).

This passage should give you the key for clearing up the whole matter. After saying: *for, behold, I create new heavens and a new earth,* he immediately goes on to elucidate this by adding: *for behold, I create Jerusalem a rejoicing and her people a joy.* After this introduction he says, in effect: those states of mind, faith and joy in it, which I have promised to you to bring about, are perpetually existing. For faith in God and joy in that faith are two states of mind which can never cease to exist or be altered in anyone who has achieved them. He says, therefore: Just as the state of faith and joy in it, of which I have promised that they will become general all over the earth, is everlasting and perpetual, so your progeny and your name shall be everlasting. That is the meaning of the passage that follows: *For as the new heavens and the new earth which I will make, shall remain before me, saith the Lord, so shall your seed and your name remain* (66, 22). It occurs sometimes that the *seed* remains but the *name* does not. Thus you find many nations who are no doubt the descendants of the Persians or the Greeks, but are not known by any special name, being included in another community. This is in my opinion also an indication of the perpetuity of the Law, for whose sake we have a *name* of our own.

We have been beating about the bush a good deal, but meanwhile our conclusion has become quite apparent: the idea that this world will perish or change from its present state, or that some of its nature will change and that it will persist in this change – that idea is not expressly stated in the text of any prophet.[51] Nor is it contained in the words of the Sages. True, they say 'Six thousand years the world will exist, and one thousand it will be waste' (Rosh Hashanah 31a), but this does not imply the cessation of the universe as a whole, for the words 'and one thousand years it will be waste' indicate that time, at any rate, will continue. Moreover, this is the opinion of one individual, and only refers to a definite form (of the world).

The opinion of all Sages throughout, and a fundamental principle which is adduced in argument by every one of the teachers of the Mishnah and the Talmud, is the phrase: *there is no new thing under the sun* (Ecclesiastes 1, 9). There is thus no innovation of any kind and for any reason. Even those who take 'new heavens and a new earth' literally, say: 'even the heavens and the earth that are going to be created, already are created and kept in reserve, as it is said *they remain before me*. It is not said *they will remain before me*, but *they remain*' (Bereshith Rabba I), and this contention is supported by: *there is no new thing under the sun*. You need not take this as contradicting my former explanations. Possibly the author of this statement intended that the natural conditions designed to bring about the promised circumstances have been existing from the six days of Creation, which is quite correct.

When I said that nothing in the *nature* of the world would change and persist in that changed condition, I did so to exclude miracles. True, the staff turned into a snake and the water into blood, and the pure and noble hand of Moses became white with leprosy without any natural cause necessitating all this. However, these and similar happenings did not persist or become a new nature. Instead, as our Sages said: 'the world continues according to its custom' (Abodah Zarah 54b). This is my opinion, and is the one that ought to be adopted. The Sages, however, have made a very peculiar statement about miracles, which you can find in full in Bereshith Rabba (V) and in Midrash Koheleth (*ad* 3, 14). Its gist is that they consider the miracles also in some way part of nature. They say, in effect, that when God created this universe and imprinted this nature on it, He made it part of those natural dispositions that all the miracles that happened should take place within them at the appointed time when they did take place. The wonder performed by the prophet consists in the fact that God informs him of the time when he should make his announcement. Then that event takes place exactly as was implied in its natural disposition when that disposition was originally given to it.[52]

This statement, if it is to be understood as I have summed it up, testifies to the high moral character of its author, and shows that he found it exceedingly difficult to accept that any natural disposition should alter after the act of creation, or that any divine will should supervene after things have been settled in this way. He holds, for instance, that God laid it into the nature of water that it should always form a continuous mass and run downwards except at the moment when the Egyptians were drowned in it, and then only that particular mass of water should divide itself. I have directed your attention to the spirit of that statement, namely that it is due to fear of admitting any possibility of innovation. It is said there:

'R. Jonathan says, God made an agreement with the sea that it should be torn apart before the children of Israel. That is the meaning of *and the sea returned to its former place* when the morning appeared* (Exodus 14, 27). Said R. Jeremiah b. Eleazar, not with the sea alone did God make such a covenant, but with everything that was created in the six days of creation. This is the meaning of: *I, even my hands, have stretched out the heavens, and all their host have I commanded* (Isaiah 45, 12). I then and there commanded the sea to divide itself, the fire not to hurt Hananiah, Mishael, and Azariah, the lions not to harm Daniel, and the fish to vomit out Jonah' (Bereshith Rabba, v, 5).

The same would, of course, apply to other miracles.

Thus the matter is clear from this short summary of our position. We agree with one half of Aristotle's theory, in so far as we believe this universe to be perpetual and everlasting, always possessing this nature which God has willed, without anything ever changing in any way except in a matter of detail through a miracle – though God has power to alter all of it, or terminate its existence, or terminate the existence of any natural feature He wishes. But – we say – the world had a beginning. There was nothing at all in existence apart from God, and His wisdom decreed that creation should come into being when He brought it into being, and also that that which He had brought into being should not cease to be, and that none of its natural features should change except in such matters of detail as He desired, some of which we know, and in other respects which

---

*Thus Targum Yerushalmi and the Vulgate. A.V. (with Onkelos): 'to its strength'.

we have not yet experienced but which will happen at some future time.

This is our view and the dogma of our faith. Aristotle holds that just as the world is everlasting and does not perish so it is eternal and has not come into being. We have said clearly that this does not make sense except on the assumption of automatic necessity, and that the assumption of automatic necessity implies, as we have explained, a certain contempt for the authority of God.

CHAPTER XXXII

THE opinions of men about prophecy are like their opinions about the eternity – or otherwise – of the world. I mean to say, just as those who acknowledge the existence of God hold three different opinions on the eternity or otherwise of the world, as we have explained, so there exist three different views about prophecy. I shall not detain myself with the view of Epicure, for he does not believe in the existence of God, leave alone the existence of prophecy. I only intend to mention the views of those who believe in God.

The first view is that of the ignorant mass,* as far as they believe in prophecy. Some of the common people of our own faith also believe in this view, which is that God chooses any man He wants, turns him into a prophet and sends him forth. It does not make any difference in their opinion whether that person is a learned man or an ignoramus, old or young. They make it, however, a prerequisite that he should also possess a certain degree of goodness and righteousness of character, for so far people have never said yet that God might make a prophet out of a wicked man, unless He first makes him good, in accordance with this view.

The second view is that of the philosophers. It says that prophecy is a kind of perfection in human nature. This perfection cannot be attained by a person except after training which brings the potential faculties of the species into actuality; that

*Or: heathen; perhaps: barbarians (Plessner).

is if there is no temperamental obstacle to this or some external reason to prevent it. It is in this respect like every other perfection which can exist in any species. Such a perfection will not actually be found in its full extent in every individual of that species, but inevitably and necessarily only in some individuals. If that perfection is such as to require an agent to bring it out, such an agent must first be there.

According to this view it is impossible for an ignorant person to become a prophet. Also a man cannot go to bed as an ordinary person and wake up as prophet, as if he had found something, but the process takes place in the following way. If a man is virtuous and perfect in both his logical and moral qualities, if his imaginative faculty is as perfect as can be, and he undertakes the preparation of which you will hear, he must necessarily become a prophet, since that perfection is natural to us. According to this view it is not possible that a man should be fit for prophecy and prepare himself for it and yet not become a prophet, any more than that a healthy man should eat wholesome food without it forming sound blood, or similar cases. [53]

The third view is that of our faith, in fact a principle of our religion. This is exactly the same as the philosophical view, except in one respect: we believe that a person who is fit for prophecy and has prepared himself for it may yet not become a prophet. That depends on the divine will, and is in my opinion like all other miracles and runs according to their pattern. The natural thing is that everyone who is fit by reason of his natural disposition and trained by reason of his education should become a prophet. One who is prevented from it is like one who is prevented from moving his hand like Jeroboam (1 Kings 13, 4) or from using his sight, like the army of the king of Syria when he wanted to get at Elisha (2 Kings 6, 18). That our dogma demands by necessity proper preparation and perfection in moral and logical qualities, is proved by the saying 'prophecy only dwells upon him who is wise, strong, and rich' (Shabbath 92a).* We have explained this in our commentary on the Mishnah and in our greater work (Mishneh Torah,

*In the Talmud: 'the divine presence . . .'. (Cf. also Nedarim 38a.)

Yesode Hatorah vii), where we stated that the 'sons of the prophets' were those constantly occupied with such preparation. That he who has prepared himself may sometimes not become a prophet is proved by the story of Baruch ben Neriah. He was a disciple of Jeremiah, and the latter trained him, taught him, and prepared him, and he ardently desired to become a prophet, but he was not allowed to become one, as he says: *I have laboured in my sighing and I find no rest* (Jeremiah 45, 3). Through Jeremiah the answer was given to him: *thus shalt thou say unto him, the Lord saith thus*, etc. *And seekest thou great things for thyself? seek them not* (ibid. 4, 5). It is indeed possible to say that this was a declaration that prophecy was too great for Baruch. It might also be said, with reference to the verse: *her prophets also find no vision from the Lord* (Lamentations 2, 9), that this was by reason of their being in exile, as we shall explain later. However, we find many passages, both in the Bible and in the words of the Sages, all of which consistently support this view: that God makes prophet whomever He wants and whenever He wants, but only a wholly perfect and virtuous person. As for an ignorant vulgar person, it is in our opinion utterly impossible that God should make him a prophet, any more than it would be possible that He would make a prophet out of an ass or a frog.

This, then, is our dogma: nothing can be done without training and perfection. It is this which provides the possibility of which divine power can take advantage. Do not be misled by the passage: *Before I formed thee in the belly I knew thee; and before thou camest forth out of the womb I sanctified thee* (Jeremiah 1, 5). This applies to every prophet, who requires some natural preparedness in his essential natural disposition, as will be shown later. As to the phrase: *I am a child* (ibid. 6), you know that the Hebrew language calls Joseph a child at a time when he was thirty years old* and calls Joshua a child at a time when he was nearly sixty; cf. the verse, referring to the story of the golden calf: *but his servant Joshua the son of Nun, a child, departed not*

---

*Genesis 41, 12. According to the Rabbis, Joseph was 18 years old when in Potiphar's house and spent 12 years in prison.

out of the tabernacle (Exodus 33, 11). Moses was at the time eighty-one and lived to 120. Joshua lived for fourteen years after his death and reached the age of 110. This proves that Joshua was at the time at least fifty-seven years old, and yet He called him a child.

Neither should you allow yourself to be misguided by the phrase in the Divine Promises: *I will pour out my spirit upon all flesh; and your sons and your daughters shall prophesy* (Joel 3, 1). The verse itself explains in what that prophecy was to consist, by saying *your old men shall dream dreams, your young men shall see visions.* Everyone who gives information on divine secrets, be it by clairvoyance or guesswork, or by true dreams, is also called a prophet. This is why the prophets of Baal and Asherah can be called prophets. Compare also the passage: *If there arise among you a prophet or a dreamer of dreams* (Deuteronomy 13, 2). In the events before Mount Sinai, where all of them witnessed the mighty fire and heard the terrible and frightening voices in a miraculous manner, the rank of prophecy was only attained by those who were fit for it, and that in different degrees, as is proved by the verse: *Come up unto the Lord, thou and Aaron, Nadab and Abihu, and seventy of the elders of Israel* (Exodus 24, 1). Moses himself was in the highest rank, for it is said: *And Moses alone shall come near the Lord, but they shall not come nigh* (ibid. 2). Aaron was beneath him, Nadab and Abihu beneath Aaron, and the seventy elders beneath Nadab and Abihu, while the rest of the people were inferior to them in proportion to their degrees of perfection. The Sages express this by saying: 'Moses had a partition to himself and Aaron had a partition to himself' (Mechilta on Exodus 19, 24).

CHAPTER XXXV

I HAVE made clear to everyone in my commentary on the Mishnah (on Sanhedrin x) and in the Mishneh Torah (Yesode Hatorah vii, 6) the four general features by which the Prophet-hood of Moses is distinguished from that of other prophets, and have there adduced full proofs. There is thus no need to repeat this, nor has it any connection with the subject of this treatise. What I want you to understand is that all statements I am making about prophecy in the course of this treatise refer to the type of prophecy given to all the prophets coming before or after Moses. The prophethood of Moses himself I do not discuss in these chapters either directly or by implication, nor do I refer to it with one word. In my opinion the name of prophet is only applied to Moses as well as to others by way of amphibological homonymy. The same is in my opinion the case with his miracles and those of others: his miracles are not in the same category as those of other prophets.

The Scriptural proof that his prophethood was distinguished from that of all those who preceded him is to be found in the verse: *And I appeared unto Abraham . . . but by my name YHWH I made me not known to them* (Exodus 6, 3). It is thus obvious that his perception of God was not like that of the Patriarchs, but greater, not to speak of the perception of others that had preceded him. The distinction between his prophethood and that of all who followed him is to be found plainly stated in the passage: *And there did not arise a prophet again in Israel like unto Moses whom the Lord knew face to face* (Deuteronomy 34, 10). It is thus clear that his perception of God was different from that of all that arose after him in Israel, who were *a kingdom of priests and an holy nation* (Exodus 19, 6), *and the Lord is among them* (Numbers 16, 3), leave alone those that arose in other nations.

CHAPTER XXXVI

It must be understood[54] that the true character of prophecy is that of an emanation flowing from God by means of the Active Intelligence first upon the rational faculty and thence upon the imaginative faculty. This is the highest rank attainable by man and the utmost degree of perfection which can be found in his species. That state is the highest degree of perfection of the imaginative faculty. Such a process can by no means take place in every man. It cannot be achieved by perfection in the speculative sciences or by improvement of character to the highest possible pitch of goodness and nobility, unless there is added to these the perfection of the imaginative faculty in the very core of one's natural disposition to the highest possible degree.

You are aware, of course, that the perfection of these physical faculties, to which the imaginative faculty belongs, is consequent upon the organ which carries that faculty having the best possible constitution and proportions and the purest substance possible. In such matters as these it is impossible to make up for any deficiencies or faults by any kind of physical training. When the constitutional disposition of an organ is bad, then the most one can hope of any regime designed to cure it is to preserve it in a healthy state, not to restore it to its most perfect state. If its defect is due to its proportions or its position or its substance – I mean the substance of the matter that makes it up – there is no cure for it.

You know all this, and there is no need to explain it at length. You are also, no doubt, acquainted with the activities of the imaginative faculty, such as retaining and combining the impressions of the senses (the sensibilia), and its natural propensity to imitation, as well as the fact that its greatest and noblest activity takes place just when the senses are at rest and do not function.[55] Then some kind of emanation flows upon it, according to its preparation; this is the cause of true dreams, and at the same time the cause of prophecy. The difference is only one of degree, not of kind. You probably know the dictum of the Sages which implies this similarity: 'dream is one sixtieth of prophecy' (Berakhoth 57b). No proportion could have thus been expressed between things different in kind. It would hardly make sense to say: the perfection of man is so many times that of a horse. The same thought is repeated in Bereshith Rabba (xvii, 5), where we find: 'the windfall of prophecy is dream'. This is an excellent comparison. The windfall is just the same as the fruit except that it has fallen off unripe and before its proper time. In the same way the activity of the imaginative faculty in the state of slumber is just the same as in the state of prophecy, except that it is incomplete and does not reach the final stage.

But why are we telling you about the sayings of the Rabbis and neglect the verse of the Torah: *If there be a prophet among you, I the Lord will make myself known to him in a vision and speak to him in a dream* (Numbers 12, 6)? Here God informs us of the true nature of prophecy. He tells us that it is an accomplishment that comes in a dream or a vision. The word *vision* (*mar'eh*) is derived from *videre* (*ra'ah*) 'to see'. It means that the action of the imaginative faculty becomes so perfect that you can see a thing as if it were outside you, and that the thing which is produced by it appears as if it had come to it by way of external sensation. In these two classes, vision and dream, are all the stages of prophecy, as we shall explain later.

It is well known that the matter with which a man is intensely occupied in his waking time and while in full possession of his senses and in which he is interested and to which he is drawn, will be the one on which the imaginative faculty will act during sleep, when the (Active) Intelligence emanates upon it according to its preparedness. It would be superfluous to give instances of this or talk about it at length, since it is an obvious thing which everyone knows. It is practically the same as the perception of the senses, about which no man of sound intellect holds any divergent opinion.

Having made these introductory remarks, I want you to imagine a human individual, the substance of whose brain by its essential natural disposition is perfectly balanced as regards purity of matter, the mixture proper to each part, proportion, and position, and who is not hampered by any defects of mixture in any other organ. Let such a man study and be educated until his potential abilities become realized in actuality and he attains a perfectly accomplished human reason, as well as a pure and balanced human character, and all his desires are concentrated upon seeking the knowledge of the secrets of this universe and the understanding of its causes. His thoughts are constantly directed towards noble subjects and his chief interest is the knowledge of God and the understanding of His actions, and what beliefs he should hold about them. He has given up all thought and desire for the animalic things, I mean the enjoyment of eating, drinking, and carnal intercourse, and with them the sense of touch, which Aristotle discusses in his *Ethics* (iii, 10) and of which he says that it is something for us to be ashamed of. How well said, and how true that it is a disgrace! We possess it in so far as we are mere animals, like the beasts. There is nothing in it of the concept of humanity. In the other sensual pleasures, such as smell, hearing, and sight, though they are physical, man can occasionally experience an enjoyment in so far as he is a human being, as Aristotle shows.

Our discussion has led us into things which do not belong, strictly speaking, to our subject. It requires them, though, since most of the thoughts of the outstanding men of learning are concerned with the pleasures of that sense (of touch) and they long for them. At the same time they wonder how it is that they do not prophesy, since after all prophecy is something natural.

It is also required of such a person that his thought of, and desire for, sham ambitions should have ceased. I mean by that the search for power or honour among the vulgar crowd and courting their respect and partisanship for the sheer lust of it. He must regard all men according to their circumstances. Seen from this point of view they are either like cattle or like wild beasts of prey, about whom the perfect and unworldly person only thinks, if he thinks of them at all, either to escape harm from them, if he happens to have any commerce with them, or else to get some benefit from them if he needs this for some of his purposes. If a person is of that type, there is little doubt that when his imaginative faculty, being of the utmost perfection, is active, and inspiration flows upon it from the Intellect, according to its speculative accomplishments, he will perceive nothing but very wonderful metaphysical matters, and will see nothing but God and His angels. He will not become aware of, or obtain any knowledge of, any matters but such as are true opinions or general rules of conduct for beneficial relations among men.

We have thus enumerated three points: the perfection of the rational faculty through education, perfection of the imaginative faculty through natural disposition, and perfection of character through stopping to think of all corporeal pleasures and dispelling one's desire for foolish and wicked honours. It is obvious that perfect individuals will differ greatly with regard to these three. According to the differences in each of these three matters will be the different degrees of all prophets. You know that every faculty of the body sometimes is blunted and weakened and disturbed, and at other times is sound. This imaginative faculty is certainly a faculty of the body. For this reason you find that the prophecy of prophets stops in times of grief or anger and the like. You are no doubt acquainted with the saying: 'Prophecy does not dwell upon a person either in sadness or in indolence' (Shabbath 30b), and with the fact that no revelation came to our father Jacob throughout the period of his grief because his imaginative faculty was occupied with the loss of Joseph (Pirqe R. Eliezer 38). You also know that Moses did not receive revelations as he used to from after the affair with the spies until the whole generation of the wilderness had gone (Taanith 30b, Pesachin 69b), because he suffered so deeply from their violent allegations* – and this in spite of the fact that the imaginative faculty played no role in his prophecy, but the flow of inspiration from the Intellect took place without its mediation. We have mentioned repeatedly that he did not prophesy in metaphors like other prophets. In the same way you will find that other prophets prophesied for a while and then prophecy was taken from them, as it could not continue owing to some incident that interfered with it. This was no doubt the immediate essential cause for the cessation of prophecy during the exile. What 'sadness' or 'indolence' can be worse for a man in any situation than being a slave subjected to wicked idolaters who combined the lack of true reason with full possession of all bestial lusts, *while there is no might in thy hand* (Deuteronomy 28, 32). This is exactly what we were foretold. This is what he meant by saying: *they shall run to and fro*

*Or: from their enormous sin.

to seek the word of the Lord, and shall not find it (Amos 8, 12), and
*her king and her princes are among the gentiles, the instruction of the
law is no more, her prophets also find no vision from the Lord*
(Lamentations 2, 9). This is quite true and the reason for it is
obvious: the instrument had become impaired. For this reason,
too, prophecy will come back to us in its normal form in the
days of the Messiah – may He reveal Himself speedily! – as we
have been promised.

CHAPTER XXXVII

IT is worth taking some trouble to get quite clear about the
exact manner in which we are subject to this divine emanation*
which reaches us and by which we achieve reason and our
minds are differentiated. A person may obtain some of it, just
enough to make him accomplished, but no more. The quantity
that reaches another person may be big enough to overflow
after having made him accomplished, so as to work for the
accomplishment of others. It is with this as with all things in
the world: some are so perfect as to guide others, and others get
just enough perfection to be guided by others,** as we have
explained before.

After these introductory remarks, it must be understood that
there are several possibilities: the stream of emanation from the
Intellect may flow only upon the rational faculty, without anything flowing from it upon the imaginative faculty. The reason
for this may be either because the quantity of the flow is too
small or because of some defect in the natural disposition of the
imaginative faculty, so that it cannot receive the emanation of
the Intellect. Such people form the class of scholars of a speculative bent. The inspiration may flow upon both faculties, the
rational and the imaginative, as I and other philosophers have
explained, and the imaginative faculty be of the utmost natural
perfection. That is the class of prophets. The emanation may
also flow only upon the imaginative faculty, the defect of the

*For Maimonides' opinion of the term, see p. 85.
**Other reading: to guide himself, but not others.

rational faculty being due either to its natural disposition or to lack of training. That class comprises administrators of states, lawgivers, soothsayers, augurs, and prophetic dreamers, as well as those that perform wonders by strange tricks and secret skills, although they are not possessed of any real knowledge. All these belong to this third class.

Here it is necessary to insist upon the fact that some men of that third-named class have, on occasion, experienced wonderful imaginations and dreams and trances in a waking state, which resemble the prophetic vision so much that they themselves think that they are prophets.[56] They are so impressed by what they perceive in those imaginations that they think they have obtained wisdom without study. They put forward horribly confused ideas on important speculative matters, and mix up in the most astonishing way true ideas and illusions. All this is due to the power of their imagination and weakness of their reason, in which nothing ever happens, I mean, which never becomes actual.

There are, of course, in each of these three classes great differences of degree. Both the two first classes are, as we have explained, divisible into two groups, because the emanation that reaches each class may either be of a quantity sufficient to make that man alone accomplished or be more than is needed for his personal perfection so that he can use it to perfect others. In the first class, the scholars, the emanation flowing upon the rational faculty may be sufficient to make that person able to investigate and understand, to know and to discern, without his making any move to teach others or to write; for he feels no desire for it nor is he able to do it. On the other hand the flow may be so powerful as to force him to write or teach.

The same applies to the second class. Some may receive just enough revelation so as to perfect themselves, and no more, others so much that they feel an urge to preach to people and teach them and to pass on to them some of their own perfection. You will see that but for that excess of perfection the sciences would not have been laid down in books, nor would any prophets have preached to men the knowledge of truth.

No scholar ever would write a book for himself in order to teach himself what he knows already. The nature of that Intellect is such that it flows continually and overflows from one recipient of the emanation to another successively, until it reaches an individual from whom the flow cannot pass on to another, but is just sufficient to effect his perfection.

The nature of this situation compels him who has received such an excessive quantity of emanation to preach to men, willy-nilly, whether they accept his teaching or not, and even if he suffers bodily harm. This goes so far that we find some prophets preached until they were killed, because that divine inspiration moved them and did not allow them to stop or tarry, though they were greatly afflicted. For this reason we find Jeremiah admitting openly that because of the contempt he suffered from those evildoers and unbelievers of his own time, he would have been glad to hide his prophecy* and not to preach to them the truth which they rejected; but he was unable to do so. He says: *because the word of the Lord is made a reproach unto me and a derision, all the day. Then I said, I will not make mention of him, nor speak any more in his name. But there was in my heart like a burning fire shut up in my bones, and I weary myself to hold it in, but cannot* (Jeremiah 20, 8–9). This is the meaning of the other prophet's saying: *the Lord God hath spoken; who can but prophesy?* (Amos 3, 8). Keep this well in mind.

CHAPTER XXXVIII

It must be fully realized that there is necessarily in every human being some aggressive faculty. But for it, he would not be moved in his mind to repel that which harms him. I hold that this faculty takes the same place among psychological forces as the power of repulsion among natural forces. The force of this aggressive faculty varies like that of other faculties. You may find some man who will attack a lion and another who will run away from a mouse, one who will attack an army and fight them, and another who will tremble and fear when a

*Other reading: to put a stop to his prophesying.

woman shouts at him. There certainly must be some temperamental disposition rooted in one's nature, which can be increased by methods designed to make actual that which is
potential and by a certain mental attitude. Similarly it can be
diminished by lack of occasion and by a different mental
attitude. You can observe the differences in degree of this
faculty in boys right from their childhood.

In the same way this faculty of divination is found in all
human beings, only in different degrees. It works in particular
in matters in which a man is intensely interested and round
which his mind turns, so much so that you may feel in your
own mind that a certain person has done or said a certain thing
in a certain affair, and it really turns out to be so. You will find
some people possessing a very powerful and sure gift of surmise and divination, so strong that they hardly ever imagine a
thing to take place but that it takes place wholly or partly as
they imagined it. There are many causes for such an event,
dependent on a variety of circumstances before, after, and during the event, but owing to these powers of divination the
brain reviews all these premises and draws conclusions from
them in the shortest possible time so that it might be thought
to have been done in no time. By means of this faculty some
men can give warning of important impending events.

These two faculties, the aggressive and the divinatory, must
of course be very strong in prophets. When the Intellect inspires
them, these two faculties become very much intensified until
they produce the well-known results: a single man with his
stick approaches a powerful king in order to free a people from
slavery; and this man is neither frightened nor apprehensive,
because he has been told: *I will be with thee* (Exodus 3, 12). They
possess this quality, too, in different degrees, but all must have
it, as was said to Jeremiah: *Be not afraid of them . . . be not dismayed of them . . . for behold I have made thee this day a fortified
city* (Jeremiah 1, 8, 17, 18), and to Ezekiel: *be not afraid of them,
nor of their words* (Ezekiel 2, 6). Thus you will find all of them
to be men of a strongly aggressive spirit and endowed with
ample gifts of divination so that they can tell of impending

events in the shortest possible time. In this respect, too, they differed, as you are no doubt aware.

It must be fully understood that true prophets without any doubt attain to speculative perceptions of such a kind that no man by mere speculation could have perceived the causes that necessarily led to that conclusion. Similarly they announce events that no man could have foretold by mere common surmise and intuition. The reason is that same emanation, which flows upon the imaginative faculty until it perfects the latter to such an extent that it functions so as to foretell future events, and perceives them as if they were events perceived by the senses and had reached the imaginative faculty through the senses – that same emanation also perfects the functions of the rational faculty so that it functions in such a way as to know things as they truly are, and obtains that perception as if it had deduced them from speculative premises. This is the truth which everyone believes who wishes to be just, for each of these things bears out the correctness of all the others.

It stands to reason that all this applies especially to the rational faculty. After all, this faculty is the one which is the recipient of the emanation from the Active Intelligence and which is brought into actuality by it, and only from the rational faculty does the emanation pass on to the imaginative faculty. How then can it be explained that the perfection of the imaginative faculty reaches such a pitch that it apprehends things that have not been communicated to it through the senses, if the rational faculty were not to gain similar advantages in being able to apprehend things it could not have apprehended through reflection and logical deduction from premises? This is the true meaning of prophecy, and those the features which distinguish prophetic teaching.

CHAPTER XXXIX

HAVING thus spoken of the nature of prophecy, and having discovered its true character and made clear at the same time that the prophethood of our teacher Moses was different from that of all others, let us state that this conclusion in itself is sufficient ground for proclaiming the validity of the Law.* Nothing like the mission of Moses to us ever took place in any society known to us from Adam until Moses, nor has any similar mission ever been accorded after him to any of our prophets. It is, indeed, the foundation of our Law that no other will ever take place. Therefore, according to our opinion, there never was nor ever will be more than one Law, namely that of Moses.[57]

The evidence for this, as put down in the Bible and later writings is that none of the prophets that preceded Moses, such as the patriarchs, Sem, Eber, Noah, Methuselah, and Enoch, ever said to a group of people: 'God sent me to you and commanded me to tell you this and that; He forbids you to do thus and thus and commands you to do thus and thus'. Neither the text of the Torah nor any reliable tradition ever said such a thing. What happened is that these men received revelations from God in the way we have explained before, and those whose share of the divine emanation was strong, like Abraham, gathered people around them and preached to them by way of instruction and communication of the truth they had apprehended. Thus Abraham would instruct people and explain to them with speculative proofs that there was one God in the world, who had created all other things, and it was not right to worship images, or any created thing. He would enjoin people to keep to this and would attract them by well-chosen words and kindness; but he never said: 'God has sent me to you and has enjoined on me certain positive and negative commandments'. Indeed when he was commanded to circumcise himself, his sons, and those attached to him, he did circumcise them, but did not call upon people in general to do so, after the manner of prophetic preaching. This can be seen from the very words of Scripture: *For I know him, that he will command his children and his household after him, and they shall keep the way of the Lord, to do justice and judgment* (Genesis 18, 19). From this it is obvious that he did so only by way of moral persuasion.

*Or: that his perception was sufficient to cause him to proclaim the Law.

The same applies to Isaac, Jacob, Levi, Kohath, and Amram, who were preaching to people in this manner. The Sages say of the prophets who preceded him: 'the law court of Eber, the law court of Methuselah, the homiletic teaching of Methuselah'.* All of these – may peace be upon them – were prophets who taught people in the manner of instructors, teachers, and moral guides, not by saying: 'God said to me, speak to the sons of so-and-so'.

This was the state of affairs before Moses. As for Moses himself, you well know what was said to him, what he said, and that all the congregation said of him: *we have seen this day that God doth talk with man, and he liveth* (Deuteronomy 5, 24**). To come to the prophets that arose after Moses, you are aware of all their stories as told, and know that their position was that of warners to the people, whom they called to the Law of Moses. They threatened those that turned away from it and made promises to those that were steadfast in observing it. We further believe that this will always be so, as it is said: *It is not in heaven that thou shouldst say, Who shall go up for us to heaven and bring it unto us,* etc. (Deuteronomy 30, 12), and *those things which are revealed belong to us and to our children for ever* (Deuteronomy 29, 29***).

This is just as it ought to be. If a thing is as perfect as it can possibly be within its own species, then anything existing within that species cannot but fall short of that degree of perfection, either by excess or deficiency. For instance, if a thing possesses the most perfectly balanced mixture possible within that species, then every mixture deviating from this perfect balance will have either too much or too little. This is the case with this Law, in view of its perfect balance which is clearly stated in the words *equitable laws and statutes* (Deuteronomy 4, 8). You know, of course, that equitable (*tzaddiq*) is the same as well-balanced. It consists of acts of worship not implying any burden or exaggeration, such as monasticism §

*Cf. Bereshith Rabba xliii.
**In Hebrew vs. 21.
***In Hebrew vs. 28.
§Other reading: as that of the Brahmins.

or itinerant dervish life and the like, nor a lack of religious duties which leads to gluttony or indulgence and ultimately to a decline of man from his moral and intellectual perfection, as happened with the religions of the nations of antiquity.* When we shall, later in this treatise, discuss the reasons for the laws, you will obtain a sufficient idea of its equability and wisdom. This is why it is said of it: *the statutes of the Lord are perfect* (Psalm 19, 8).

Only this Law do we call a divine law. The other systems of political constitution, such as the laws of the Greeks and the puerilities of the Sabians and others, are all the work of human planners, not of prophets, as I have repeatedly explained.

CHAPTER XL

It has, I think, been made perfectly clear that man is by nature sociable. His nature is to live in a community; he is not in this respect like other animals, for whom life in a community is not a necessity. This is due to the high degree of compositeness in this species. As you know, man is the most composite being, and therefore there are great differences between human individuals. You will hardly ever find two persons alike in any class of moral characteristics any more than you will find them alike in their external appearance. The reason for this is the difference of mixture. Both the substances and the accidents pursuant to the form differ. Every natural form is associated with certain accidents peculiar to it and pursuant to it, which are distinct from the accidents pursuant to the substance. Nothing like this immense range of individual differences is to be found in any species of animal. The differences between the individuals of any species of living beings are small, except in man. You will find that any two of us are so different as if they were of different species in every feature of character. The harshness of one person may reach such a limit that he will kill his youngest son in anger, while another feels sorry for killing a

*Other reading: of the heathen.

gnat or other insect and becomes depressed over it. The same applies to most other features.

Seeing that the nature of man brings with it such enormous differences between individuals and at the same time requires life in society, it would be impossible for any society to come about except through a leader who co-ordinates their actions, supplements what is imperfect and restrains exaggeration, and lays down standards for their activities and behaviour so that they can always act according to the same standard. Thus the natural differences will be masked by the large degree of conventional co-ordination, and the community will be well-ordered. For this reason I say that the Law, though it is not part of nature, yet is closely interwoven with nature. It is part of the wisdom of God in maintaining this human species – since He willed its existence – that He made it part of their nature that some individuals possess the faculty of leadership.[58]

To some of these leaders the content of their mission is directly communicated. These are the prophet and the law-giver. Others have power only to enforce in practice what the former two have laid down,* to follow it up and to bring it into actuality. They are the ruler who adopts the laws and the pretender to prophethood who adopts the religious law of the prophet, either in its entirety or in part. He may choose the latter course either because it is easier for him, or in order to make people believe that these things came to him in a revelation and that he is not a mere follower of someone else. They do this out of jealousy, for there are men who are attracted by certain accomplishments and experience a desire and longing for them; they wish people to imagine that they possess that accomplishment, though they themselves know that they have nothing of it. For instance, you often find people claiming other people's poems or plagiarising them. The same happens in some scientific publications and with many details of various sciences when an envious and lazy person gets hold of a new idea of someone else's and claims that he thought of it first.

The same thing happens also with the accomplishment of

*Other reading: what the prophet has proclaimed.

prophecy. We find that some people claimed prophethood and said things which had never been revealed by God at all, such as Zedekiah, the son of Chenaanah.* Others, we find, claimed prophethood and said things which God most certainly had said – I mean to say, these things had been revealed, but not to them, as in the case of Hananiah, the son of Azzur** – and they appropriated them and used them for their own aggrandisement.

All these things are obvious and easy to distinguish. I am only explaining them to remove any doubts in your mind and to provide you with a standard by which you can differentiate between systems of law based on human agreement, those based on divine Law, and lastly those promulgated by men who have taken some prophetic utterances, and by way of plagiarism claim them as their own. In those cases where the originators of laws have clearly stated that they had made them up from their own minds, no further arguments are needed in face of this admission by the party itself, which dispenses with all need for evidence. What I want to discuss are those systems of law concerning which it is claimed that they are of prophetic origin. Of these some are prophetic, i.e. divine, others are human laws (*nomoi*), others again stolen. You may find that the whole purpose of a system of law and the intention of its administrator who directs its functions, is solely to order the affairs of the state and to free it from injustice and dissension, but there is in it no striving for speculative accomplishments or any attention to the development of the rational faculty. Such a system does not care about people's opinions, be they true or faulty, but its only aim is to regulate the relations of people amongst each other, in some way or other, and to provide for them some imaginary*** happiness according to the views of that administrator. You will, of course, realize that that law is of human origin, and that its originator is, as we have shown, of the third class, namely of those perfected only in their imaginative faculty.

*I Kings 22, 11.
**Jeremiah ch. 28.
***This word is missing in some MSS.

Then you may find another system of law, all of whose ordinances have regard to the proper management of physical matters as described above, but also to the establishment of proper beliefs, and which makes it its business to implant true ideas about God and the angels in the first instance, and which aims to make man wise, knowledgeable, and mentally active, so that he obtains a true idea of the whole universe. You will know that this ordinance is from God and this law is divine.[59]

It remains for you to discover whether the alleged originator is that accomplished person to whom it was revealed or an individual who merely appropriated those ideas and pretended they were his own. The method for examining this is to investigate the character of that person, to follow up his actions, and to study his life. Your most important indication is the rejection and contempt of bodily pleasures, for that is the first stage of achievement of scholars, how much more so of prophets. This applies specially to the senses, which, as Aristotle says, are shameful for us,[60] and more particularly to the filth of sexual intercourse. This is why God used just this to disgrace all pretenders, so that truth might become known to those who seek it and they might be neither deceived nor misled. Just consider how Zedekiah, the son of Maaseiah, and Ahab, the son of Kolaiah, claimed prophecy and men followed them when they uttered revelations which had been received by others. Then they became involved in vile sexual lust, so that they committed adultery with wives of their colleagues and followers, until God brought their crimes to light as He had disgraced others before them, and the king of Babylon had them burned, as Jeremiah says: *And of them shall be taken up a curse by all the captivity of Judah which are in Babylon, saying, The Lord make thee like Zedekiah and like Ahab whom the king of Babylon roasted in the fire; Because they have committed villainy in Israel, and have committed adultery with their neighbours' wives, and have spoken words in my name falsely, which I have not commanded them; even I know and I am a witness, saith the Lord* (Jeremiah 29, 22–3). Get this point quite clear.

CHAPTER XLII

W E have made it clear that wherever seeing, or being addressed by, an angel is mentioned, this refers to prophetic vision or to a dream. [61] It makes no difference whether this fact is explicitly stated or not, as we have said before. Take this to mind and carefully consider it in all its implications.

It is all the same whether the particular passage says first that he saw the angel, or the phrasing implies that he thought at first it was a human being and then in the end he realized it was an angel. Whenever it turns out in the end that what he saw, and was addressed by, was an angel, you must accept it as true that this was from the outset a prophetic vision or a prophetic dream. In such a prophetic vision or prophetic dream the prophet sometimes sees God speaking to him, as we shall mention later, or he may see an angel who speaks to him, or hear someone speak to him without seeing anyone speaking, or he may see a human being speaking to him and afterwards he realizes that the one who spoke to him was an angel. It is with reference to this latter type of prophecy that it is said that someone saw a man say or do something and then knew that it was an angel.

This great principle was enunciated by one of our Rabbis, one of the greatest among them, namely R. Hiyya the Elder, when discussing the verse: *And the Lord appeared unto him in the plains of Mamre*, etc. (Genesis 18, 1). After the introductory sentence, which is that God appeared to him, Scripture explains what form this appearance took. It states that first he saw three men, and ran, and *they* said, and he said to *them*,* etc. The Sage who gives this explanation says that the words of Abraham: *My Lord, if now I have found favour in thy sight, pass not away, I pray thee, from thy servant* (ibid. 3) were also a description of what he said in a prophetic vision to one of them. He specifies: 'he said it to the greatest among them' (Bereshith Rabba xlviii, 3). Take good note of this story, for it is one of the mysteries.

I give a similar explanation of the story of Jacob, where it

*Reading *wa-qála* (Hirschfeld).

says: *and there wrestled a man with him* (Genesis 32, 25). I say that it belongs to the category of revelation, since in the end it turned out that it was an angel. It is just the same as the story of Abraham: the latter is introduced by a general statement *and God appeared to him,* etc., and then only it is explained how this took place. So too in the case of Jacob. He says: *and the angels of God met him* (ibid. 2), then goes on to explain what happened until they met him. He states that he sent messengers, and did this and that, *and Jacob was left alone* (25). These, then, are the same angels of God of whom it is said in the beginning: *and the angels of God met him.* All this wrestling and conversation took place in prophetic vision.

Similarly in the story of Balaam: the happenings on the way and the speech of the she-ass, all took place in a prophetic vision, since in the end it turns out to be the angel of God speaking to him. I hold the same with regard to the incident with Joshua: *he lifted up his eyes and looked, and behold there stood a man over against him* (Joshua 5, 13), namely that it took place in a prophetic vision, for in the end it transpires that it was *the captain of the Lord's host.* On the other hand, as regards the passage: *And an angel of the Lord came up from Gilgal . . . and it came to pass when the angel of the Lord spake these words unto all the children of Israel . . .* (Judges 2, 1-4), our Rabbis have already said that the angel of God mentioned here was Phineas. They say: 'this was Phineas, for while the Divine Presence was dwelling upon him, he resembled an angel of the Lord' (Wayyiqra Rabba i). We have explained before that the word 'angel' (*mal'akh*) is homonymous, and that a prophet, too, may be called 'angel' (messenger), as in the passage: *and He sent an ANGEL and brought us out of Egypt* (Numbers 20, 16), and in: *then spake Haggai the Lord's messenger* (*mal'akh*) *in the Lord's message* (*mal'akhuth*) *unto the people* (Haggai 1, 13).

From the instances I have quoted inference may be made to other cases I have not mentioned.

BOOK III

CHAPTER XII

IT frequently occurs to popular imagination that the evil things in the world are more numerous than the good things. This idea is implied in many of the sayings and songs of most nations. They say that it is a wonder if something good is found once in a while, but the evils of fate are many and persistent. This erroneous opinion is not only current among the vulgar, but also among those who think they know something. There is a well-known book by Rhazes, entitled *The Theology*, in which he put together many of his mad and foolish ideas.[62] Among these is an assertion of his own invention: that more evil exists than good, i.e. when you compare the quiet times a man enjoys and the pleasure he derives from them with the pains and severe accidents, bodily defects, paralyses of limbs, terrors, worries and afflictions which he experiences, you find that man's existence is a scourge and a terrible evil inflicted upon him. To prove the truth of this view he sets about enumerating all those evils, so as to contradict all that men of truth have said concerning God's mercy towards His world and His manifest goodness, and His being without any doubt the absolute good, as well as that all things derived from Him are absolutely good. The cause of the error is that this fool and his fellows from among the vulgar look upon the world only from the point of view of a human. Every fool thinks the whole world exists for his sake, as if there were nothing but he himself: if things turn out contrary to his desires he concludes that all the universe is bad. If man would but examine the universe and picture it to himself, and realize clearly his small importance within it, he would understand the truth in all its clarity.

For this interminable drivel of men about the great number of evils in the world does, as they themselves admit, not apply to the angels, the spheres and stars, the elements and the minerals and plants composed of them, or even the various kinds of animals. All their thoughts are concentrated on some individuals of the human species. When a man goes on eating noxious food until he develops elephantiasis, they wonder how this great evil befell him and how it comes to exist at all. Similarly they find it strange if someone has practised excess in cohabitation until his eyes grew weak, and find it hard to understand why this man should have been stricken by blindness, and so in other cases. The truth of the matter is that all men alive, leave alone other animals, are in no way commensurable with the whole of the universe in its continuity, as is clearly stated in the verses: *Man is like to a whiff of air* (Psalm 144, 4); *How much less man that is a worm, and the son of man that is a maggot?* (Job 25, 6); *How much less they that dwell in houses of clay?* (Job 4, 19); *Behold the nations are as a drop of a bucket, and are counted as the small dust of the balance* (Isaiah 40, 15). More passages occur in the books of the prophets on this important topic, which is most useful to teach man his own value and to dispel the erroneous idea that the universe exists for his sake alone.

On the contrary, in our opinion the universe exists because of God's will alone. In it the human species is unimportant in comparison with the higher universe, i.e. spheres and stars. As for the angels, no comparison with man is at all possible. Man, however, is the most important among those things that have come into being, namely, in this lower world of ours. I mean to say he is the noblest among the creatures that are composed of the elements. Therefore, his existence is a great benefit and act of grace towards him on the part of God, seeing that he singled man out and gave him perfection. Most evils that befall individuals are due to themselves, that is to say to imperfect individuals. Because of our own imperfections we wail and ask to be delivered. When we suffer from the evils we have brought upon ourselves by our own free will, we attribute them to God – far be it from Him! – as He says in His own Book: *Is corruption His? No; His children's is the blemish** (Deuteronomy 32, 5), and as Solomon explains: *The foolishness of man perverteth his way* (Proverbs 19, 3).

---

*Thus the *American Jewish Version*, which seems of all translations of this difficult verse to come closest to the sense intended here.

CHAPTER XIII

THE minds of accomplished men often are bewildered by the search for the purpose of this universe. I shall explain here why this investigation is pointless, whichever view we take.

Every maker works with some aim or object. The thing which is made must necessarily have some purpose for the sake of which it is made. This is obvious and does not require any proof by philosophical speculation. It is also obvious that the thing thus made for some aim must have come into being, not having existed before. It is furthermore obvious and generally agreed that something that exists by necessity, and therefore never was nor will ever be non-existent, does not require a maker, as we have explained before. Since it is not made, the question about its purpose is pointless. Therefore one cannot say, 'what is the purpose of the Creator?', as he is not a created thing.

From these premises it is clear that a purpose can only be sought with reference to something non-eternal which has been made by the design of a being gifted with reason. Where a thing has a rational principle we cannot but inquire after its final cause. In the case of an uncreated thing, however, no purpose is to be looked for, as we have said before.

After this introduction, I claim that there is no point in the search for a purpose of the universe as a whole, either according to our view that the world is created, or according to the view of Aristotle that it is uncreated. If one accepts Aristotle's view that the world is uncreated, no ulterior purpose can be sought for any part of the world; for in accordance with his system it is not permissible to inquire what is the purpose of the existence of the heaven, why is it of those proportions or numbers, or why matter is of that particular nature or what is the purpose of any particular kind of animal or plant. With him, everything exists by eternal necessity which persists uninterruptedly and will never cease. Natural science may, of course, inquire after the purpose of any natural object, but that is not the ultimate purpose with which we are concerned in this chapter. It is made clear in the *Physics* (ii, 8) that every natural object must have some purpose. This final cause, which is the most important of the four causes, is unknown for most species. Aristotle constantly stresses that 'nature does nothing in vain', i.e. that every natural occurrence must needs have a purpose. Aristotle also states that the plants were created because of the animals. With regard to some objects it is clear that they exist for some definite purpose, especially with the organs of animals.

You must understand that the existence of such purpose in natural processes led the philosophers of necessity to the belief in another, extranatural principle, which Aristotle names the rational or divine principle. It is the principle which causes the existence of some things for the sake of others. I should like to remark here that one of the most important arguments for a created world in the eyes of an unprejudiced person is the proof that every natural object has a purpose and that things exist for the sake of each other, as this points to design, and no design can be imagined except where something is newly brought into being.

To come back to the subject of this chapter, the discussion of purpose: Aristotle has shown that in nature effective, formal, and final cause may be one, i.e. one in kind. Thus the form of John, for example, is the effective cause of the form of the person of Jack, his son. What it effected is the bestowal of a form of its own kind upon the matter constituting Jack. The purpose of Jack is that he should bear human form. The same applies in his view to every individual of the natural species that have recourse to procreation: the three causes are in their case of one kind.[63] All this is, however, only the primary cause. As to the existence of an ultimate purpose of every species, every one who discusses nature asserts that there must be such a one, but to discover it is a difficult matter, leave alone discovering the purpose of the universe as a whole. From the words of Aristotle it appears that he holds the ultimate purpose of these species to be, on the one hand, the perpetuation of generation and corruption, which in turn is necessary for keeping the process of being going in this prime matter, whose individual aspects cannot be permanent; on the other hand, that the ultimate thing should arise from them that can possibly arise, i.e. the most perfect thing possible. For the ultimate aim is the attainment of perfection. It is obvious that the most perfect thing that can arise out of this matter is man, and that he is the most composite being as well as the most perfect one, so much so that if we say that all things existing beneath the sphere of the moon are for his sake, this would be true from this point of view, i.e. in the sense that the movement implied in the change of things takes place because of the tendency towards evolving the most perfect thing that can exist.

For Aristotle, with his view of an uncreated world, there is no need to ask what is the purpose of the existence of man. With him, the immediate purpose of every emerging individual is the perfection of the generic form. Every individual in which the functions connected with that form are perfectly developed, has fulfilled its purpose perfectly and completely. The ultimate purpose of the species is the perpetuation of that form so as to carry on the cycle of generation and corruption, in order that there may always be a cosmos in which the most perfect possible thing can be striven for. It is thus obvious that in accordance with the view of an uncreated world there is no point in the search for an ultimate purpose of the universe as a whole. [64]

In accordance with our own theory and view that the world in its entirety came into being out of non-existence, it might be thought that this inquiry about the purpose of this whole universe would be logically consistent. It might also be thought that the purpose of the whole universe was nothing but the existence of man so that he might serve God, and that all that was made was made for him, so that even the spheres only revolve for his benefit and the provision of his needs. This idea is strongly supported by the apparent meaning of certain passages in the Prophets: *He formed it to be inhabited* (Isaiah 45, 18); *But for my covenant of the law, which is to be studied day and night, I should not have appointed the ordinances of heaven and* *earth* (Jeremiah 33, 25);* or *that stretches out the heavens as a curtain and spreadeth them out as a tent to dwell in* (Isaiah 40, 22). If the heavenly spheres exist for the sake of man, how much more does this apply to other species of animals and to plants.

If this theory is followed up, as learned men should follow up any theory, it will become plain how unsound it is. Let us assume that one who believes in it would be asked: is the Creator able to bring about this purpose, viz. the existence of man, without all these preparations, or is it only possible for man to exist after these have been provided? If someone should reply that this is possible, and that God is able to create man without, for instance, there being a heaven, we should ask: what object did He then pursue with** all these things, which are not a purpose in themselves, but only exist for the sake of another thing which could perfectly well exist without them all? What is more, even if all things exist for the sake of man, and the purpose of man, as they say, is to engage in worship, the problem remains, namely, what is the purpose of His worship, since God's perfection is not increased even if everything He has created worships Him and apprehends Him to the utmost possible degree, nor is it at all diminished if there is nothing in existence beside Him? Let our interlocutor say now that this worship is not for the sake of the perfection of God but for our own perfection, because it is the finest thing for us and constitutes our ultimate perfection. Then we must repeat the same question: what is the purpose of our existence in possession of this perfection? Whatever we say, the discussion will end with our admission, on the subject of purpose, that God willed it thus or that His wisdom decreed it thus. This is the correct answer.[65]

You will find that the Sages of Israel expressed it thus in their prayers: 'Thou hast set man apart from the beginning and acknowledged him that he should stand before Thee, Yet who shall say unto Thee, 'What dost thou?', and if he be righteous,

---

*Rendered according to the Midrashic interpretation on which its use here is based (Pesachin 68b, cf. Rashi there).

**Thus all Arabic MSS.; Tibbon: what is the use of . . .

what boon is that to Thee?' (Ne'ilah Amidah, Service of the Synagogue, Day of Atonement, II, 251). They clearly say that there is no purpose here, only will and will alone. Since this is so, and the necessary result of our belief in a created world is the admission of the possibility that the universe, with all its causes and effects, might have existed in a different or even contrary form, we arrive at the absurd conclusion concerning the existence of all that exists apart from man, that it exists without any purpose whatsoever, since the only purpose envisaged, viz. man, could exist without any of it.

For this reason I hold that the view which is correct, and in accordance both with our religious beliefs and the above philosophical considerations, is not to believe that all things exist for the sake of the existence of man, but that all other things were intended for their own sake, not for the sake of any other thing. Thereby any investigation of the purpose of all species of things becomes pointless, even according to our own view, that the world is created. We say that He created all individual objects of the world according to His will; some of them are intended for their own sakes, others for the sake of something else, which in its turn is intended for its own sake. Just as God willed that the human species should exist, so He willed that the heavens and the stars on them should exist, and likewise He willed that the angels should exist. With every thing He intended that thing itself. Whenever a thing could not exist but with another thing as a premise, He brought that other thing into existence first, as when He created the senses as a preparation for the logical faculty.

This notion is also expressed in the Bible: *Everything hath the Lord wrought for its destined end* (Proverbs 16, 4). The pronoun may refer to the object. If it is taken as referring to the subject, the meaning of *lema'anehu* is 'for His own sake', i.e. His will, since this is His substance, as has been explained in this treatise. We have shown that His essence is also called His Glory in the verse: *Let me see, I beseech thee, thy glory* (Exodus 33, 18). Therefore, the expression used here, 'Everything hath the Lord wrought for His own sake' means the same as: *Every*

*one that is called by my name and whom I have created for my glory,
I have formed him; yea, I have made him* (Isaiah 43, 7). He says
there: all those things whose creation is attributed to me I made
for the sake of my will and for no other reason. The phrase 'I
have formed him; yea, I have made him' refers to the point
mentioned above; viz. that there are things which cannot exist
except following upon the existence of certain other things.
He therefore says: I have called into being that first thing which
is needed as a premise, as, e.g., matter, for everything consisting
of matter; then I made out of, or after, that earlier thing that
which I had intended to bring into existence. There is nothing
here but will, and will alone.

If you study that book which guides everyone who accepts
guidance – for which reason it is called *Torah*, guidance,* –
you will clearly see the idea which we are trying to evolve here
appearing in the story of Creation from beginning to end. It is
not declared there of any thing that it exists because of some
other thing, but with regard to every single object it is stated
that He brought it into being and that its existence conformed
to His intention. This is the meaning of the phrase 'and God
saw that it was good'. You will, no doubt, remember our
interpretation of the saying 'the Torah speaks according to the
language of men';** how the word 'good' expresses with us
that something is in conformity with our intention. Of the
whole it is said: *And God saw every thing that he had made, and
behold, it was very good* (Genesis 1, 31). Thus, everything had
come about in conformity with His intention and will never
be upset, as is shown by the use of 'very'; for it sometimes
happens that a thing is good and in conformity with our intention for a while, but then fails in its purpose. We are, therefore,
informed that all those things which were made turned out
according to His purpose and intention and permanently
remain as they were intended. You must not allow yourself to
be misled by the passage about the stars, *to give light upon the*

*For this rendering, cf. the lexicon by David b. Abraham of Fez (ed. Skoss, i, 8),
where the root-meaning is given as *hidâya*, the word used by Maimonides here. That
lexicon is largely based on the work of Saadiah, which Maimonides certainly knew.
**Yebamoth 71a, discussed Guide of the Perplexed Book I, ch. xxvi.

earth, and to rule by day and by night (Genesis 1, 17-18), into thinking that it means they were created for the sake of this function. It is a statement about their nature: it pleased Him to create them thus, i.e. giving light and ruling. In the same way He said to Adam: *and have dominion over the fish of the sea* (ibid. 28), which, of course, does not mean that man was created for this purpose, but is a statement about the nature which God bestowed upon him.

We are thus necessarily led to the belief that this whole universe was intended by God according to His will, and we shall not in any way seek for it another reason or purpose. As we shall not inquire into the purpose of the existence of God, so we shall not inquire into the purpose of His will, according to which everything past and future is happening in the way it happens. Do not allow yourself to be misled into thinking that it is because of us that spheres and angels exist. Our own value is clearly stated in the verse: *behold, nations are as a drop out of a bucket* (Isaiah 40, 15). Just visualize your own substance and that of the spheres and stars and incorporeal intelligences, and the truth will become clear to you. You will understand that man is the most perfect and noble being created out of matter, but no more. If his mode of existence is compared with that of the spheres, leave alone of the incorporeal things, he will appear exceedingly unimportant.[66]

This is what we ought to believe. Only if a man knows himself and has no illusion about himself and understands every existing thing in relation to itself, he will find real rest. Then his mind will not be disturbed by searching for a purpose in something which has not that kind of purpose, or no purpose at all except its own existence, which depends upon the will of God.

CHAPTER XVI

WITH regard to the question whether God knows what exists beside Himself, the philosophers have produced some reckless, self-confident nonsense,* and have come to grief in such a way

* Reading *iftāta,*

that no one can help them any more to pick themselves up, nor those who follow them in this theory. I shall tell you exactly what erroneous processes of thought have enmeshed them in their reckless assertions, and shall then tell you the views of our religion concerning these things and our defence against their evil and absurd statements on the subject of God's knowledge.

The factor which most contributed to their becoming involved in those errors and indeed first caused them to conceive them was the impression, so easily gained by a superficial approach, that there is no order in the affairs of human individuals. Some men of good character lead lives of lowliness and suffering, while some wicked people enjoy an agreeable existence. This has led our philosophers to posit the following alternatives: either God is unaware of these personal conditions and does not perceive them, or He knows of them and perceives them. If He does know and perceive them, then there are three alternatives: either He arranges them and directs them along the best and most perfect lines, or He is restrained by outside forces from arranging them and has no power over them, or He knows the proper way to arrange them and is able to carry it out, but neglects to do so either through contempt and scorn or out of jealousy.

Having posited these alternatives, they cut the discussion short and decide off-hand that two of these three alternatives – which could with equal cogency be stated of every one who is gifted with knowledge – are inadmissible in the case of God, namely that He should have no power, or that He should have the power and not be interested, since these two imply wickedness or lack of power, and He is above such things. There remains thus only the one possibility, that He knows nothing of those conditions at all, or else that He knows them and arranges them in the best possible way, but it is we who find them badly arranged and contrary to logic and incompatible with what should be expected. This they consider a proof that God is in no way or manner aware of those conditions.

It is this train of thought which trapped them first so as to fall into that reckless assertion. You will find all the details of those alternative propositions which I have here described in detail, as well as proof of my assertion that this was the point at which their argument went wrong, in the work on *Providence*, by Alexander of Aphrodisias. [67]

You may well consider with amazement how they have fallen into something worse than that which they wanted to avoid, and how they have ignored the very thing which they constantly point out to us and never tire of explaining to us. As for their falling into something worse than what they sought to avoid: they tried to avoid attributing negligence to God, and without further ado credited him with ignorance, saying that all that belongs to this lower world is hidden from Him and impossible for Him to perceive. As for ignoring what they themselves constantly point out: they consider the universe from the point of view of the conditions of human individuals, whose misfortunes are either due to themselves or necessarily arise from the nature of matter, as they themselves perpetually state and explain; we ourselves have explained this point above as far as it is needed here.

Having established this principle which bids to destroy every decent moral principle and to sully the good name of every true belief, they further attempted to hide its absurdity by declaring that knowledge of those things was inadmissible in the case of God for a number of reasons. One of these is that individual objects or events can only be apprehended by the senses, not by reason, but God does not perceive by any sense. Another is that individual objects or events are infinite in number, while knowledge is something that encompasses; what is infinite, however, cannot be encompassed by knowledge. A third argument is that knowledge of happenings – which are, of course, individual events – implies some change because individual acts of knowing occur one after another. *

They arrive at many contradictory guesses. Some of them say that God only knows species, not individuals. Others say that He knows nothing at all outside His own substance, so as to

*Or: because new knowledge constantly supersedes former knowledge.

avoid ascribing to Him any plurality of knowledge. Some philosophers held the same belief as we ourselves, namely* that God knows every thing and that nothing whatsoever is hidden from Him. These were some great men who lived before Aristotle. Alexander mentions them in his above-mentioned treatise, but rejects their view. As its main short-coming he mentions the trite fact that the good suffer and the wicked prosper.

To cut the matter short, you will have realized by now that all these thinkers would not have become involved in any speculation of this sort if they had found some consistent order in human affairs, the kind of order that the common people see in life, nor would they have made any such reckless state-ments. Their prime motive in undertaking this speculation was their observation of the fate of good and wicked men, which they assert to be inconsistent, just as ignorant people among ourselves say: *the way of the Lord is not equitable* (Ezekiel 33, 17).

Having thus proved that the discussions about God's know-ledge and providence are closely bound up with each other, I shall proceed to set forth the views of those who speculated on the subject of providence. I shall then go on to resolve the doubts prevalent concerning the knowledge of God about individual acts and events.

CHAPTER XX

IT is generally agreed that it would be incorrect to ascribe to God the acquisition of new knowledge, i.e. that He should now know something He did not know before. It would be equally incorrect to ascribe to Him manifold and multiple acts of cognition, even according to the view of those who believe in divine attributes. Assuming this as proven, we, the believers in the Divine Law, say that He knows many and manifold things by the same act of knowledge and that His acts of cognition do not vary according to the variation of things known, as it would be the case with us. We further say that all

*Reading *annahu* for *wa-annahu*,

things that emerge anew were known to Him before they existed, and He knew them continually. For this reason He does not acquire any new knowledge whatsoever. He knows that so-and-so does not exist now, but will exist at such-and-such a time and will remain alive for so-and-so much time and will then be non-existent. When that person comes into being, as God knew he would, no new piece of knowledge has been added. It was not as if something hitherto unknown to Him had occurred, but something occurred which He continually knew would occur just in the way it did.

A consequence of this belief is that knowledge should pertain to non-existent things and should encompass the infinite. That is exactly what we do believe. We say, in effect, that with regard to non-existing things, whose creation pre-exists in God's knowledge – since His is the power to create them – there is no reason why His knowledge should not extend to them. Those things, however, which essentially cannot exist are with regard to His knowledge in a state of absolute non-existence, to which His knowledge cannot extend any more than our knowledge can extend to something that does not exist for us.

The idea of knowledge encompassing the infinite raises a number of difficulties. Some thinkers assume that (divine) knowledge attaches to the species and in some way is extended over all the individuals of the species. This is the belief of everyone who accepts the Divine Law in so far as the requirements of speculative thought demand it.

The philosophers, however, declare without further ado that God's knowledge cannot extend to the non-existent or that any knowledge can encompass the infinite. Therefore, since He does not acquire new knowledge, it is absurd that He should know anything of those things that emerge anew, and thus God does not know anything except permanent things that do not change. Some of them have still another doubt. They say, even if God knows only the permanent things, this would still imply many acts of knowing, since the acts of knowing vary according to the things known, because to every knowable object belongs a particular act of knowing. Therefore,

God cannot know anything except His own substance.[68]

My own opinion is that the reason for falling into all these errors is that they treat God's knowledge as something comparable with our own. Each school of thought contemplates things which would be impossible with our own cognitive processes and concludes that the same restrictions should also apply in the case of God, or that he should experience the same difficulties. For their failure in this matter the philosophers deserve more reproach than anyone else, for it is they who proved that His essence does not allow of any plurality and that He possesses no attributes outside His essence and that His knowledge is identical with His essence; it is they who proved that our minds are insufficient to apprehend His true essence as it is, as we have explained before. How then can they assert that they apprehend God's knowledge when it is not something outside His essence? That same insufficiency of our minds to apprehend His essence also prevents us from apprehending His knowledge of how things exist. It is not a knowledge of the same species as our own so that we could treat it analogically, but it is something as different from it as can be. Just as there is a necessarily existing essence from which all existence results, as they say, or which has produced all that is outside it out of non-existence, as we say – in the same way we claim that this essence apprehends everything that is outside it and nothing whatsoever that exists is ever hidden from it. There is nothing in common between our knowledge and His, just as there is nothing in common between our essence and His. What misled them is the homonymous nature of the word knowledge, for there is something common only in nomenclature, but complete difference in nature. This is why absurd conclusions will be reached if we imagine that necessary features of our own cognitive processes are also necessary in His case.

From various phrases in the Scriptures I conclude that God's knowledge with regard to a possibility that it will take place does not deprive that possibility in any way of its nature as a possibility. The nature of a possibility remains attached to it, and God's knowledge of what is going to happen in the case of possible alternatives does not imply the necessity of one or the other of the alternatives happening. This is another principle of the law of Moses concerning which there can be no doubt or scepticism. Had it been otherwise, the Law would not have said: *thou shalt make a battlement for thy roof* (Deuteronomy 22, 8), or *lest he die in the battle and another man take her* (Deuteronomy 20, 7). Similarly the entire law with its commands and prohibitions is based upon this principle, namely that God's knowledge of what is going to happen does not change the contingency from its nature. This is very difficult for our imperfect minds to grasp.

According to our view, who say that God's knowledge is not a thing superadded to His essence, it is really impossible to avoid the conclusion that between His knowledge and ours there exists the same difference of substance as between the substance of heaven and earth. This has been clearly stated by the prophets: *For not my thoughts are your thoughts, and not your ways are my ways, saith the Lord. For as high as the heavens are above the earth, so high are my ways above your ways, and my thoughts above your thoughts* (Isaiah 55, 8–9).

The sum total of the idea I am trying here briefly to explain is the following: we cannot apprehend the true nature of God's essence; yet we know that His existence is the most perfect, without any admixture of imperfection or change or affection in any way. Similarly, though we do not know the true nature of God's knowledge, because it is His substance, yet we know that He does not sometimes apprehend and at other times remain unaware, i.e. that He never acquires any new knowledge; also that His knowledge is not of a multiple nature, nor finite, that nothing of all existing things is hidden from Him and that His knowledge of them does not change their nature, but the possible retains its nature as a possibility. Anything in this enumeration that appears contradictory, is so only owing to the structure of our knowledge, which has nothing in common with His knowledge except the name.

CHAPTER XXI

WHATEVER we know, we know from observation of reality. Therefore our knowledge does not extend to what will be or to that which is infinite, and we constantly acquire new and manifold items of knowledge according to the things from which we derive them. It is otherwise with God: He does not derive His knowledge of things from the things, so that His knowledge would be multiple and ever new, but those things themselves are a consequence of His knowledge, which precedes them and establishes them as they are, whether this be as an incorporeal being, as a perpetually existing individual composed of matter, or as a thing possessing matter passing through various individuals according to some consistent law.

This is the reason why in the case of God there is neither a multiplicity of items of knowledge, nor acquisition of any new or different knowledge. Through knowing the true nature of His own unchangeable essence, He knows everything that results from all His works. For us to desire to understand how this takes place, is the same as to desire that we were He and that our perception were the same as His. The proper belief for a person who seeks truth and justice, is to hold that nothing whatsoever is hidden from God, but everything is accessible to His knowledge, which is identical with His substance; further, that it is out of the question for us to know anything of this type of perception. If we knew how it works, then we should ourselves be possessed of that intelligence with which that type of perception is achieved. This, however, is not possessed by anyone in the universe except God alone, whose essence it is.[69]

Take these remarks to heart, for I maintain that it is very wonderful and a sound opinion. When it is followed up, no trace of erroneous or misleading ideas will be found in it, nor will it lead to any absurd conclusions or to the attribution of any shortcomings to God. We must accept it, since in dealing with those momentous and sublime subjects no demonstrative proof of any kind can be brought, be it according to the opinions of ourselves, who believe in revelation, or of the philosophers, whatever their opinions on this subject. In all subjects which do not allow of demonstrative proof, however, the same method must be followed which we have applied in dealing with this subject, God's knowledge of that which is outside Him. It should, therefore, be given full consideration.

CHAPTERS XVII–XVIII
(COMBINED)

INTRODUCTORY REMARKS

[Chapter xvii enumerates five views about Providence:

1. That of the Epicureans, who do not acknowledge any influence of God upon the world, and therefore no providence. They derive all happenings from chance meetings of atoms.

2. That of Aristotle. He maintains that all cosmic happenings proceed by way of necessity from God. Providence is therefore the same as the eternal order of things established by God. In the sublunar world – where, in contrast to the celestial spheres, the individuals are subject to generation and corruption, and the species alone are eternal – divine providence extends solely to the species. It is thus only another expression for the general purposeful arrangement of things. The fate of human and animal individuals is a product of mere chance.

3. That of the Ash'arites, a group within the Moslem theological school of the Mutakallimun. They reduce all happenings to divine predestination. This even determines the will of each man, turning the one into a pious person, the other into a sinner. It bestows upon one man benefits and upon the other misfortunes. The divine will is not bound by any reasons or laws of causality.

4. The Mu'tazilites, another Moslem school. They, too, accept the idea of individual providence, but at the same time recognize the free will of man. Providence, for them, is determined by God's wisdom, which provides for the needs of the creatures. It does not inflict suffering on innocent men or animals without recompensing them for it in the world to come.

5. The view of the Torah, according to its usual interpretation. This, again, teaches free will, and sees in all human fate dispositions of divine justice. All benefits accorded to man are by way of reward, all misfortunes by way of punishment. Some teachers of the Talmud mention also 'chastisements of love', i.e. sufferings which do not constitute a punishment, but are to purify man so as to make him deserving of higher happiness. This resembles the teaching of the Mu'tazilites.

Maimonides points out the difficulties inherent in each of these theories. He attempts to remove these in his own teaching which now follows, and in which he sees also the true interpretation of the words of the Torah.]

MY own beliefs on this principle, namely divine providence, are those that I shall now expound. In this belief I do not base myself upon conclusions reached by demonstrative proof, but upon what I have come to recognize as the meaning of the Pentateuch and the prophetical books. My own belief is in any event freer from absurdities than the beliefs previously described, and agrees more closely with rational methods of deduction.

I believe that divine providence extends, in this lower sublunar world, only and alone to human individuals. The human species is the only one in which all conditions of individuals and the good and evil that befalls them are according to deserts, as it is said: *for all his ways are justice* (Deuteronomy 32, 4). With regard to other animals, and still more so to plants and other things, my view is identical with that of Aristotle: I do not believe in any manner whatsoever that this leaf has fallen because of any providential act, or that this spider has caught that fly through the personal and actual decree and will of God, or that Jack's spittle, in moving so that it descended upon this particular gnat at a particular spot and killed it, was directed by decree and destiny, or that the fact that this fish snapped that worm from the surface of the water was due to an act of the personal will of God. All this I hold to be pure chance, just as Aristotle does. Divine providence, in my opinion, follows in the wake of divine emanation. It is the species which is affected by this rational emanation, so that it possesses reason, and everything that is accessible to a rational being becomes accessible to it – it is that species, I say, which divine providence constantly attends and whose every action it assesses for reward and punishment. Though the sinking of a ship and the death of its passengers, or the collapse of the roof upon those who are in the house, may be due to pure chance, yet the fact that the ones travelled in that ship or the others sat in that house cannot in our opinion be anything but a result of divine will in accordance with their deserts, as dictated by His judgments, the principles of which our minds are insufficient to know.

The reason which led me to accept this belief is that I have never yet discovered a passage in any prophetic book relating that God exercised any providence with regard to any individual animal, but only with regard to humans. The prophets even have expressed wonder that providence should be exercised towards human beings, since man is too small that any interest should be taken in him. How much more so should this apply in the case of other living beings. Thus Scripture says: *What is man that thou takest cognizance of him* . . . (Psalm 144, 3), *What is the mortal that thou rememberest him* . . . (Psalm 8, 5). Scripture, however, is quite unequivocal with regard to the fact that providence attends all human individuals and that all their deeds are taken into account, e.g.: *He fashioneth their hearts altogether; he hath regard to all their works* (Psalm 33, 15); *Whose eyes are open over all the ways of the sons of man, to give unto every one according to his ways* (Jeremiah 32, 19); *For his eyes are upon the ways of man, and all his steps doth he see* (Job 34, 21). The Pentateuch, too, contains passages showing providence for individual human beings and examination of their deeds, e.g.: *On the day when I visit I will visit their sin upon them* (Exodus 32, 34); *Whosoever hath sinned against me, him I will blot out from my book* (ibid. 33); *I will destroy that person from among his people* (Leviticus 23, 30); *Then I will set my face against that person* (ibid. 20, 6); and many more. All the stories of Abraham, Isaac, and Jacob are lucid proof of personal providence.

With regard to other living beings the position is without any doubt as Aristotle saw it. For this reason it is not only permitted, but positively commanded to slaughter them, and we may use them for our purposes as we wish. Proof that the animals do not enjoy providence except in the way indicated by Aristotle, may be found in the words of the prophet who, upon contemplating Nebuchadnezzar's rise to power and the great slaughter he committed, said: *O Lord, it is as if man had* been disregarded and forsaken like fishes and creeping things – thereby implying that those species are in fact disregarded. These are his words: *And thou makest men as the fishes of the sea, as the creeping things that have no ruler over them? All of them he bringeth up with the angle, etc.* (Habakkuk 1, 14–15). Moreover the prophet explains that this is not the case; it is not a question of forgetting or withdrawal of providence; but of punishment for those people because they deserved what came upon them, as he says: *O Lord, thou hast ordained them for judgment, and o Rock thou hast established them for correction* (ibid. 12).

Do not presume that the idea put forward here is contradicted by verses such as: *Who giveth to the beast its food, to the young ravens which cry* (Psalm 147, 9); *The young lions roar after their prey, and ask from God their food* (Psalm 104, 21); *Thou openest thy hand and satisfiest the desire of every living thing* (Psalm 145, 16); or the saying of the Rabbis: 'He sits and nourishes everything, from the horns of wild oxen to the eggs of lice' (Shabbath 107b, Abodah Zarah 3b). You may find many other passages like these. There is, however, nothing in them to controvert my view, since they all refer to providence for the species, not for the individual. They describe, in other words, God's generosity in providing for every species the food it requires and the material basis of its existence. This is, of course, self-evident. Aristotle, too, holds that this kind of providence must of necessity be available. Alexander of Aphrodisias even states this explicitly on the authority of Aristotle, namely that there is provision for the existence of the proper food of each species in sufficient quantities for its individuals. Were it not so, there is little doubt that the species would cease to exist. All this will be easily understood after a little reflection.

True, the Rabbis have said that 'the prohibition of causing suffering to animals is derived from the Torah' (Baba Metzi'a 32b), taking their authority from the verse: *wherefore hast thou smitten thine ass?* (Numbers 22, 32)*. This, however, is intended to perfect our own character, by preventing us from acquiring

*The Talmud passage quotes, however, not this verse but Exodus 23, 5.

habits of cruelty. We should never inflict suffering needlessly and without purpose, but should endeavour to show mercy and kindness even to every animal, except when our needs demand otherwise, as in the case indicated by: *when ... thy soul longeth to eat flesh* (Deuteronomy 12, 20). This means that we should not slaughter animals merely out of cruelty or for sport.

There is also no need to deal seriously with the question why God's providence should extend to individual human beings and not extend in the same manner to individual animals. He who asks thus ought to ask himself first why God gave reason to man and did not give it to other species of animals. The proper reply to the latter question is, of course, that God willed it thus, or that His wisdom decreed it thus, or that nature so required it, whichever of the three views discussed earlier on you care to choose. The same answers dispose also of the first question.

Follow up this theory in your own mind into its ultimate implications. I do not believe that anything is hidden from God, or ascribe to Him any lack of power, but I do believe that providence goes with reason and is a necessary consequence of its possession. This is because providence is exercised by a rational being, namely the One who is reason so perfect that no greater perfection is thinkable. Therefore, providence extends to every one who is affected by this emanation to the extent that that being is gifted with reason.[70]

(Ch. xviii.) This means that divine providence does not extend to all individuals of the human race in the same way, but to a degree varying in proportion to their share of human perfection. From this consideration it necessarily results that God's providence for the prophets is particularly intensive, graded again according to their prophetic rank. His providence for the men of virtue and the pious will also correspond to the degree of virtue and piety they possess, since it is that quantity of divine emanation which makes the prophets speak, and produces the good deeds of the pious, and perfects the knowledge of the men of virtue. As for the ignorant and impious, the less they possess of this emanation, the less attention will they enjoy and the more they will approach the order of individuals of animal species: *he is like the beasts that perish* (Psalm 49, 12*). For this reason killing them is considered a small matter; if it is to the public benefit it is even commanded.

This rule constitutes one of the basic principles of the Law. Indeed the Law can be said to be founded on this concept, that different human individuals enjoy the benefits of providence to a varying degree.

(End of xvii.) This then, in my opinion, is the view which agrees both with reason and with the express statements of Scripture. The other views discussed before say either too much or too little: either they exaggerate so much as to produce utter lunacy,** estrangement from reason and obstinate denial of the evidence of the senses; or they fall into immense underestimation which leads to evil beliefs about God, corruption of the proper order of human existence, and effacement of the moral and intellectual superiority of man. I refer here, of course, to the theory of those who deny individual providence to man and place him upon one level with the animals.

CHAPTER XXIII

INTRODUCTORY REMARKS

[The problem of Divine Providence is further discussed in chapters xxii and xxiii, taking the book of Job as its text. Chapter xxii interprets the story of Job; chapter xxiii discusses the opinions of Job and his friends. It finds in these the views of the philosophers and theologians as expounded in chapter xvii, though with some additions and modifications. The opinions of Job himself, as interpreted in the following extract, are of particular importance for Maimonides' own theory.]

JOB's view about the fact that the most perfect and upright man is afflicted with the greatest and most acute pain was that this is proof that the just and the wicked are equal in the eyes of God, owing to His contempt for, and lack of interest in, the

*Hebrew vs. 13.
**Thus Tibbon; Harizi translates 'confusion'.

human race. This is expressed in His utterance:* *And I say, it is all one thing; therefore I say, the innocent and the wicked both he can bring to their end. Be it by a torrent** that slays unawares, he will mock at the trial of the guiltless**** (Job 9, 22–23). He says that if the torrent comes suddenly and kills and carries off everyone it meets in its way, God mocks at the trial of the guiltless. He reinforces the argument by saying: *This one dieth in the fullness of his health, all his life being restful and safe; his veins§ are full of milk, and his bones bathed in marrow. And another dieth with an embittered soul, and has never partaken of anything good. Yet together they must lie upon the dust, and decay shall cover them* (21, 23–6). He attempts to draw similar inferences from the prosperity of the wicked and their success in life. He speaks about this at great length, and says: *And yet when I think of it I am terrified, and shuddering takes hold of my body. Wherefore do the wicked live, become stout, yea, are mighty in wealth? Their posterity is established in their sight with them, and their progeny in their presence* (21, 6–8). Having described this complete success, he turns to his two interlocutors and says: If it is as you assert, that the children of that prosperous sinner will perish after his death and their traces be effaced – what does it matter to this man, in the midst of his own prosperity, what will befall his family after his death; *for what care hath he of his household after him, when the number of his months is all accomplished to him?* (21, 21). He proceeds to explain that there is nothing to hope for after death. The only possible conclusion is that all this is due to neglect. Now, however, he expresses astonishment that God did not neglect the original work of bringing man into being and fashioning him, yet neglects to govern him: *Hast thou not poured me out as milk and curdled me like cheese?* etc. (10, 10).

*To get nearer the flavour which the verses had for Maimonides, our translation, unless demanded otherwise by the context, is based on the translation of Job by Saadiah, which was also used by Maimonides. Owing to the peculiar difficulties of the book, each age has its own Job.

**Maimonides' interpretation here is peculiar to himself. Apparently it is based on comparison with Isaiah 28. 15, 18 (cf. Targum there).

***Saadiah: so that therein the reward of the innocent turns into mockery.

§ Thus Saadiah; true meaning unknown.

All this is in effect the same as one of the (above-mentioned) beliefs and theories about divine providence. You know well that the Rabbis pronounced these opinions of Job's heretical in the extreme and said: 'Dust into the mouth of Job! – Job wished to turn the bowl upside down – Job was one of those who disbelieve in the resurrection of the dead – Job began to curse and blaspheme' (Baba Bathra 16a). Yet God said to Eliphaz: *for ye have not spoken before me the thing that is right concerning my servant Job* (42, 7).* The Rabbis, however, justify this by saying that 'no man is punishable for things done in grief' (Baba Bathra 16b), i.e., he was excused because of his intense pains.

This kind of talk, however, has no real bearing upon this parable. The reason for those words (of God) is another one, which I shall now explain, namely that Job subsequently gave up this opinion, which is indeed erroneous in the extreme, and adduced logical proofs to dispose of his error. After all,** this is the idea that most readily at first suggests itself to one's mind, especially to one who has been affected by misfortunes, though he knows of himself that he is guiltless. This is a fact which no one will dispute.*** This is why this opinion is attributed to Job. However, he only said these things as long as he was not in possession of true knowledge, but knew of God by hearsay, as most adherents of revealed religions do. As soon as he obtained reliable knowledge of God he realized that true happiness, which consists in knowing God, is in store for all those who know Him, and none of all those afflictions can dull it. Job had imagined that those imaginary kinds of happiness such as health, possessions, and children, were the true aim of life, as long as he knew of God only by report, not by his own thinking. This is why he fell into all those perplexities and said such things. That is what he means when he says: *I had heard of thee by the hearing of the ear, but now mine eye hath seen thee. Therefore*

*Maimonides follows here Saadiah. A.V.: for ye have not spoken of me the thing that is right, as my servant Job hath.

**Reading (with Tibbon) *ammâ inna.*

***Perhaps one should read *yunkar* and translate: No one would wonder at such an attitude.

I abhor and repent upon the dust and ashes (Job 42, 5–6). Completed according to the meaning this should read: 'I abhor all that I desired before and repent for having been in dust and ashes', * as his state allegedly was *while he was sitting down among the ashes* (2, 8). Because of this last utterance, which indicates that he had grasped the truth, it is subsequently said of him 'for ye have not spoken before me the thing that is right concerning my servant Job'.[71]

CHAPTER XXVII

Two things are the purpose of the entire Law: the welfare of the soul and the welfare of the body.[72] The welfare of the soul is achieved through communicating to the mass of the people correct beliefs within their intellectual grasp. Some of these have to be imparted by explicit statements, others by parables, since on the whole the nature of the multitude is not so as to allow them to grasp those things as they are. The welfare of the body is achieved by setting aright the way they live together. This purpose is attained by two things. One of them is to remove injustice from their midst. This means that no man is permitted to do what he wants and has power to do, but is constrained to do only such things as are for the common benefit. The second means is to train every individual in socially useful habits so that the affairs of the state run smoothly.[73]

You will appreciate that without any doubt one of these two purposes is the nobler, namely the achievement of welfare of the soul by imparting correct beliefs, while the other precedes it both in the order of nature and of time, I mean the welfare of the body, which is the administration of the state and the happy arrangement of the conditions of its inhabitants as far as this is in our power. This second aim is the more urgent; in the exposition of this subject and its details much effort has been expended, since the first purpose cannot be achieved before the second is attained. For it is proved that man can achieve perfection in two respects, firstly in his body and secondly in his soul.

*This is in fact Saadiah's rendering, which Maimonides treats somewhat like a Midrash.

The first concerns his being as healthy and fit in his body as possible. This cannot be unless he finds his needs whenever he requires them, namely food and other requisites of his body, such as shelter, baths, etc. However, no man can succeed in this alone, but every individual can only achieve all this by combining into a state. As is well known, man is social by nature.

The second form of perfection is attained when he becomes actually rational, i.e. acquires an intellect in actuality, by knowing of all existing things everything man has the power to know in accordance with his ultimate state of perfection. It is obvious that this ultimate perfection does not carry with it any actions or moral qualities, but consists in opinions alone to which one has been led by speculation and compelled by investigation. It is also obvious that this glorious ultimate perfection cannot be attained unless the first form of perfection has been achieved. Man is unable to conceive clearly an idea, even if it is explained to him, leave alone arrive at this idea through his own efforts, when he is affected by pain, violent hunger, thirst, heat, or violent cold. Only after attaining the first form of perfection is it possible to achieve the ultimate perfection, which is doubtlessly the nobler one and is alone the cause of everlasting life.

The true law, which, as we have explained, is the only and unique one, namely the Law of Moses, has been given so as to bestow upon us the two kinds of perfection together. It provides for the improvement of human relationships by removing injustice and inculcating good and generous habits, so that the community will last without any disturbance of its order, and thus every member of it attain to his first stage of perfection. At the same time it ordains for the improvement of men's beliefs and the instilling of correct opinions by which man can attain to ultimate perfection. The Torah expressly mentions these two stages of perfection and informs us that the aim of the entire Law is to attain these: *And the Lord commanded us to do all these statutes, to fear the Lord our God, that it might be well with us at all times, and that he might preserve us alive, as it is at this day* (Deuteronomy 6, 24). In this passage the ultimate perfection is mentioned first, in keeping with its importance, since we have explained that it is the ultimate purpose. It is contained in the words 'that it might be well with us at all times'. You know well what the Rabbis have said in discussing the verse: *that it may be well with thee and that thou mayest prolong thy days* (Deuteronomy 22, 7); 'That it may be well with thee – for a world which is wholly good, and that thou mayest prolong thy days – for a world which is eternally extended' (Qiddushin 39b, Yalqut I, 930). Similarly the intention of 'that it may be well with us at all times' here is the attainment of the world that is wholly good and eternally extended, i.e. everlasting life, while the words 'that he might preserve us alive as it is at this day' refer to the first, corporeal existence which lasts only a certain time, and which does not achieve its perfect order except in society, as we have shown.

CHAPTER XXIX

IT is a well-known fact that our father Abraham was brought up in the religion of the Sabians, [74] who believed that there was no God other than the stars. When I shall have finished telling you in this chapter about their books – which we now possess in Arabic translations – and their ancient tales, and exposing their beliefs and history to you from those sources, you will realize that they openly asserted that the stars are God* and that the sun is the supreme God. They also claimed that the other planets were gods, but considered the two luminaries to be the greatest. You will also find that they expressly asserted that the sun is the one that governs the upper and the lower world. These are the actual words they used.

You will also find that in those books and tales of theirs they mention our father Abraham and say literally the following: As for Abraham, who was brought up at Kutha, when he proclaimed opinions contrary to the general belief and asserted that there was a Maker other than the sun, they adduced such-

---

*So, not 'gods', most Arabic MSS.

and-such arguments against him. Among their arguments they mentioned a number of effects of the sunlight such as are plainly perceived. Abraham then said to them: You are quite right; the sun is like the axe in the hand of the carpenter. Then they go on to mention some further arguments he employed against them. In the end of that story they tell how the king imprisoned our father Abraham and how he continued to argue with them in prison for some days. Finally the king became afraid that Abraham would make orderly government impossible for him and turn people away from their accustomed beliefs. He therefore exiled him to the other end of Syria, having first confiscated all his property. Thus they relate. You can find this story in full detail in the *Nabataean Agriculture*. They make no mention of the events related in our more reliable documents or of the revelations he received, because they deny the truth of his words, for the reason that he contradicted their pernicious doctrine. I have little doubt that when he came out in opposition to the beliefs of all his compatriots, those poor misguided people reviled and reproached him, and spoke ill of him. When he bore all this for the sake of God and preferred truth to honour, it was said to him: *And I will bless those that bless thee, and him that curseth thee I will curse, and in thee shall all families of the earth be blessed* (Genesis 12, 3). The outcome of his story was that, as we can see to-day, most of the inhabitants of the earth are agreed in holding his memory dear and blessing themselves with his name. Even those who are not of his progeny derive their origin from him. No one now is against him or ignorant of his greatness, except for the last remnants of that extinct religion, who have remained in the remote corners of the earth, like the heathen Turks in the far north, and the Indians in the far south. These are the last remnants of the Sabians.

The highest peak the philosophers of those times reached in their speculations was the following phantasy: God is the spirit of the heavenly sphere, i.e. the heavens and the stars are the body and God its spirit.[75] Abu Bakr as-Sa'igh mentions this belief in his commentary on Aristotle's Physics.[76] For this reason all Sabians believed in the uncreated world, since God in their view was identical with the sky.

They also assert that Adam was a person born from a male and a female like all other men, but they hold him in high esteem and say that he was a prophet, the emissary of the moon, and that he preached the worship of the moon; also that he wrote books about agriculture. The Sabians further maintain that Noah was an agriculturist and did not approve of idolatry. All Sabians disparage Noah because of this, saying that he never in his life did obeisance to any idol. They also say in their books that he was beaten and imprisoned for his worship of God, and suchlike stories more.

And because of those Sabian ideas they put up statues for the stars: golden statues for the sun and silver statues for the moon, etc., and divided the metals and the climes among the stars, saying this or that region had as its god to this or that planet. They built temples and placed images in them. They claimed that the powers of the planets were emanated onto those images, and those images spoke, understood what was spoken to them, reasoned, gave revelations (oracles) to people and gave them useful information. They said similar things about the trees which belonged to the division of those planets. If such a tree were dedicated to that particular planet and was planted in its name, and certain things were done for it and with it, the spirituality of that planet would emanate onto that tree. It would then give oracles to people and speak to them in their dreams. You will find all this in their books, which I shall name later on.

These then were the prophets of Baal and the prophets of Asherah, who are mentioned in our books, and in whose minds those ideas had got such hold that they *forsook the Lord* (Isaiah 1, 4) and cried: *O Baal, answer us* (I Kings 18, 26), all this because such views were then generally held. At that time ignorance was widespread, and much nonsense and phantasy of that kind was current in the world, and all kinds of ideas arose, and there rose among them *one who useth divination, one who is an observer of times, an enchanter, a conjurer, a charmer, a con-*

sulter with familiar spirits, a wizard, and one who inquireth of the dead (Deuteronomy 18, 10–11). In our major work, *Mishneh Torah*, we have explained that our father Abraham set about combating these ideas by argument and mild preaching, by friendly persuasion and by attracting them by means of kind deeds to the worship of God. Then the prince of prophets (Moses) was sent forth and completed the work, commanding to kill those people, to wipe out their very traces, and to extirpate their progeny: *their altars shall ye pull down*, etc. (Judges 2, 2). He issued a prohibition against following any of those customs of theirs, saying: *and ye shall not walk in the customs of the nation*, etc. (Leviticus 20, 23).

You know well from the express statements of the Torah in a number of passages that the first purpose of the whole law is to remove idolatry and to wipe out its traces and all that belongs to it, even its memory, and everything that leads to carrying out some action connected with it, such as consulters of familiar spirits, wizards, passing through fire, diviners, observers of times, enchanters, conjurers, charmers, and inquirers from the dead, and to warn of doing anything that is like any of their deeds, leave alone imitating them. It is clearly stated in the Torah that all the things which they considered acts of devotion to their gods and means of obtaining their favour are things hated and loathed in the sight of God: *For every abomination to the Lord, which he hateth, have they done unto their gods* (Deuteronomy 12, 31).

This is the thing regarding which the true prophets say: *for after vain things which cannot profit, they have gone** (cf, I Samuel 12, 21). How immense therefore is the benefit of every commandment that liberates us from that terrible heresy and guides us back to the path of true faith, namely that there is a God who created all this and that it is He who must be worshipped and loved and feared, not those imaginary divinities, and this true God does not require for coming near to Him and gaining His favour anything onerous, only love for Him and fear of Him, which are the highest degree of worship,

---

*A conflation of two verses, 1 Sam. 12. 21 and Jer. 2. 8.

as we shall show: *And now, o Israel, what doth the Lord thy God require of thee, but to fear the Lord thy God, to walk in all His ways, and to love Him* ... (Deuteronomy 10, 12). We shall follow up this subject later on.

Now, however, let me return to my present subject. I say that the meaning and causes of many laws became fully clear to me only when I studied the beliefs, views, actions, and methods of worship of the Sabians, as you will see when I come to explain the motives of those commandments which are wrongly assumed to have no reason. I shall now enumerate the books from which you will be able to learn all I know about the Sabians' beliefs and views, so that you will be able to convince yourself of the correctness of my statements concerning the motives of those laws. The most extensive book on the subject is the *Nabataean Agriculture*, translated[77] by Ibn Wahshiyya. That book is full of the figments of the idol-worshippers and of such things to which the common people feel somehow attracted and attached, such as the fabrication of talismans, the attraction of star-spirits to earth, magic, jinns and ghouls who populate the deserts. More such fables are spread abroad in that book which make sensible people laugh. Their purpose is to discredit the clear signs and wonders by which the people of the world know that there is a God who judges the inhabitants of the earth, as it is said: *in order that thou mayest know how that the earth is the Lord's* (Exodus 9, 29), and *to the end thou mayest know that I am the Lord in the midst of the earth* (Exodus 8, 22).*

All those that I have mentioned to you[78] are books of idolatry which have been translated into Arabic. No doubt they are only a small proportion compared with those that have not been so translated, or do not exist any more, but have perished and been lost in course of time. Those that we possess now, however, contain most of the views and actions of the Sabians. Some of these are still known to-day in the world, such as the building of temples, the placing of statues of cast metal and stone inside them, the building of altars on

*In Hebrew vs. 18.

which either animal sacrifices or various kinds of food are offered, festive rites and meetings for prayer and other forms of worship in those temples – in which they institute some very sacred spots which they call temples of intellectual forms – the placing of statues *upon the high mountains*, etc. (Deuteronomy 12, 2), the worship of Asheroth, the erection of Masseboth, and other things about which you may inform yourself from those books which I have indicated. The knowledge of those views and actions is an important step in the enterprise of finding reasons for the commandments. The very root and linch-pin of our law is the extirpation of those ideas from our minds and the erasing of those monuments from existence. To wipe them from our minds, as it is said: *that your heart be not deceived* (Deuteronomy 11, 16), and *whose heart turneth away this day from the Lord our God* (Deuteronomy 29, 18);* to erase them from existence, as it is said: *their altars shall ye destroy and their Asheroth shall ye cut down,* etc. (Deuteronomy 7, 5), and *ye shall destroy their name out of the same place* (Deuteronomy 12, 3). These two points are repeated in a number of passages. This was the primary and general aim of the whole law, as our Rabbis teach us in the comment handed down in their name to the verse: *All that the Lord hath commanded you by the hand of Moses* (Numbers 15, 23), where they say 'thus you learn that everyone who acknowledges idol-worship denies the whole law, while everyone who denies idol-worship acknowledges the whole law' (Horayoth 8a, etc.). Take good note of this.

CHAPTER XXXII

W HEN you consider the works of God as seen in nature, you will become conscious of God's subtlety and wisdom in creating the animal body with the interlocking functions of its organs and their complicated layout. You will also realize how wisely and subtly He arranged for the successive stages of development of the whole individual.

Many items in our Law exhibit the same careful planning,

*In Hebrew vs. 17.

being, of course, the work of that same planner, God. It is impossible to pass all at once from one extreme to another; it is therefore not in keeping with human nature for man to abandon suddenly all he has been used to. This was so when God sent Moses to make us a *kingdom of priests and a holy nation* (Exodus 19, 6) through the knowledge of God – as has been explained before – and said: *Unto thee it was shewed, that thou mightest know, that the Lord he is God, there is none else beside him* (Deuteronomy 4, 35) and *Know therefore this day and consider it in thine heart, that the Lord he is God in the heavens above,* etc. (ibid. 39). He also sent him to invite us to devote ourselves exclusively to His worship, as it is said: *and to serve him with all your heart* (Deuteronomy 11, 13); *And ye shall serve the Lord your God* (Exodus 23, 25); *and him shall ye serve* (Deuteronomy 13, 4).* At that time the generally accepted custom all the world over, and the common method of worship in which we ourselves had grown up, was to offer sacrifices of various animals in those temples in which the statues had been placed, to prostrate oneself before them, and to burn incense before them. The religious and godly men of that time were those who dedicated themselves to service in those temples which had been erected for the stars, as we have related. This being so, God's wisdom and subtlety, evident in all His creation, did not decree that He should proclaim in His law a complete ban on all these kinds of worship, and their abolition. It would in those days have been quite inconceivable that such a thing should have been accepted, seeing that human nature is always happy only with that to which it is accustomed. Such a step at that time would have been as if a prophet should appear in our own time to preach the worship of God, and would say: God enjoins upon you not to pray to Him, not to fast, and not to call upon His help in misfortune, but to let your worship consist in thought only, to the exclusion of all works.

For this reason God permitted those methods of worship to continue, but instead of their being directed to created beings and figments of the imagination devoid of any reality, He

*In Hebrew vs. 5.

caused them to be directed to Himself and enjoined us to carry them on in His name.[79] He commanded us to build Him a temple: *And let them make me a sanctuary* (Exodus 25, 8), in which the altar should be dedicated to His name: *An altar of earth shalt thou make unto me* (Exodus 20, 24). The sacrifices were to be offered to God: *If any one of you wish to bring an offering unto the Lord* (Leviticus 1, 2). Also prostration and incense-burning were to be carried out only before Him. He prohibited that any of these acts should be done for anyone else: *He that sacrificeth unto any God, save unto the Lord only, shall be utterly destroyed* (Exodus 22, 20);* *For thou shalt not prostrate thyself to another God* (Exodus 34, 14). He also set aside priests for the service of the Sanctuary, and said: *that they may be priests unto me* (Exodus 28, 41). It was, of course, necessary that dues should be paid to them in sufficient quantities for their livelihood, because their own time was taken up by the service of the temple and the sacrifices; these are the tithes payable to Levites and Priests. By this subtle disposition on the part of God the very memory of idolatry was in course of time wiped off the earth. The essential and real principle of our faith, the existence and Unity of God, was thus established without people being shocked and dismayed by the abolition of the forms of worship to which they had been accustomed, since no other form of worship was then known.

This type of worship, i.e. the sacrifices, was for a secondary purpose, while private and public prayer and such like acts of worship were closer to the primary purpose and indispensable in attaining it. Therefore an important difference has been made between the two types. The first type of worship, viz. the sacrifices, though carried out in the name of God, was not made obligatory upon us to the extent that it had been practised before. Sacrifices were not to be brought in every place and at every time, neither was a temple to be erected wherever accident would have it, nor was anyone who happened to be present entitled to offer sacrifices, *whosoever desired it he consecrated* (I Kings 13, 33). All this was forbidden. One temple was to be

*In Hebrew vs. 19.

established *unto the place which the Lord shall choose* (Deuteronomy 12, 26), and no sacrifices were to be offered anywhere else, *that thou offer not thy burnt-offerings in every place which thou mayest see* (ibid. 13). No one was to be a priest but the descendants of a particular family. All this was designed to diminish this type of acts of worship and to prevent there being any more of it than divine wisdom had thought inadvisable to abolish altogether.

Private and public prayer, on the other hand, were to be offered in every place and by whoever happened to be there. The same applies to the Fringes, the *Mezuzah*, the Phylacteries and other forms of worship of that kind. Because of this distinction which I have just pointed out to you, there are found in the books of prophets so many passages of reproof for the people because of their zeal in sacrifices. They were told that these were not in themselves of any essential value and that God had no need for them. Thus Samuel said: *Hath the Lord as much delight in burnt-offerings and in sacrifices, as in obeying the voice of the Lord?* (I Samuel 15, 22). Isaiah said: *For what serveth me the multitude of your sacrifices, saith the Lord* (Isaiah 1, 11). Jeremiah said: *For I spoke not with your fathers, and I commanded them not on the day of my bringing them out of the land of Egypt, concerning burnt offering or sacrifice; but this thing did I command them, saying, Hearken to my voice, and I will be unto you for a God and ye shall be unto me for a people* (Jeremiah 7, 22–23). This passage has been a source of difficulty for every one whom I have so far read or heard. They ask how Jeremiah could assert that God did not command us concerning burnt offering and sacrifice, since a large part of the commandments deal with just this matter? The meaning of the passage is as I have explained it to you: namely, that the primary purpose was that you should apprehend Me and not worship any one but Me, 'and I will be unto you for a God and ye shall be unto me for a people'. All those laws concerning sacrifices and pilgrimages to the Temple were merely in order to achieve that principle. For its sake I have transferred those acts of worship to Myself, until the traces of idolatry should be extinguished and the principle of My unity established. You, however, have come to dismiss that purpose, and cling to those things that were merely instituted for its sake. You have attached doubt to My existence: *They have denied the Lord and said, he existeth not* (Jeremiah 5, 12). You have worshipped idols: *will ye . . . burn incense to Baal and walk after other gods . . . and then come and stand before my presence in this house?* (Jeremiah 7, 9–10): you still visit the temple of God and offer sacrifices, though these were not intended as a primary purpose.

That very same idea which is here expressed by Jeremiah, is also put forward in the Psalms as a reproof for the whole people, because they ignored at that time the primary purpose and made no clear distinction between it and the secondary purpose: *Hear, o my people and I will speak; o Israel and I will testify against thee: God, thy God, am I. Not because of thy sacrifices will I reprove thee, and thy burnt-offerings are continually before me. I will not take a bullock out of thy house, nor he-goats out of thy folds* (Psalm 50, 7–9). Wherever this idea is expressed it has this meaning. Think this well over and take it to heart.

CHAPTER LI

THE chapter that now follows does not contain any new ideas other than those found in the preceding chapters of this treatise. It is a kind of conclusion or summary. At the same time it discusses the manner of worship proper for those who have apprehended the truths relating particularly to Him after apprehending what He is, and guides such men towards achieving this worship, which is the highest purpose of mankind. It further informs them how divine providence affects them in this world until they are gathered into the *bundle of life* (I Samuel 25, 29).

I shall open this chapter with a simile: A prince is in his castle; his subjects are partly dwelling in the city and partly without. Of those in the city, some have turned their backs towards the prince's house and face another way. Others are making for the house of the prince and are directed towards it, seeking to obtain entry to it to have audience with the prince; but to this moment they have not yet seen the walls of the palace. Some of those who are going towards it have reached the palace and are wandering round it in search of the gate. A few have entered through the gate and are passing through the forecourt. Others again have got so far as to enter the inner courtyard of the palace and thus are in the same locality as the prince, i.e. in the palace itself. Penetrating as far as the inside of the palace does not yet mean that they see the prince or speak to him. Far from this, after entering the palace further efforts are required: then only does one reach the presence of the prince and see him from afar or nearby, hears him speak, or is allowed to address him.

I shall now explain this simile to you which I have invented: those who are outside the city are all those human beings who possess no religious belief whatever, be it of a speculative or of a traditional nature, such as the outlying tribes of the Turks in the distant north and the negroes in the distant south, as well as those in our own part of the world who resemble them in this respect. These are like animals devoid of reason; in my view they are not to be classed as human beings, but among the beings below the humans and above the apes, since they possess human shape and outline and higher intelligence than the ape.

Those who are in the city but turn their backs to the prince's palace are men of thought and speculation who have arrived at false opinions, be this due to some major error that crept into their reasoning or to their acceptance of erroneous ideas of others. Because of these opinions they are in such a position that with every step they become further removed from the palace. These are much worse off than the first group. It is they whose killing and the utter extermination of whose ideas is at times required by necessity, lest they cause others to go astray.[80]

Those who are making for the palace and aim at entering it, but have never seen the palace yet, are the great mass of those who obey the Law, or in other words the 'men without learning who occupy themselves with religious duties'.

Those who have arrived at the palace and are walking round it are those possessed of religious learning, who accept the right opinions as traditional beliefs and study the detailed ordinances of the works demanded in the service of God, but have never made an attempt to speculate on the principles of their faith or inquired in any way into the justification of any item of faith.

Those who have embarked on speculation concerning the principles of religion have entered the forecourts. No doubt the people there are of varying ranks. Those finally, who have succeeded in obtaining demonstrative proof of everything that can be demonstratively proved, and have reached certainty with regard to all those metaphysical matters on which certainty can be reached, and have almost reached certainty wherever no more than this was possible, those, I say, have penetrated to the presence of the prince in the inner parts of the palace.

Know, my dear son, that as long as you are occupied with the mathematical sciences and the technique of logic, you belong to those who walk around the palace in search of the gate, as our Sages have expressed it metaphorically: 'Ben Zoma is still outside' (Hagiga 15a). As soon as you learn the natural sciences you enter the palace and pass through its forecourts. When you complete your study of the natural sciences and get a grasp of metaphysics, you enter unto the prince *into the inner courtyard* (Ezekiel 44, 21, 27) and have achieved to be in the same house as he. This is the rank of the learned, though they are of different degrees of perfection. But as for the man who after having reached full perfection in metaphysics exercises his mind independently and inclines with his whole being to God, leaving aside everything else, and devotes all activities of his intellect to contemplation of the universe in order to find in it guidance towards God, so as to learn how God governs it – such men are those who have obtained admission to the audience-chamber of the prince. This is the rank of prophets.[81] One among these, through the high degree of his perception and his complete abstraction from everything else, got so far that it was said of him *and he was there with God* (Exodus 34, 28).

There he was, in that sacred place, asking and receiving replies, speaking and being spoken to. Owing to the supreme happiness caused by that which he perceived, he *did neither eat bread, nor drink water* (ibid.); for the intellect had grown so strong that every crude force in the body, that is the manifestations of the sense of touch, was put out of action. Other prophets only saw from nearby and others again only from afar, as it is said: *the Lord hath appeared from afar* unto me (Jeremiah 31, 3**). We have spoken above (part ii, ch. xl) of the different degrees of prophecy.

Let us now return to the subject of this chapter, which is the obligation*** of exercising one's independent power of thinking on the subject of God alone after having obtained the knowledge of Him, as we have explained before. This is the form of service to God which is reserved for those who have apprehended Truth. The more they think about God and let their minds dwell upon Him, the more intensive their service to Him.[82]

Those, however, who think of God and mention Him frequently§ without any knowledge, but just following some imagination or a belief taken over on the authority of others, are in my opinion not only outside the palace, but¶ far removed from it, and neither really mention God nor think of Him, since that idea which is in their imagination and which they mention with their lips does not correspond to any reality whatsoever. It is merely a figment of their imagination, as we have shown in our chapter on Attributes.§§ Such a form of service to God can be undertaken only after intellectual ideation. It is only after having apprehended God and His works according as the intellect requires it, that you can attempt to devote yourself to Him and strive to come near Him and to broaden the bond that links you with him, i.e. the intellectual

*Maimonides' interpretation agrees with the Peshitta, and possibly the Septuagint, against Jewish tradition. A.V.: 'of old'. Cf., however, Sotah 11a.

**Hebrew vs. 2.

***For this meaning of *ta'kīd* cf. Guide iii. 125.a.6 (Munk).

§ A quotation from Koran iii. 41?

¶Reading *ba'īdan*.

§§Cf. p. 65.

function. It is said: *Unto thee it was shewed that thou mightest know that the Lord he is God* (Deuteronomy 4, 35); *Know therefore this day and consider it in thine heart that the Lord he is God* (ibid. 39); *Know ye that the Lord he is God* (Psalm 100, 3).

The Torah has made it quite clear that this ultimate form of service, to which we draw attention in this chapter, is possible only after God has been apprehended: *to love the Lord your God and to serve Him with all your heart and with all your soul* (Deuteronomy 11, 13). We have on several occasions shown that love is proportionate to the degree of apprehension. After love follows that service, to which also our Sages allude (with reference to this verse): 'this is service in one's heart' (Taanith 2a, etc.).* In my view it (the service) consists in exercising one's power of thinking with regard to the First Intelligible (πρῶτον νοητόν) and in concentrating upon Him as far as this is possible.[83] For this reason you find that David in his last will enjoined upon Solomon these two duties, zeal in apprehending God and zeal in His service after apprehending Him: *And thou, Solomon my son, know thou the God of thy father, and serve him . . . if thou seek him, he will be found of thee* (I Chronicles 28, 9).

The stress is in every instance on intellectual apprehension, not on imaginations, for thinking about imaginations is not called 'knowing' but *that which cometh into your mind* (Ezekiel 20, 32). It has also become clear that, after apprehending, the aim should be complete devotion to God and perpetual exercising of intellectual thought in His love. This succeeds mostly in a state of solitude and seclusion; which is why every man of virtue secludes himself as much as possible and keeps company with others only when this is unavoidable.

EXCURSUS

WE have shown to you earlier on that this intellect which has come to us as an emanation from God is the bond that exists between us and Him.[84] It is up to you: if you wish you can

*In the Talmud: 'which is service in one's heart?'

strengthen and broaden this bond, or you can weaken it and make it gradually thinner until you cut it off altogether. This bond is strengthened by exercising the intellect in the love of God, which is achieved in the way we have described before. Its weakening and thinning is the result of employing your powers of thinking on other things. Even if you were the most learned of all men in the truths of metaphysics, the moment that you empty your mind of God and are with your entire being engaged in some unavoidable act of eating or other necessary business, you thereby cut off the bond between yourself and God. You are at that moment not with Him, nor is He with you. The relationship which exists between you and God is at that time actually severed. For this reason the people of virtue begrudge the times during which they are occupied with other things and warn us against this mistake: 'do not remove God from your thoughts' (Shabbath 149a). David says: *I have set the Lord always before me; since he is thus my right hand I shall not be moved* (Psalm 16, 8).* He says, in effect: I have never let Him out of my mind, He is therefore in a way like my right hand, which I never for a moment can dismiss from my consciousness because of its rapid movement; for this reason I shall not be moved, i.e. shall not fall.

You must clearly understand that all acts of service to God, such as the Reading of the Law, prayer, and the performance of other commandments have as their sole purpose to train you to busy yourself with God's ordinances rather than with worldly affairs, or in other words to be too much taken up with God to pay any attention to anything else. If you pray with your lips, with your face to the wall, and all the while are thinking of your business; or if you utter the words of the Law with your tongue while your mind is occupied with the building of your house, so that you attach no meaning to what you read; and likewise each time you perform a commandment by acting with your limbs in the manner of one who digs a

---

*Thus Saadiah. The following interpretation, which seems to be Maimonides' own is given by David Kimchi, in his commentary on Psalms, in the very words of Ibn Tibbon's rendering, but not in Maimonides' name.

ditch or cuts firewood in a copse, without giving yourself any account of the meaning of your action, from whom it emanates, or what is its purpose – if you do any of these, then don't imagine that you have achieved any purpose. You are at that moment very much like those of whom it is said: *Thou art near in their mouth, and far from their reins* (Jeremiah 12, 2).

Now I shall start to instruct you in the correct method of training through which you will achieve this noble aim. The first thing to which you must accustom yourself is to free your mind from every thought while you recite the *Shema'* and the *Amidah*, instead of being satisfied if you have fully concentrated during the first verse of the *Shema'* and the opening benediction of the *Amidah*. When you have for a number of years been successful in this and have control over yourself, accustom yourself further, whenever you recite the Law or hear it recited, to concentrate uninterruptedly with your whole being and all your thoughts upon the meaning of what you hear or read. When you have mastered this for some time you should train yourself to apply your mind wholeheartedly to whatever you recite of other passages from the prophets. In all benedictions, too, you should aim at pondering what you utter and realizing its meaning.

When you are able to perform all these forms of service with a pure intention, and your mind, while you are performing them, is free from all thought of worldly affairs, train yourself to direct your thoughts to the necessities or luxuries of your life, and generally to *negotia mundi*, only at times when you eat or drink or follow the call of nature or talk to your wife or your little children, or while you converse with common people. Thus I have provided you with ample time during which you may think over anything you need in the way of money matters, the management of your house, and your physical needs. At those times, on the other hand, when you are busy with religious matters, your mind should not be engaged on anything but the act you are performing, as we have indicated above. However, when you enjoy complete solitude or lie awake upon your couch, you ought to be extremely careful not to allow your thoughts in those precious moments to dwell on anything but that worship with the intellect. This is the nearness to God and the true method of appearing before Him which I have taught you, not the way through emotions based on imaginations.

It is, to my mind, perfectly possible for an educated person who trains himself in the way indicated, to get as far as that. It is also thinkable that a man should achieve such a degree of perception of the Truths, and of happiness through such perception, that he is able to talk to people and to occupy himself with the actions necessary for his life while at the same time his intellect is turned towards God and he is with his heart constantly before God, though his outer form is with men, as is said in those poetical similes intended to describe this state: *I sleep, but my heart waketh, it is the voice of my beloved that knocketh* ... (Canticles 5, 2). I should, however, not like to assert that this was the case with all prophets; all I can say is that it was the position of Moses, of whom it is said: *and Moses alone shall come near unto the Lord, but they shall not come nigh* (Exodus 24, 2); *and he was there with the Lord* (ibid. 34, 28); *but as for thee, stand thou here by Me* (Deuteronomy 5, 31).* We have explained the meaning of those verses in former chapters. This rank was also held by the Patriarchs, who were so close to God that His name became known to the world through their name** as *God of Abraham, God of Isaac, and God of Jacob. ... This is my name forever* (Exodus 3, 15). Their intellects were so completely taken up with the perception of God that He concluded with each of them an eternal covenant: *Then will I remember my covenant with Jacob*, etc. (Leviticus 26, 42). For these four, Moses and the three Patriarchs, were distinguished by a high degree of preoccupation with God, i.e. perception of Him and love for Him, as witnessed by Scripture, and likewise God's providence for them and their descendants was very great indeed; yet at the same time they would be occupied with managing other people, increasing their fortune, and tending their property.

*Hebrew vs. 28.
**Or: through them.

This, in my view, is a clear proof that while engaged in these pursuits they were attending to them with their limbs only, while their intellect was constantly in the presence of God.

It further appears to me that I can state the reason why these four remained constantly perfect before God and enjoyed His uninterrupted providence even while they were engaged in increasing their wealth, i.e. in the labours of stockbreeding, agriculture, and house-management. It was that their purpose in all these pursuits was to come nearer to God. And what a nearness that was! For the purpose of all their efforts during their lifetime was to bring into being a nation that would know God and serve Him: *For I have known him, that he will command his children and his household after him, that they may keep the way of the Lord, to do righteousness and justice* (Genesis 18, 19). It has been shown earlier in this book that all their labours were directed towards the purpose of spreading 'the exclusive worship of God in the world' and to guide men towards the love of Him. This is why they were worthy of reaching that rank: for all those worldly occupations were a magnificent and pure form of service to God. This is, of course, not the rank which a man like me can presume to teach you to attain; but that degree of achievement which I have described before can be aimed at and attained by the method of training which I have indicated. The right attitude towards God is humility: then He may remove the obstacles that lie between us and Him – though most of those obstacles are due to ourselves, as we have shown in former chapters of this treatise: *Your iniquities have separated between you and your God* (Isaiah 59, 2).

In this connection a most remarkable speculation has occurred to my mind, through which various doubts are resolved and divine secrets laid open. We have shown in the chapters on Divine Providence that the degree of providence extended to every intellectual being is proportionate to its intellect. Therefore a person of perfect perception whose intellect never severs its bond with God will enjoy constant providence.[85] In the case of a person of perfect perception whose intellect sometimes for a time departs from God, providence rests upon him only while he thinks of God and departs from him while he is other-wise occupied. It does, however, not withdraw from him to the same extent that it is withdrawn from one who never exercised his intellect. It merely diminishes, since that person of perfect perception does at the time when he is busy not possess an actual intellect, but he only perceives potentially, though to a degree close to actuality. He may thus be compared to a skilful scribe who is not actually writing.[86] The one who has never comprehended God, however, is like him who is in darkness and has never seen any light, as we have explained when discussing the verse: *and the wicked shall be silent in dark-ness* (I Samuel 2, 9),* while he who perceives and directs his whole being to the object of his intellect is like one who is in the full light of the sun; the one who perceives but is otherwise occupied resembles, while he is occupied, a man on a dull day, when the sun does not shine because of the clouds that veil it from his sight.

For that reason it appears to me that every one of the prophets or men of perfect virtue who was afflicted by a worldly mis-fortune, was so affected at such a moment of distraction; and the gravity of his affliction was in proportion to the length of that distraction or the sordidness of the matter which caused that preoccupation. If this is correct, then it offers a solution for the tremendous problem which has caused the philosophers to deny Divine Providence as applying to individual human beings and to put men on the same footing as individuals of other animal species. Their proof for this assertion, as we know, was the fact that virtuous and good men are suddenly over-whelmed by terrible misfortunes. Now the secret of this has become clear, even if we admit their general argument. It results that Divine Providence is constantly guarding those who have obtained a share of that emanation which is granted to all who make an effort to obtain it. When a man has achieved purity of thought, clear perception of God by the proper methods, and beatitude through that which he per-ceives, it will never be possible for evil of any kind to befall

*Cf. Book iii, ch. xviii.

this man, because he is with God and God is with him. However, when he averts himself from God, in which state he is
hidden from God and God is hidden from him, he is a target
for every evil thing that happens to come his way. The thing
which induces Providence and saves man from the raging sea
of chance happenings, is just that intellectual emanation. It
may fail to reach that virtuous and good man for a limited
time, or it may never reach at all that other imperfect and evil
man, and for this reason they are affected by chance happenings.

The philosophers have proved that in youth the bodily
forces prevent the attainment of most ethical virtues. This
applies more emphatically to that pure thought which results
from the perfect development of the concepts which lead man
to love God. It is absurd to believe that this can be achieved
at a time when the bodily humours are at boiling point. However, to the extent that the bodily forces become weaker and
the fire of the lusts dies down, the powers of the intellect
become stronger, its lights more extensive, its perception
clearer, and it derives enjoyment from that which it perceives.
When an accomplished person reaches a ripe old age and
approaches death, that faculty of perception increases greatly,
and his joy in perception, and love for what he perceives
becomes overpowering, until his soul finally leaves his body in
that state of happiness. This is what the Sages meant when they
said of Moses, Aaron, and Miriam that 'all three of them died
as through a kiss'. In commenting upon the verse: *So Moses the
servant of the Lord died there in the land of Moab through the
mouth** of the Lord* (Deuteronomy 34, 5), they say: 'hence we
learn that he died through a kiss'. Similarly it is said of Aaron
. . . at the mouth of the Lord, and died there (Numbers 33, 38).
They also say about Miriam that she, too, died through a kiss,
but the phrase 'through the mouth of the Lord' is not employed
in her case because she was a woman and it would not be
decorous to use this simile with regard to her (Baba Bathra
17a). The intention is that the three of them died in the happiness of that perception, caused by their intense love. In this

*A.V.: 'according to the word'.

statement the Sages employ the well-known poetical image which refers to the perception derived from intense love to God as a kiss, as in the verse: *Let him kiss me with the kisses of his mouth, for thy love is better than wine* (Canticles 1, 2).

This kind of death, which is in truth escape from death, is only mentioned by the Sages as having been accorded to Moses, Aaron, and Miriam. The other prophets and people of virtue did not reach this rank, but with all of them the faculty of perception in their intellect grew stronger at the moment of the separation (of body and soul), as it is said: *when thy righteousness goes before thee, the glory of the Lord shall gather thee in* (Isaiah 58, 8).* Once it has entered upon eternal life, that intellect remains permanently in one state, for the obstacle which separated it at times from its object is now removed. Its eternal survival is in that state of immense happiness which is not comparable with the pleasures of the body, as we ourselves in our various works and others before us have shown.

Train yourself to understand this chapter, and make every effort to increase the number of occasions when you are with God or at least striving towards Him, and to diminish the occasions when you are with things other than He and not striving towards Him. This guidance is sufficient for the purpose of this treatise.

CHAPTER LII

W HEN a man is in the presence of a mighty king, he will not sit, move, and behave in the same way as he would when he is alone in his own house; nor will he speak in the king's audience chamber in the same easy-going manner as he would in his own family circle or among his relatives. Therefore, any man who is keen on attaining human perfection and wishes to be a true 'man of God' must awake to the fact that the great King who constantly protects him and is near to him is mightier than any human individual, even if it were David or Solomon. That

*Cf. Abodah Zarah 5a. A.V.: 'and thy righteousness shall go before thee; the glory of the Lord shall be thy reward'.

King and constant guardian is the intellect emanated upon us which is the bond between us and God. Just as we perceive Him in that light which He emanates upon us – as it is said: *In thy light we see light* (Psalm 36, 9)* – so God looks down upon us by the same light. Because of it God is perpetually with us, looking down upon us from above, *Can any hide himself in secret places that I shall not see him? saith the Lord* (Jeremiah 23, 24).

Make an effort to understand the full significance of this. You will then appreciate if I tell you that the men of perfection, once they understood this fact, were inspired with such terror of sin, humility, fear and awe of God and shame before Him – and that by way of Truth, not of imaginations – that it caused their private conduct with their wives and in their privy to be the same as their public conduct with other people. Thus you find that our Sages, in their intercourse with their wives, were 'uncovering a hand-breadth and covering up another hand-breadth' (Nedarim 20a, b). Elsewhere it says: 'who is modest? He who eases himself at night-time in the same (modest) manner as he would by day' (Berakhoth 62a). You may remember the prohibition to walk with an erect body because it is said 'the whole earth is full of His glory' (Isaiah 6, 3; Qiddushin 31a). This is sufficient to establish the point which I am putting forward, namely that we are constantly before God and in the presence of His Majesty, whether we walk or are at rest.** The greatest among our Sages shrank from uncovering their heads because man is in intimate contact with the Divine Majesty. For the same reason they also talked little. In our commentary on *Pirke Aboth* we have given the necessary explanations on the subject of restraint in talking: *For God is in heaven and thou upon earth; therefore let thy words be few* (Ecclesiastes 5, 2).***

This idea to which I have drawn your attention is also the point of all religious practices. From those individual actions

---

*In Hebrew vs. 10.
**For this rendering, cf. Koran iii. 196.
***In Hebrew vs. 1.

and by their constant repetition the outstanding men of virtue receive such training that they attain human perfection, that they fear God and are in terror and awe of Him and are aware in whose presence they are, and in consequence do what is right. God Himself has made it clear that the purpose of all religious practices is the achievement of that emotion, the absolute necessity of achieving which we have clearly demonstrated in this chapter to all who know the truth – viz. fear of God and awe of His command. He says: *If thou wilt not observe to do all the words of this law that are written in this book, that thou mayest fear this glorious and awful name, the Lord thy God* (Deuteronomy 28, 58). Consider carefully how clearly it is put there that the purpose* of 'all the words of this law' was to achieve a single aim, namely 'to fear this glorious and awful name'. That this purpose is achieved by practical acts of religious observance, this you can know from the phrase in this verse 'if thou wilt not observe to do', which shows clearly that it is achieved by the positive and negative commandments.

The ideas, on the other hand, which the Law inspires in us, viz. the perception of God's existence and Unity, are designed to instil into us Love, as we have shown on several occasions. You know no doubt the specification which Scripture attaches to Love: *with all thy soul and with all thy power* (Deuteronomy 6, 5). For those two purposes, fear and love, result from these two (soul and power): love is produced by the doctrines of the Law, which include apprehending God's existence as it really is, while fear is induced by the observance of all religious practices, as we have just shown.[87] Endeavour to understand this fully from this brief account.

CHAPTER LIV

ANCIENT and modern philosophers have shown that four types of perfection are attainable for man:[88]

The first and lowest is the one for which the inhabitants of

---

*Literally: the purpose at the time (when the Law was given).

the earth destroy each other, i.e. the perfection of wealth. It comprises the property, clothes, instruments, slaves, lands and suchlike which a man owns. If a man is a powerful king, this also falls into this class. This is a perfection which has no real connection of any kind with that person, but only a relation. The pleasure derived from it is in any event for the most part purely imaginary, i.e. the pleasure of saying: this is my house, or this is my slave, or this property is mine, or this is my army. If he were to look at himself he would discover that all this is outside his own self and that every single one of these possessions exists on account of itself. Therefore, as soon as the relation ceases, that individual who was a powerful king, may one bright morning find that there is no difference between him and the lowliest of mankind, though no change has occurred in any one of those things that had stood in a relation to him. The philosophers show that he who devotes his energy and efforts to the acquisition of this kind of perfection strives for something purely imaginary, for it is a thing which has no permanence. Even if the wealth remains in his possession throughout his life, no perfection in his own self will ever result from it.

The second kind of perfection is more closely connected with man's own self. This is the perfection of physique and appearance, as when a man's constitution is perfectly balanced and his limbs and organs are in proper proportion and of the requisite strength. This kind of perfection is also not considered to be a final purpose, because it is physical perfection which is given to man not in so far as he is human, but in so far as he is animal, and he shares it with the lowest beasts. Moreover, if a man were to reach the utmost degree of strength possible for him it would not be equal to that of a strong mule, leave alone that of a lion or elephant. The only purpose of this perfection, even if it reached the degree just described, would be to carry a heavy burden or break a thick bone, or similar things in which there is not even great profit for the body; as for any spiritual benefit, that is entirely lacking in this class.

The third kind of perfection affects the substance of the

person more deeply than the second. It is the perfection of ethical virtues, when a man's character is of its most virtuous constitution. Most religious prescriptions are designed for the attainment of this kind of perfection. This kind of perfection is, however, merely a prerequisite to something else, not a purpose in itself, because all ethical qualities refer to relations between a person and others. In a way this perfection in his ethical qualities is nothing but a prerequisite for the benefit of society. It thus becomes an instrument for something else. Just suppose that a man is all alone and has no business with anyone: in that case all his ethical qualities will be found to be vain and void. There would in such a case be no need of them and they would in no way contribute to his personal perfection. It is only with regard to others that man needs them and receives any benefit from them.

The fourth kind is the true human perfection; that is the attainment of rational virtues. By this I mean, of course, the conception of ideas which lead to correct opinions on metaphysical matters.[89] This is the ultimate purpose, and this is the one which bestows upon man true perfection, being peculiar to him alone. It brings him eternal life,[90] and by it man is man. Consider each one of the three preceding types of perfection, and you will discover that they belong to others, not to yourself – or if you must needs have it according to the conventional view, they belong to you and others at the same time. This last perfection, however, belongs to yourself exclusively, and no one else has any share in it: *Let them be only thine own, and not strangers' with thee* (Proverbs 5, 17).

For this reason it is only proper that you should be eager to acquire that which remains your own instead of toiling and suffering for others. Woe to you, if you are oblivious of your own soul until its former splendid white colour turns black under the domination of the physical instincts, as it says in the opening lines of those well-known poetical allegories which describe just this subject: *my mother's sons were incensed against me; they made me keeper of the vineyards, but my own vineyard have I not kept* (Canticles 1, 6). On that very same matter it is said: *Lest thou give thy vigour unto others, and thy years unto strangers** (Proverbs 5, 9).

The prophets, too, have explained to us those selfsame matters and have elucidated them for us in the same way as the philosphers have done. They have stated unambiguously that neither the perfection of wealth, nor that of health, nor that of ethical qualities is the kind of perfection in which one can glory or which one should desire, but that the only perfection worthy of glory and desire is the knowledge of God, which is the only true knowledge. Jeremiah says on the subject of these four kinds of perfection: *Thus saith the Lord, Let not the wise man glory in his wisdom, neither let the mighty man glory in his might, let not the rich man glory in his riches; But let him that glorieth glory in this, that he understandeth and knoweth Me* (Jeremiah 9, 23-24).** Note how he enumerates these things according to their rank in the mind of the vulgar. The greatest perfection for them is the rich man in his riches; below him is the mighty man in his might, and below him again the wise man in his wisdom, i.e. the man possessed of ethical qualities. Still, the latter, too, is honoured by the multitude, who are here addressed, and for that reason they have been arranged in that order.

The Sages have discovered exactly the same meaning in this verse as we have mentioned. The latter also clearly state the same as I have expounded in this chapter, namely that wherever Wisdom is mentioned in a general way as being the highest purpose, the perception of God is meant. They also state that the wealth man acquires, such as the treasures which men so ardently desire and consider a form of perfection, is not a perfection at all; neither are the religious practices, that is the various forms of worship, nor the moral rules which are so useful to all men in their dealings with each other – all this has nothing to do with the ultimate purpose or is equal to it in value, but is only a series of preparatory steps for that purpose. But we must let them speak to us on all these subjects in their

---

*Rendered according to the Targum.
**In Hebrew vss. 22-23.

own words, as expressed in Bereshith Rabba (xxxv, 16 end):

> One verse says: *and all things desirable are not to be compared unto her* (Proverbs 8, 11), while another says: *And all the things thou canst desire are not to be compared unto her* (ibid. 3, 15). 'Things desirable' are religious actions and good deeds, while 'things thou canst desire' are precious stones and pearls. Both 'things desirable' and 'things thou canst desire' are not to be compared unto her, 'but let him that glorieth glory in this, that he understandeth and knoweth me'.

Note how concisely this is expressed and what an accomplished man its author is; how he has incorporated the essence of our lengthy arguments and preliminary remarks.

Having discussed the wonderful thoughts contained in this verse and the observations of the Sages upon it, let us deal in full with its contents. For this verse, in indicating the noblest purpose, does not restrict itself to telling us that it is the perception of God. If that were its intention, it would have said 'but let him that glorieth glory in this, that he understandeth and knoweth me' and stopped there, or would have said 'understandeth and knoweth that I am One' or 'that I have no image' or 'that there is no one like me', or something to that effect. In fact the verse says that the cause for glory is comprehending Me and knowing My attributes, i.e. God's actions – as we have shown when commenting on the verse: *shew me now thy ways* (Exodus 33, 13, cf. above p. 72). In this verse we are informed that the actions one must know and imitate are 'mercy, justice and righteousness'.

Then Jeremiah adds another important idea by saying *in the earth*. This is the pivot of the Law. It is not so, as the destructive critics think, that divine providence stops short at the sphere of the moon and that the earth with all that is on it receives no attention, *the Lord hath forsaken the earth* (Ezekiel 9, 9). No, it is as God has informed us through the Prince of the Learned, *that the earth is the Lord's* (Exodus 9, 29). He means by this that His providence extends to the earth, corresponding to its needs, as it extends to Heaven according its needs. This is indicated by Jeremiah in the words: *that I am the Lord who exercise mercy, justice, and righteousness in the earth.* Finally, he completes the thought by saying, *for in these things I delight, saith the Lord,* meaning, thereby, that it is My purpose that you should exercise mercy, justice, and righteousness in the earth, similarly as we have explained before, when speaking of the Thirteen Dispositions, that the intention was that we should imitate them and that they should form our model of conduct. The full purpose of the exposition contained in this verse is thus to inform us that the perfection of man in which he can truly glory is that achieved by him who has attained comprehension of God to the extent of his powers, and knows in what manner God provides for His creatures in creating them and governing them, and who after comprehending this aims in his own conduct at mercy, justice, and righteousness, so as to imitate God's actions, as we have repeatedly explained in this treatise. [91]

This, then, is all that I intended to lay down in this treatise, believing that it would be of great benefit to the likes of you. I hope for your sake that after thorough study you will grasp every idea which I have included in this book with the help of God. May He grant me and all our brethren in Israel what He hath promised us. *Then the eyes of the blind shall be opened and the ears of the deaf shall be unstopped* (Isaiah 35, 5). *The people that walked in darkness have seen a great light; they that dwelt in the land of the shadow of death, upon them hath the light shined* (Isaiah 9, 2).

Amen.

To each who calls Him, God is near indeed,
If he but call in truth nor turn away.
By each who seeks Him He is found with ease,
If straight to Him he strives and does not stray.*

---

*This poem (in Hebrew) is apparently by Maimonides himself.

COMMENTARY

COMMENTARY

NOTES TO THE INTRODUCTION

1. Homonymous terms are those which denote different objects which have nothing in common, as e.g. the word 'dog' which denotes both the animal and the Dog-star. Ambiguous (amphibological) are words denoting different objects which agree only in unessential features. Metaphorical are words possessing a fixed meaning, but used occasionally, for the sake of analogy, of other things. Thus a hero may be called a lion. Cf. Maimonides' treatise on the logical terms, *Milloth ha-Higgayon*, ch. xiii.

2. The reason why Maimonides starts his work with the discussion of words with several significations, and of Biblical passages to be taken allegorically, is that the apparent contradiction between the statements of Scripture and the teachings of philosophy rests on the misunderstanding of such terms and the literal interpretation of such passages, and is removed by their correct explanation.

3. The Description of the Heavenly Chariot by Ezekiel, (*Ma'aseh Merkabah*), and the Story of Creation (*Ma'aseh Bereshith*) were for the Talmud mystical secret teachings concerning the world beyond the senses, described allegorically in the image of the Chariot, and the cosmogonical processes which represent the rise of the world from God. Maimonides identifies these two with metaphysics and the natural sciences, the philosophical theory of the world beyond the senses and the scientific ideas of the elements and laws of nature.

4. Elsewhere Maimonides explains the use of imagery in the Bible and the allegorical presentation of metaphysical truths in the prophetic writings as a concession to the masses, who could not understand those truths in all their profundity and for whom such similes and allusions must suffice. Here he deduces the need for such a method of presentation from the character of metaphysical knowledge itself. This it is not possible to obtain by a systematic and gradual process, like the knowledge of other sciences, but it comes as a sudden illumination, only to vanish again as suddenly. It can therefore not be transmitted in conceptual formulations. This is true not only for prophetic insight, which transcends the limits of philosophical thinking and is to be compared with flashes of lightning. It applies equally to philosophical knowledge itself, which Maimonides compares with light emanating from a jewel; this is an illumination of a lower grade. Maimonides does not tell us how this fits in with his general idea of the dialectic character of metaphysical knowledge. It is evident that he refers to some transformation of conceptual apprehension into intuitive perception of metaphysical objects, without which these cannot be known.

5. Maimonides declares here that he propounded contradictory state-

ments on some problems in different places of his treatise because he did not wish to pronounce openly his ultimate opinion about those problems, but wished to rouse the attention of the more profound readers by those very contradictions. Coupled with his foregoing remark that for proper understanding statements in different parts of his work must be combined so that their connection – not indicated by himself – could be grasped, this has led some old and modern commentators to search for the hidden meaning of his teachings. These attempts are fully justified in themselves, but have frequently resulted in arbitrary reinterpretations of his system. Thus some commentators draw from a contradiction in the exegesis of a biblical passage the conclusion that his whole polemics against the teaching of the eternity of the world is not meant to be taken seriously, and that in reality he shared the opinion which he combated with such emphasis. There is no need to stress how arbitrary such an interpretation is. We are justified in looking for an esoteric teaching of Maimonides only in those cases where he merely alludes to the solution of a problem or where his discussion of the problem contains such essential and profound contradictions that they must be considered to have been intentional.

BOOK I

CHAPTER I

6. It is a commonplace of Jewish exegesis that man is not described as being in the image of God because of his physical form. The novelty of Maimonides' explanation lies in two features: 1. For him the Hebrew word *tzelem* 'image' is equivalent to the Aristotelian concept of form; 2. the form of man is his intellect. Aristotle taught that all physical things, and particularly the objects of the corporeal world which are subject to generation and corruption, are composed of matter and form. Matter is the substrate which persists throughout all generation and corruption. It remains unaffected by the transition from one thing to another; thus it has the possibility of becoming one thing as well as becoming another. The realization, in each case, of one of these possibilities requires another factor, form. Generation and corruption are due to matter divesting itself of one form and accepting another. Form is, therefore, that which is responsible for the nature of each thing. Each species of things possessing identical nature has also identical form. This specific form, according to Maimonides, is denoted by *tzelem*. Aristotle further taught that the form of all organisms is their soul, hence the form of man is the human soul. Since this is distinguished from the soul of any other living being by its rational faculty, some followers of Aristotle, among them Maimonides, identify this rational faculty and the active intelligence that springs from it with the nature of man. Maimonides claims that it is the rational faculty which makes man the image of God. The peculiarity of man's soul, which is the essence of his nature and for which he is counted as the image of God, is his intellect. Here this intellectualist conception of the nature of man is interpreted into the Bible.

CHAPTER II

7. Maimonides takes as his point of departure the view of Aristotle that the principles of ethics do not form part of the realm of intellectual knowledge, but are to be looked upon as opinions held by general consent. He concludes that in his original state of intellectual perfection man considered things only as true and false, not as good and evil. This latter attitude he adopted only when he became subject to his sensual desires. Maimonides does not explain how it was possible for man in his original state to receive a divine precept which, as he says, was given to him because of his intellect. It is, however, clear that he distinguishes between this intellectual precept and the later ethical categories of good and evil. Spinoza (Ethics IV, 68 note) adopted this interpretation of the biblical account in a somewhat altered form.

8. Maimonides obviously means that the judgment of things as good and evil resulted from the necessity for man to deal with his sensual urges and to

master them. According to the, probably correct, view of many inter-
preters, Maimonides wishes to imply that the Biblical tale applies not to
Adam alone, but that man as such only distinguishes between good and
evil because his reason must hold its own against his sensual impulses.

CHAPTER XXXI

9. Alexander of Aphrodisias is the well-known commentator of Aristotle
who lived in the 2nd and 3rd centuries C.E. By saying that Alexander does
not name the power of habit and upbringing among the causes restraining
man from recognizing truth because this influence was not strong in his
time, Maimonides means to say that in the pagan world popular beliefs had
no effect upon philosophical thought. In the monotheistic religions, however, the adherence to the traditional literal interpretation of holy books is a
hindrance to the perception of truth.

CHAPTER XXXIV

10. God, and the world beyond the senses in general, can be known only
by deduction from the world of the senses. For this reason the study of the
science of nature, in its widest sense, is a necessary preliminary to metaphysics. One must know mathematics, because it is an auxiliary science of
the natural sciences and because it helps to formulate the idea of the Unity of
God in its strictest sense; logic, because it guides the mind to methodical
recognition of truth as such. Maimonides not only wishes to show that it is
inadmissible to start straight away on the study of metaphysics, but also that
knowledge of other sciences is indispensable for the achievement of the
final goal of religion, the knowledge of God.

11. Because of the difficulties of metaphysics and the manifold preparatory studies necessary for it, religious truths must also be communicated
by way of revelation, so that they become accessible to everyone. This
necessity of publishing the truths of reason also by way of revelation is a
commonplace of Jewish religious philosophy. With it, Maimonides com-
bines the further conclusion that the Bible offers religious truth in a form
suitable for the understanding of the people, and that its deeper meaning
must be communicated only to those prepared for it.

CHAPTER XXXV

12. The prohibition of communicating the deeper meaning of the Bible
to the masses is here most decisively limited in its scope. It is instructive to
compare Maimonides' view with that of his contemporary, the Moslem
philosopher Averroes. The latter says that because the Koran represents God
in bodily terms, it is not permissible to tell the common herd that God is
incorporeal. Only those trained in philosophy may be acquainted with the
metaphorical sense of those expressions. Maimonides, on the contrary,

considers it necessary to inform the people that God is incorporeal, above all external influence, and not comparable with any being, for only then will the object of their worship really be God. Thus the difference between the beliefs of the people and that of the philosophers is only relative, not absolute. Religious necessity requires the communication of certain elements of the philosophical idea of God to the common people.

13. Every body is composed in a double sense, firstly from the elements constituting the essence of the body, viz. matter and form, which are present equally in all parts of the body; secondly from its real parts, into which it can be divided *ad infinitum*.

CHAPTER L

14. The discussion of the nature of faith in this chapter serves as an introduction to the treatment of the divine attributes in the following chapters. Following the Arab Aristotelians, Maimonides defines faith as conviction of the truth of that which is a notion in the mind. For this reason no one can believe in the Unity of God unless in his notion of God nothing is contained which posits some multiplicity in God. Since, however, a plurality of attributes inherent in the nature of God nullifies such Unity, no one who ascribes to God a plurality of such attributes can possibly be said to believe in Unity, even though he may profess his faith in it by words.

15. The theory mentioned in the text is one of the various compromise formulas which are intended to combine Unity of God with the assumption of essential attributes. For Maimonides it is as contradictory as the Christian idea of the Trinity, which tries to maintain unity of God in spite of His threefold character. The same comparison is frequently found in Arabic and Jewish literature.

CHAPTER LI

16. This refers to Aristotle's rebuttal of the denial of movement by the school of Elea and of the atom theory of Democritus.

17. One of those self-evident truths which have to be defended only because, in spite of their obvious nature, they have been denied, is the fact that every attribute superadded to the essence of God posits a plurality in God. It is different with such attributes as are not superadded to God's essence but in themselves constitute that essence and belong to its definition. Maimonides declares such attributes in this chapter to be permissible; in the next chapter he is going to demonstrate that for other reasons they, too, are inadmissible.

CHAPTER LII

18. In the preceding chapter Maimonides had provisionally admitted the two first classes of attributes: those in which a thing is described by its definition or by part of its definition. Now he demonstrates that such

attributes are also impossible with reference to God. God cannot be described by His definition because an absolutely elementary being cannot be defined; nor can one think of a part of His definition, since otherwise His essence would contain a plurality of elements. This is just as impossible as a plurality of attributes superadded to His essence.

19. The definition of time which Maimonides here employs, is that of Aristotle. Since, according to it, time is the measure of movement, and movement exists only for corporeal things, God has no relation to time. God's eternity does not mean existence in a time long past, but existence without time.

20. The distinction between the two kinds of relation is as follows: correlation denotes a real connection between two objects, such as that existing between master and slave. Such a mutual relationship exists only between things belonging to the same grade of existence. What Maimonides describes as 'a certain kind of relationship' is not a real connection, but a relation which rests on the comparison of two things. Such a relation between God and world seems at first blush possible, but in fact is impossible, for only such things can be compared as possess some properties in common, whatever those may be.

CHAPTER LIV

21. This chapter is intended to demonstrate not only that in the Torah, too, the essence of God is said to be outside human knowledge, and only His works can be known. It is also meant to explain how on this assumption one should understand those statements of the Bible regarding God which in their literal sense predicate certain qualities of Him. According to Maimonides these do in reality not apply to the essence of God but to His works, which they indicate by attributing to God that quality which in man would produce corresponding activities. The thirteen Dispositions which were revealed to Moses are then interpreted in this sense. When God is called compassionate, this does not mean that He feels compassion, but that He works deeds with regard to His creatures similar to those which with us would proceed from the feeling of compassion. Evidently the idea of God loses in this manner much of its personal character. Some of it is, however, preserved in so far as God's works proceed from His free decision and are directed towards certain definite aims, in particular the wellbeing of His creatures.

22. The idea that it is man's aim to resemble God as far as possible, was taught by Plato (Theaetetus, 176), and thence has passed into many works of late Greek philosophical literature. From the latter the maxim became known to Arab and Jewish philosophers, who saw in it a confirmation of the harmony of philosophy and revelation.

CHAPTER LVII

23. In his discussion of the relation of God's existence to His essence, Maimonides follows the Moslem philosopher Avicenna (980–1037). According to the latter all things – except God – can in themselves either exist or not exist. Their existence is due to an exterior cause. Hence with them existence is a property superadded to their essence. Only in the case of God does His essence include existence. Since His existence is identical with His essence, it cannot be considered a separate attribute. The same, as will be shown later in the chapter, is true of His Unity. With God this again is identical with His essence, while with all other beings it is superadded to their essence; hence it cannot be treated as a separate attribute of God. While it may seem in this chapter that these attributes can be used of God as descriptions of His homogeneous essence, it will be demonstrated in the following chapter that when applied to God they have only a negative meaning.

CHAPTER LVIII

24. In the example cited before, the negative statements lead to some extent to a positive description, since after deduction of all other possibilities only one definite possibility is left. The last sentence states that this is not always true, particularly not of statements regarding God.

25. Having found in the preceding chapter that with God there is no distinction between essence and existence, Maimonides now concludes that existence cannot be applied to Him as a positive attribute. We cannot assert existence, only negate non-existence. Similarly all other attributes relating to His essence merely deny some imperfection which is to be removed from His essence. The explanation of statements which seem to describe God with positive attributes, begun in ch. LIV, is here continued. Having shown there that part of these statements do not apply to the essence but to the works of God, Maimonides now says of those statements which apply to the essence of God, that they are positive only in form, but negative in meaning.

26. Even the basic attributes of the personal conception of God: Power, Wisdom, and Will, are divested of their positive character. Yet even with their negative interpretation it remains a fact that God's activity is free and directed towards certain definite purposes.

27. This means that all negative statements about God must be understood to mean that the attributes denied of God are absolutely inadmissible of Him, just as it is absolutely impossible that the wall should see.

CHAPTER LXIX

28. Having shown that the reason for which the Mutakallimun refused to call God Cause and admitted only the name Doer is invalid, Maimonides now proceeds to demonstrate that the term Doer is not sufficient for describ-

ing the causal relation of God to the world. He starts from the Aristotelian division of four causes: material, formal, effective, and final. God cannot be the material cause of the world; He can only have produced matter. He is, however, the ultimate cause of the world in the three other senses, which already Aristotle treated as closely connected.

29. While the effective cause is responsible for bringing a thing into being, the continued existence of every thing is due to its formal cause. By describing God, with the Mutakallimun, only as Doer, we merely say that He once called the world into being, and would leave room for the possibility that after its creation the world stands no longer in need of God, much as a house, once constructed, goes on existing independently of its builder. In order to express that the world is constantly dependent on God for its existence (a fact which, of course, the Mutakallimun fully appreciated) we must at the same time consider Him the ultimate formal cause, which maintains the world in being as the form maintains the thing of which it is the form. Of course, God is not bound up with the world in the same way as a form with its objects. God exists outside the world, but is its formal cause in so far as He maintains it in being.

30. The argument here is based on the above-mentioned theory of Aristotle, which includes final cause or purpose among the causes of things. For Aristotle this final cause was to account for the immanent purposefulness of things, particularly the purposeful structure of organisms. Maimonides, however, goes on to ask after the purpose of that purpose, and thus arrives at the question of an ultimate purpose, which can be found only in God's will or God's wisdom. Clearly the concept of ultimate purpose, as just now of ultimate form, has undergone a shift of meaning. Strictly, God is not the ultimate purpose of things, but is final cause only in so far as the purposeful arrangement of the world has been instituted by Him. This is the view Maimonides puts himself forward in book III, ch. XIII, where he reaches the same results as in the present chapter, but contradicts it in the argumentation.

31. (Propositions 19 and 20.) These two propositions serve to provide the sharpest possible conceptual formulation for the proof that there must be some first world cause which is above generation and corruption. Their point of departure is the difference between things whose existence is possible and things whose existence is necessary. The necessity of existence can be external or immanent, *i.e.*, it may be due to external causes or to the essence of the thing itself. Things whose existence is necessitated by an external cause are essentially possessed only of possible existence, as conversely things of merely possible existence require for their existence an external cause. If there were no being whose existence is necessitated by its essence, then all things would essentially be only possibly existent. It would then be possible that none of them should exist. There must thus be a supreme cause which exists by immanent necessity, i.e. whose essence includes existence. This connection of essence and existence, which here appears as a mere postulate, is in the ontological proof for the existence of God in Western philosophy deduced from the concept of God.

32. (Propositions 21 and 22.) In these two propositions the transition is made from the necessary existence of God to His absolute simplicity and incorporeality, thus arriving at the conception of God which forms the basis of the theory of the attributes.

33. This proof for the existence of God does not, as Maimonides says, derive from Aristotle (where we find, at most, some vague suggestion of such an argument) but from the Moslem philosopher Avicenna, though the latter's argumentation is rather freely adapted by Maimonides. He concludes that because it is possible for everything subject to generation and corruption to pass at some point into non-existence, there must be some being that cannot come into being or perish because its essence excludes every change.

34. This proof derives from Aristotle himself. It is based on the principle that the series of causes cannot be infinite, but that there must be a first cause. While elsewhere the happening of the effect, which in Aristotle's system is defined as a transition from potentiality to actuality, presupposes a corresponding change in the cause, the supreme cause works without any change in itself; otherwise a further cause would be needed. Its working is not bound up with any process within it.

35. In Aristotle's system the form of all things belonging to the same species, e.g. of all human beings, is identical. That there are several beings possessing the same form is due to the fact that the same form realizes itself again and again in different matter. With incorporeal beings such plurality is impossible, there can be only one immaterial substance of any one species. With regard to God it follows that there can be only one being of necessary existence, i.e. only one God.

36. This proof of the unity of God is an emended form of a proof

advanced by the Mutakallimun. The latter had refuted the assumption that the world was the work of two Gods by pointing out that it would then be possible for the two Gods to restrain and disturb each other in their activity. In his presentation and critique of the views of the Mutakallimun, Maimonides had found fault with this refutation of dualism because it did not envisage the possibility that the different parts of the world may be the work of different creators. The argumentation of the Mutakallimun becomes in his view conclusive only if we know that the world is a homogeneous whole, all parts of which are connected. Only the unity of the world permits us to draw a cogent conclusion as to the unity of its creator. Hence he gives in another chapter of the Guide (Part I, ch. LXXII, not included in this selection) detailed proof for the unity of the world, on which he here bases his proof of the Unity of God.

CHAPTER XIII

37. This discussion of time is directed against the argumentation of Aristotle. The latter demonstrates first that time has no beginning, and from this concludes that movement, too, has no beginning, since time cannot exist without movement (cf. Phys. VIII. 1; Metaph. XII. 6). Maimonides reverses the argument. From the Aristotelian definition of time as measure of movement (note 19, p. 210) he concludes that the question whether time had a beginning or not depends on whether movement had a beginning or not. If the world is created, then time itself is one of the created things. The idea that the creation of the world includes the creation of time goes back to Plato (Timaeus 37, 38). Galen's sceptical pronouncement that we cannot understand the nature of time, mentioned earlier in the text, is in keeping with the sceptical attitude of that thinker on all problems belonging to, or touching on, metaphysics.

38. The view that the omnipotence of God does not attain what is essentially impossible was in this form first enunciated by the Aristotle commentator Alexander of Aphrodisias (De Fato, ch. XXX) who also adduces similar instances. Those who asserted that matter is uncreated, saw also in the emergence of a thing without being preceded by matter an absolute impossibility. Maimonides accepts the principle as such, but distinguishes between that which is absolutely impossible, e.g. that which contains within itself a logical contradiction, and that which is in conflict with the actual laws of our universe. The creation of matter he reckons as a case of the latter kind.

39. Here the idea that the world is created but founded upon eternal matter is rejected with the same emphasis as Aristotle's idea of the eternity of the world. Later on (ch. XXV) Maimonides admits that it is not in conflict with the Biblical conception of God, though he still insists on *creatio ex nihilo* because the eternity of matter cannot be proved.

CHAPTER XIV

40. Movement must here be understood in the widest sense, in which every change is a movement. From this conception of movement it results that there cannot be a first movement, since the emergence of movement is in itself a movement which precedes the alleged first movement; thus a *regressus ad infinitum* would arise. This argumentation goes back to Aristotle (Physics VIII. 1), but reproduces only part of his demonstration, and that in a rather free form.

41. This proof derives from Aristotle (Physics I. 9). It is based on Aristotle's theory, mentioned here frequently, that the generation and corruption of things is due to existing matter accepting one form instead of another. This view excludes any possibility of new matter or form themselves coming into being.

42. The idea that the immutability of God excludes a beginning of the world in time is of Neoplatonic origin. In Arabic literature it is quoted under the name of the Neoplatonic philosopher Proclus (cf. Shahrastani, German trsl. by Haarbruecker, II. 199 seq.).

CHAPTER XVI

43. Since prophecy is also possible on the assumption of the eternity of the world, our decision in favour of creation in time can be supported by the teachings of the prophets without moving in a vicious circle.

CHAPTER XVII

44. Maimonides distinguishes three stages: that which preceded the creation of the world, that of creation, and that in which the world has been since its creation. The laws valid in the world since the conclusion of the creative process have no validity either for the stage before its creation nor for the process of creation itself. The error of the philosophers consists in their attributing absolute validity to the laws valid within the world, for which reason, as mentioned in ch. XIII, they reckon *creatio ex nihilo* among the absolute impossibilities, which are not attained by the power of God.

CHAPTER XVIII

45. Both arguments in our chapter aim at proving that action which emanates from God can have a beginning without any change taking place in God's essence and without any necessity of looking for a cause for such a change. True, it is difficult to visualize action starting without any happening within the cause, but the same difficulty also attaches to the emanation-theory accepted by those who think the world eternal. This also makes the world proceed from God without anything taking place within God. The

real difficulty is to think of God as cause without ascribing to Him any activity. This difficulty remains whether we take God's causality to be eternal or to have had a beginning in time.

CHAPTER XXII

46. This principle does not derive from Aristotle, to whom the emanation theory is alien, but from the Arab Aristotelians, particularly Avicenna, who took it from Neoplatonic sources. Neither are the following three principles to be found in Aristotle, though the second and fourth actually are in harmony with his system. It has not yet been discovered from where Maimonides took them in this particular form.

47. The theory of emanation, be it in its original Neoplatonic form or in that which it was given by the Arab Aristotelians, is faced with the difficulty of explaining how the manifold forms of being can proceed from the absolutely simple ultimate cause, especially if one acknowledges the first principle, that a simple cause can only have a simple effect. The Moslem Aristotelians endeavour to account for the gradual transition from unity to plurality by saying that the thinking substances proceeding from God know not only themselves but also their causes. Thus a plurality of intelligibles arises in their mind, which increases in proportion to their removal from the first cause. This plurality in the mind of those thinking substances is also made to explain the fact that from each of them emanates not only a further thinking substance but also a heavenly sphere (cf. Shahrastani trsl. II. 262 seq.). Against this bizarre theory Maimonides turns his criticism; a similar critique had been put forward by the Moslem theologian Al-Ghazzali (1059–1111).

48. The further objections of Maimonides do not refer any more to the problem of transition from unity to plurality, but are an attempt to show that the theory of emanation cannot explain why the world, and in particular the heavenly spheres emanated directly from the spiritual beings, possess the arrangement which we observe. A modern writer (Duhem, Le Système du monde V. 191 seq.) asserts that in this critique, too, Maimonides follows Al-Ghazali, who in turn develops ideas of the Mutakallimun. Maimonides himself occasionally points out a certain relationship between his own ideas and those of the Mutakallimun. However, he employs the points made by his Moslem predecessors in an entirely new sense. The Mutakallimun began by saying that the actual nature of things is entirely accidental; and a rose, for instance, might have any colour instead of red. From this they conclude directly the necessity of a creator who selected one of those possibilities. Al-Ghazzali employs this very line of thought with reference to the spheres. Maimonides does not directly deduce from the accidental character of things that they originate from a divine act of will. He merely demonstrates that their accidental character is incompatible with

the theory of emanation, by which all things proceed with logical necessity from the ultimate cause of the universe. Since it has been established before that their last cause is God, we can conclude indirectly that they do not emanate from God but are a work of His will.

CHAPTER XXV

49. Perhaps Maimonides has here in view the opinion of Avicenna that the teaching of the creation of the world in time is nothing but a presentation, adapted to the comprehension of the masses, of the eternal emanation of the world from God.

50. This passage is important for the understanding of Maimonides' basic conception of the relation between philosophy and revelation: if the eternity of the world could be demonstrated by strict philosophical proof, we should have to acknowledge it, although this would lead to the abandonment of the Torah.

CHAPTER XXIX

51. This doctrine, that God will not destroy the world He has created, nor suspend the laws of nature existing in it, and that these laws will retain their validity also in the time of Messianic redemption and the world-epoch following upon it, implies a far-reaching rationalization of eschatological ideas. All phantastic theories of a renovation of the order of nature are discarded: there remains only belief in the redemption of Israel from the oppression of the nations, the renewal of its national independence, the universal acceptance of its faith (cf. Mishneh Torah, Hilkhoth Melakhim, ch. XII). Maimonides can adduce Talmudic statements in support of his view, but in the middle ages he stands more or less alone with it.

52. In his commentary on the Ethics of the Fathers (V. 6) Maimonides adopts this view, while in this passage it is not quite clear whether he accepts it or restricts himself to assuming that the miracles were part of the divine plan of creation, but in each particular case require a special interference of God in the course of nature.

CHAPTER XXXII

53. The conception of prophecy which is here given as that of the philosophers belongs to the Arab Aristotelians. For the first time it is found in Alfarabi (d. 950; cf. Dieterici, Der Musterstaat, etc., pp. 80–4) and recurs in Avicenna. Similar ideas are to be found in late Greek philosophy, but in this particular form the theory has not yet been traced in Greek works.

CHAPTER XXXVI

54. On this explanation of prophecy, and particularly on the concept of the Active Intelligence, cf. the Introduction, para. 6.

55. The term 'imaginative faculty' is here used in a wider sense than is usual in medieval psychology. In particular it also comprises memory, which as a rule is considered a special force of the soul.

CHAPTER XXXVII

56. While Maimonides says here of the third class that with them the influence of the active intelligence attains only the imaginative faculty, not the rational faculty, he states in ch. XXXVIII that the imaginative faculty can receive the influence of the active intelligence only through the medium of the rational faculty. No satisfactory harmonization of the two statements has yet been achieved. The idea of placing statesmen and legislators on the same level as sorcerers and soothsayers is derived from Plato (Meno 99) who says of statesmen without philosophical training that like soothsayers they often hit upon the right thing without knowing why.

CHAPTER XXXIX

57. The uniqueness of Moses' prophecy has been stressed in ch. XXXV. Here it becomes clear why Maimonides attaches such importance to it. Moses is the only one ever to proclaim a divine law; a divine law could be given only through a prophet of this particular type. With this, Maimonides aims at opposing the claims of Christianity and Islam to have abrogated the Biblical revelation, as well as the theory of the Moslem philosophers that the prophet is essentially a legislator. He admits that prophecy is a natural phenomenon, but denies the sufficiency of natural prophecy for the proclamation of a divine law. For this, he asserts, a prophecy of a special kind is required.

CHAPTER XL

58. The source of this chapter is Avicenna. He, too, teaches that man can exist only in society and that for communal life man needs law. For this reason, he says, God never lets humanity lack legislators. (Cf. Avicenna's Metaphysics, German trsl. by Horten, pp. 661-6.)

59. Avicenna, too, is of the opinion that the prophet does not merely care for the external well-being of society. The purpose of prophecy is for him to guide mankind towards salvation, both in this world and in the next. He does not, however, draw from this the same conclusion as Maimonides, that a purely political legislation cannot be of divine origin. This conclusion is, of course, of particular importance for Maimonides, because he recognizes only the Torah as divine legislation. In order to prove this claim, he eliminates first the purely political legislations, and then shows that those legislations

which combine religious with political elements cannot be considered as prophetic laws because of the personality of their originators.

60. This saying of Aristotle's, quoted repeatedly by Maimonides, is from the Nicomachean Ethics (III, 10). The remark that a man of unbridled sexual lust cannot be a prophet, refers, of course, to Mohammed, as commentators were quick to point out.

CHAPTER XLII

61. Prophetic vision, in contrast to prophetic dreams, takes place in a waking state.

BOOK III

CHAPTER XII

62. The celebrated Arab physician and medical writer Rhazes (Al-Razi, d. ca. 930) composed also philosophical works, but the Aristotelian school-men did not take him seriously. In religious matters he was inclined to agnostic views, which are also the cause of his pessimism.

CHAPTER XIII

63. The terms 'effective cause' and 'final cause' have been discussed by Maimonides in Part I, ch. LXIX (cf. pp. 84, 86). That the two are identical was stated by Aristotle (Phys. II, 7 and elsewhere). The formulation, that they are identical in kind, does not occur in his works, but is in harmony with his views. When an organism is brought forth by another, the effective cause is the form of the procreating organism, which is identical with the form of the procreated organism, if not individually, at any rate in kind. Since the act of procreation has as its purpose the imposition of form, all three causes are identical in kind.

64. The inquiry after the ultimate purpose of the world presupposes that the world has its cause in a divine act of will. It is therefore impossible on the terms of the theory of emanation ascribed to Aristotle (as well as the actual theory held by Aristotle himself). According to that theory there can only be an immanent purposefulness of things, due to the fact that the effective causes of things are purposeful forms. This immanent purposefulness extends from the individual thing to the whole species, because in the continuous process of generation and corruption the form of the species is permanent (cf. Aristotle, De gener. et corr. II, 11).

65. Having demonstrated that man cannot be considered the ultimate purpose of creation, Maimonides now shows that the inquiry after an ultimate purpose of creation is altogether impossible, and that there is no other answer to it than that God willed it thus. As has been pointed out in note 30 on Part I, ch. LXIX (p. 212), Maimonides arrives in these two passages at the same results by completely different ways. There he says that every purpose must have a further purpose, so that one must arrive in the end at an ultimate purpose, which can be sought only in the will of God. Here the question after an ultimate purpose of creation is rejected because one can ask of every alleged purpose what the purpose of that purpose is, so that in the end no answer remains except that God willed it thus.

66. It is usually believed that the cosmology of Copernicus led to the view that the position of man within the universe is too insignificant to see in him the purpose of creation. It is therefore of some importance to establish the fact that Maimonides arrived at the same result on the basis of the Ptolemaic cosmology.

CHAPTER XVI

67. It is not known to which of Alexander's writings Maimonides here refers. The quotation has not been traced in any of his preserved works.

CHAPTER XX

68. The view that God knows only Himself is stated by Aristotle (Metaph. XII, 9). His commentators, however, have for the most part interpreted this as meaning that God, in knowing Himself, knows at the same time all that proceeds from His essence. One of these interpretations states that God as supreme form is cause only of the forms of things, He therefore knows only the permanent regularity of forms, while the ever changing reality of individual things is not embraced by His consciousness. Another interpretations lets the entire existence of things be caused by God and therefore be known by Him. Maimonides' polemics turns against this restriction of God's omniscience to universals. This theory is usually thought to be that of the Arab Aristotelians. However, Avicenna endeavours to show that the knowledge of universals includes knowledge of the particulars they embrace. It is doubtful whether this is not merely a concession to Moslem theology.

CHAPTER XXI

69. The theory of divine knowledge propounded here contains a difficulty which appears also elsewhere in Maimonides' theory of attributes. First he says that God's knowledge has nothing but the name in common with our knowledge: here he states that nothing escapes it, that it embraces everything, that it precedes things and is not derived from them. It is thus a form of knowledge thoroughly different from our own, but still knowledge.

CHAPTERS XVII–XVIII

70. According to this explanation individual providence is due to the natural connection of human intelligence with the Active Intelligence, and through it with God. The measure of divine providence is not conditioned by ethical perfection, as it might have appeared earlier on, but by the intellectual perfection of the individual. This, however, presupposes moral perfection. It is to be assumed that the source of this view – found in a similar form in Abraham ibn Ezra's commentary on Exodus 33, 17 – is to be sought in the Arab Aristotelians. However, the passage from Alfarabi, which Maimonides quotes on another occasion, does not lay the same stress on the intellectual factor.

CHAPTER XXIII

71. The final view of Job, which Maimonides shares, is thus this, that the sufferings of the just do not constitute a testimony against divine justice, because the just man finds his supreme happiness in the knowledge of God,

which raises him above all his sufferings. Throughout the chapter it is admitted that external sufferings can afflict even the perfectly innocent. This is in contradiction to the view put forward in ch. XVII (p. 165) as that of the Torah as commonly understood, namely that man's fate is entirely conditioned by his actions. This assumption is left untouched even by Maimonides' own interpretation as given there. Evidently this is one of the intentional contradictions of which Maimonides speaks in the Introduction (p. 48). There is, however, no reason to believe that Maimonides has now given up the theory of providence which he propounded in chs. XVII–XVIII. He merely sees that it is insufficient to explain everything that happens to man as work of divine justice. He seeks therefore to supplement his view by that of Job, an attitude frequently found in the history of theology.

CHAPTER XXVII

72. For the double purpose of divine law, cf. Part II, ch. XL (p. 145).

73. Moral conduct is in this chapter and the following considered merely as a means for the maintenance of social order, which itself serves the physical well-being of mankind. Later on Maimonides also takes into account the other aspect of morals, to bridle the lusts of man and thereby to enable his mind to develop freely. In accordance with this view he assigns to moral perfection the middle place between physical and intellectual perfection.

CHAPTER XXIX

74. In the Koran the term Sabians is applied to a religious community, identified by modern scholarship with the gnostic sect of the Mandaeans. As Mohammed speaks well of them, a remnant of a pagan community which continued into Moslem times adopted the name of Sabians. Members of that community composed in Arabic a number of works which they passed off as translations of writings of high antiquity. Their claims were accepted in Moslem and Jewish circles, and thus also by Maimonides. Hence he identifies the pagan religion of the nations of Moses' times and before him as Sabian and attributes to it the ideas contained in the Sabian writings. He assumes that these were the ideas and customs which the Torah endeavoured to combat. If he often is right with these explanations of Biblical commandments, this is no doubt due to the fact that the Sabian writings, in spite of their late origin, evidently contain much ancient material.

75. This means that God is connected with the heavenly spheres in the same way as the soul with the body. That is nothing but a philosophical disguise of the idea that the sky is the supreme God, or that the supreme God dwells there.

76. Abu Bakr al-Sa'igh, better known as Ibn Bajja (Avempace, d. 1138) was a philosopher of the Aristotelian school. He lived in Spain and later in

Morocco. He is also of some importance as an astronomer. Maimonides relates that he had studied astronomy with one of his pupils. It is to be assumed that he was also influenced by Ibn Bajja's philosophy, but too little is known of the latter's works to make an investigation of this problem possible.

77. In reality this book was Ibn Wahshiyya's own work, composed in the beginning of the 10th century. (For information on this book, cf. M. Plessner, *Der Inhalt der Nabatäischen Landwirtschaft*, Zeitschrift f. Semitistik VI (1928), pp. 27–56.)

78. We have omitted a number of other titles, which are of specialist interest only.

CHAPTER XXXII

79. While he understands the relation of other Biblical commandments to the Sabian cult customs so that those customs were abrogated by the Bible, Maimonides considers the sacrifices the only part of Biblical legislation which was included in the Torah because the Israelite people of that time would not have been able to dispense with the then generally practised form of worship by sacrifices. This view has some similarity with the assertion of some church-fathers that the entire ritual law was given to the Israelites only because of their religious immaturity. This view can hardly have been known to Maimonides. In any event it lacks the point, so characteristic for Maimonides' view of the sacrifices, that the people were accustomed to heathen customs. A most curious variation of the Christian theory is related by the Karaite writer Al-Qirqisani. He says that later Christian scholars maintained, evidently with recourse to Ezekiel 20, 25, that God gave Israel the laws in His wrath, and that the people accepted them because they were similar to the laws of the Sabians (cf. Hebrew Union College Annual, VII (1930), pp. 365–6).

CHAPTER LI

80. This apparently refers to those worshipping other Gods, who according to the Bible are punishable by death.

81. Here, where the personal relation of the prophet to God is under discussion, prophecy is taken as the highest grade of intellectual perfection.

82. The exclusive preoccupation of the mind with God, as highest form of divine service, is placed even above prayer.

83. The love to God results from the knowledge of God; on the other hand it causes the mind to concentrate ever anew upon God.

84. Cf. Part II, ch. XXXVII (p. 135) and Introduction, para. 6 (p. 22). As has been shown there, human intelligence is brought from potentiality into actuality directly by the Active Intelligence and indirectly by God. The active intelligence thus formed is, therefore, an effect of the emanation pro-

ceeding from God. The higher its development, the closer the contact of man with God.

85. The theory of providence developed in chs. XVII–XVIII (pp. 165–170) is now developed into the almost mystical idea that men whose mind is wholly in contact with God are, as long as that contact endures, lifted above all influences of the external world. It has some similarity with the teaching of Avicenna's that the miracles of prophets are due to their mind being so closely connected with the Active Intelligence that the powers of the latter communicate themselves to them; hence they are able to change the objects of the world around them in such a manner as exceeds the natural powers of man (cf. Shahrastani, trsl. Harbruecker, II, 331).

86. This passage is based on the distinction made by Aristotle between two types of potentiality. One applies as long as a man has not yet acquired a certain skill, the other when he possesses the skill, but at any given time does not exercise it (cf. De Anima, II, 5).

CHAPTER LII

87. The sharp distinction between the purpose of the Biblical laws, which is to lead to fear of God, and the Biblical truths, which is to arouse love of God, is not found elsewhere in Maimonides' writings. Indeed, it is in contradiction with his own statement at the beginning of this very chapter, that the consciousness of the permanent presence of God must produce fear and humility in man's mind. For this reason it is hardly permissible to press the argument too closely. What he wants to say is evidently, firstly, that fulfilment of the law leads only to fear of God, while love to God depends on knowledge of God, furthermore, that in the higher stages of knowledge of God the love to Him becomes the decisive factor in man's relation to God.

CHAPTER LIV

88. The following paragraphs are based on Aristotle (Nicomachian Ethics, I, 8), where it is given as common view that there are three kinds of goods: external goods, goods of the soul, and goods of the body. Among these the goods of the soul take the highest rank. In Maimonides the perfections of property and body correspond to the external goods and the goods of the body, moral and intellectual perfection to the goods of the soul. The distinction of the two latter classes, and the ranking of intellectual perfection above moral perfection also derive from Aristotle (cf. particularly Nicom. Ethics, X, 6, 7). Maimonides' exposition is formally distinguished from Aristotle's in that he speaks of types of perfection, not of classes of goods, materially, because he only recognizes as true perfection the intellectual, while for Aristotle the goods of the lower types still have a positive value. He does not hold the true happiness of mankind to lie in exterior or bodily goods, but they do form part of a perfect life. Maimon-

ides' more one-sided view is in principle, though not in detail, due to Neoplatonic influences, which with the Arabs and Jews penetrated also into the Aristotelian school.

89. As has been pointed out in the Introduction, para. 8 (p. 31), Maimonides still further narrows the true perfection and true purpose of man in so far as it does not embrace the whole field of human knowledge, but only metaphysics and in particular the knowledge of God, to which the other disciplines are nothing but preliminaries. For Aristotle, metaphysical knowledge is the highest of all, but he ascribes to the other fields of knowledge independent value.

90. According to Aristotle only the rational part of the soul is immortal. His rather involved and ambiguous statements on this point were interpreted by many Moslem and Jewish Aristotelians as meaning that human intelligence becomes immortal if it has been brought from potentiality into actuality by philosophical knowledge.

91. We have discussed in the Introduction, para. 8 (p. 35), the essential difficulty of this argument; that Maimonides first denies every independent value to moral perfection and recognizes only theoretical knowledge as true perfection, and subsequently sees the highest end of knowledge of God in our knowing His love and justice and imitating them as far as this is possible to man. Evidently Maimonides distinguishes between moral perfection, which does not rest upon philosophical knowledge, and moral conduct, which is produced by the knowledge of God. This latter is, as expression of the knowledge of God, included in that knowledge, and its value lies precisely in its being an expression of the knowledge of God.

INDEX I.

NAMES AND SUBJECTS

Aaron, 194
Abraham, 26, 96, 114, 140, 146, 167, 175–6, 178
Abu Bakr as-Sa'igh, 176, 222
action, attributes of, 71
Active Intelligence, 23, 24, 31, 107, 130, 132, 196
Adam, 177
affections, 63, 75, and *passim*
aggressive faculty, 137
aim of life, 172
Albertus Magnus, 4
Alexander of Aphrodisias, 57, 99, 114, 159, 160, 168, 208, 214, 221
Alfarabi, 107, 217, 221
ambiguous terms, 41, 205
ambition, 133
Amidah, 190
amphibological terms, 41
'ancient,' 78
angels, 21, 95, 108, 133, 145, 146, 147, 150
animalic things, 133
animals, 166–8
Aquinas, Thomas, 4
Arab Aristotelians, 12, 14, 15, 22, 130, 209, 216, 221; see Philosophers
Aristotle, 1, 2, 4, 10, 11, 12, 14, 21, 22, 30, 31, 33, 67, 90, 91, 95, 98–100, 111, 113, 115, 125, 133, 145, 151–3, 165, 167, 168, 207, 210, 211, 213, 214, 215, 216, 220, 221, 224, 225
Ash'arites, 165
Asherah, 177
astrology, 22
atoms, 67, 165
attributes, 17–20, 64, 65–82
Avempace, 222
Averroes, 208
Avicenna, 211, 213, 216, 217, 218, 221, 224

Baal, 177
Balaam, 21, 147
Baruch, 128
Batiniyya, 115
belief, 65–6, 173–4

benedictions, 190
blood, eating upon the, 28
bond with God, 187, 188, 189
Brahmins, 141

cause, 83–7, 152
chance, 165, 166, 194
Christians, 2, 4, 26, 65, 223
Code of Maimonides, *see* Mishneh Torah
Cohen, Hermann, 3
Commentary on the Mishnah, 10, 127, 129
Commentary on Pirke Aboth, 196, 217
compositeness of man, 142
Copernicus, Nicholas, 220
creation, 12, 20, 94–117, 156
Crescas, Hasdai, 6

David, King, 188
'death through a kiss,' 194
definition, 67–8
Democritus, 209
demons, 21, 28
dervishes, 142
dispositions, 73
divination, 138
divine principle, 152
'doer,' 83
dreams, 129, 131, 146

efficient cause, 84
Elea, School of, 209
emanation, 17, 22, 81, 85, 130, 131, 135, 137, 139, 166, 169, 188, 193, 196, 215, 216
embryo, 102–4
end of the world, 117–24
Epicure, 99, 126, 165
equability of the Law, 141, 142
esoteric teachings, 206
'eternal,' 81
eternal life, 195, 199
eternity of the world, 13, 14, 94–116
ethics, 27, 32, 34, 54–5, 199, 207
evils, 149
exile, 134

fasting, 181
final cause, 86
'first' and 'last', 78
First Cause, 8, 12, 83, 211
First Intelligible, 188
forces of the body, 194
form, 14, 52, 85, 142, 207, 212

Galen, 95, 214
generic form, 153
al-Ghazzali, 216
God, fear of, 196, 197
—, glory of, 72
—, goodness of, 72
—, imitation of, 77
God, our knowledge of, 9, 19, 27, 29–35,
	72, 75, 132, 181, 200
God's knowledge, 167–65
God, life of, 81
—, love of, 31–33, 188–95, 197
—, nearness to, 191–2
—, necessary existence of, 8, 15, 18, 70,
	77, 80, 90, 213
—, presence of, 196
—, proofs for the existence of, 90–2
—, proofs for the Unity of, 91–4
—, 'ways' of, 72
—, will of, 81, 86, 95, 107–8, 113, 116,
	117, 127, 154, 155
good and evil, 53–5
Greeks, 123, 142
grief, 134

habit, 57
Hananiah ben Azzur, 144
happiness, 23, 26, 30, 31, 172, 191, 194,
	195
heathen, 126, 142
heavens, 82, 97–8, 108
Hegel, G. W. F., 17
R. Hiyya the Elder (bar Abba), 146
homonyms, 41, 53, 63, 112, 162, 205
humility, 192

Ibn Bajja, 222
Ibn Ezra, Abraham, 221
Ibn Wahshiyya, 179

idolatry, 76, 178
idols, 52, 177
illumination, 7, 23, 42, 43
'image,' 51–3
imagination (imaginative faculty), 24,
	130–7, 218
immanent necessity, 213
immateriality, see simplicity
impossibility, 97
incorporeal beings, 16, 22, 106–7, 157,
	213
incorporeality, 51
Indians, 176
infinite, 159, 161, 213
intellect, 52–54
Intellectual forms, 180
— function, 188
Intelligences, 21, 22, 109, 110–11
Isaiah, 119

Jacob, 134, 146
Jeremiah, 137
R. Jeremiah b. Eleazar, 125
Job, 23, 26, 170–3
Jonathan b. Uzziel, 121
Joshua, 129, 147

Kant, Immanuel, 3
knowledge, 159, 188
Koran, 187, 208, 222
Krochmal, Nachman, 3, 6

language, 77, 118
the Law, 26–9, 140–2
law, ritual, 4, 27
lawgiver, 25, 136, 143
laws, ceremonial, 27
—, human and divine, 144–5
leadership, 143
Leibniz, G. W. von, 2
life after death, 195
'likeness,' 52
limits of human understanding, 7, 8, 55–
	6, 80, 162, 163
lunar sphere, 98, 112, 113, 166, 201
Luzzatto, S. D., 6

Maimon, Solomon, 3
Maimonides' works, *see Mishneh Torah, Commentary on the Mishnah, Commentary on Pirke Aboth, Milloth Hahiggayon*
'maker,' 84, 87, 151
man, 53, 153–5, 166–8
Mandaeans, 222
matter, 14, 97, 100, 105, 112, 205
Mendelsohn, Moses, 3
mercy, 74
Messianic Age, 135
metaphors, 41, 119, 134, 205
Milloth Hahiggayon, 205
miracles, 20, 23, 115, 116, 124–5, 127, 130, 224
Miriam, 194
misfortunes, 149, 193
Mishneh Torah, 10, 127–8, 129, 178, 217
Mohammed, 25, 219
monasticism, 141
Moses, 25, 43, 71, 114, 129–30, 134, 139 178, 181, 186–7, 191, 194
Moslems, 2, 4, 16, 24, 26, 115, 165
motion, movement, 67, 69, 95, 99, 112, 215
Mutakallimun, 13, 83, 87, 101, 165, 211, 214, 216
Mu'tazilites, 165

Nabataean Agriculture, 176, 179
nations of antiquity, 142
nature, 15, 20, 23, 124, 143, 180
negative attributes, 79–82
negroes, 185
Neoplatonism, 12, 14, 15, 17, 18, 30, 33, 215, 216, 224
'new heaven,' 'new earth', 122
Noah, 177
notion, 65

Onkelos, 53
order in human affairs, 158, 160

Paradise, 118
Patriarchs, 26, 191
perfection, 16, 19, 26, 29, 34, 44, 71, 75, 126, 131, 135, 136, 141, 153, 154, 173–4, 197–202

Persians, 123
Philosophers, 84, 96, 126, 161, 162,193, 194, 198; *see* Arab Aristotelians
Phineas, 147
Plato, 26, 97, 115, 116, 210, 214, 218
possibility, 162
potentiality, 224
prayer, 181, 182, 183, 189
predestination, 165
pretenders to prophethood, 143
priests, 182
Proclus, 215
prophecy, prophets, 4, 7, 8, 21, 24–6, 75, 102, 116, 126–39, 143–7, 169, 186, 191, 193, 218
providence, 23, 33, 157–73, 184, 191, 192–5
punishment, 75
purpose, 29, 30, 86, 151–2

Qirqisani, 223
quality, 68–9
quantity, 77
quiddity, 68

rational faculty, 130, 134, 139, 144, 207
— principle, 152
— virtues, 199
rationalism, 3, 5, 7, 9, 41
reading of the Law, 189, 190
reasons of the commandments, 180–4, 189, 196–7
relation, 69, 198, 210
repulsion, power of, 137
reward and punishment, 165–6
Rhazes, 149, 220
ruler, 75, 136, 143

Saadiah, 171, 189
Sabians, 28, 142, 175–80, 222
sacrifices, 28, 181, 223
scholars, 136, 145
sciences, 43, 60, 186
sense of touch, 133, 187
senses, 145
The Seven Nations, 75
sexual intercourse, 145, 150

Shema', 190
simplicity, 8, 16, 18, 110
society, 142-3, 173-4
solitude, 188, 190
soothsayers, 136
soul, 118, 173
space, 70
species, 153, 161, 165, 168
Spencer, John, 4, 29
spheres, 17, 21, 93, 111, 112, 150, 153, 157
Spinoza, Baruch, 3, 5, 21, 33, 207
stars, 17, 111, 112, 150, 156, 157, 175
study, 42, 59, 132
style, 119
sublunar world, *see* lunar sphere

Targum, 53, 121
temple, 177, 181, 182
Theology of Rhazes, 149
Thirteen Attributes (Dispositions) of God, 18, 34, 73, 76, 204
thought, worship through, 181, 187
Throne of Glory, 117

time, 69, 78, 93, 95, 123
training, 190-1
Turks, 176, 185

ultimate form, 85
— purpose, 87, 152, 175, 184, 200, 212
uncovering the head, 196
Unity of God, 66, 77, and *passim*
universe, 93-4, 98, 123, 145, 149-50, 151
—, purpose of, 151-7

virtues, 10, 30, 76, 194
visions, 21, 132, 136, 146

wealth, 198
welfare, 173
worship, 154, 178, 181, 184-95
worth of man, 150

youth, 194

Zedekiah b. Chenaanah, 144
— b. Maaseiah, 145

INDEX II. HEBREW WORDS

אלהים, 53
אמת, 54
דמות, 51, 52
חי-עולמים, 86
הגינה, 74
טוב, 54, 156
למענהו, 155

מרות, 73
מלאך, 147
נאמן, 73
נקה לא-ינקה, 76
מראה, 132
פקה, 55
צדיק, 141

צלם, 51, 205
רע, 54
שקר, 54
תאר, 51
תורה, 156

Genesis	page
1, 4	156
—, 17–18	157
—, 26	51
—, 27	52
—, 28	157
—, 31	72, 156
2, 16	54
3, 5	53, 55
—, 6	55
—, 7	55
—, 24	44
12, 3	176
14, 22	96
18, 1–3	146
—, 9	140
—, 19	192
21, 19	55
—, 33	96
32, 2	147
—, 25	147
33, 5	74
—, 11	74
39, 6	51
41, 12	128

Exodus	
3, 12	138
—, 15	191
6, 3	130
8, 22 (18)	179
9, 29	179, 201
14, 27	125
19, 6	130, 181
20, 5	76
—, 24	182
22, 20 (19)	182
23, 5	168
—, 25	181
24, 1–2	129
—, 2	191
25, 8	182
28, 41	182
32, 33–4	167
33, 11	129

Exodus, contd.	page
33, 13	72, 201
—, 18	155
—, 18–20	72
—, 20, 23	58
34, 6–7	73
—, 7	76
—, 14	182
—, 28	186, 187, 191
—, 29	43

Leviticus	
1, 2	182
19, 2	77
20, 6	167
—, 23	178
23, 30	167
26, 42	191

Numbers	
11, 25	43
12, 6	132
—, 7	73
15, 23	180
16, 3	130
20, 16	147
22, 32	168
33, 38	194

Deuteronomy	
4, 8	141
—, 35	181, 188
—, 39	181, 188
5, 24 (21)	141
—, 31 (28)	43, 191
6, 5	197
—, 24	174
7, 5	180
10, 12	179
11, 13	181, 188
—, 16	180
12, 2	180
—, 3	180
—, 13	183

Deuteronomy, contd.	page
12, 20	169
—, 26	183
—, 31	76, 178
12, 31	178
13, 2	129
—, 4 (5)	181
—, 16	76
18, 10–11	178
20, 7	163
—, 16–18	75
22, 7	175
—, 8	163
28, 32	134
—, 58	197
29, 18 (17)	180
—, 29 (28)	141
30, 12	141
32, 4	166
—, 5	150
34, 5	194
—, 10	130

Joshua	
5, 13	147

Judges	
2, 1–4	147
—, 2	178
8, 18	51
21, 22	74

I Samuel	
2, 9	193
6, 5	52
12, 21	178
15, 22	183
—, 29	184
—, 28, 14	51

I Kings	
13, 4	127
18, 26	177
22, 11	144
13, 33	182

II Kings	page
6, 18	127

Isaiah

1, 4	177
—, 11	183
3, 26	76
5, 20	58
6, 3	196
—, 12	120
9, 2	202
13, 10–13	120
24, 17–23	121
26, 2	51
28, 15, 18	171
29, 11	119
35, 5	55, 202
36, 1	120
40, 15	150, 157
—, 22	154
42, 20	55
43, 7	156
44, 6	78
—, 13	51
45, 12	125
—, 18	153
51, 3–6	122
—, 12	122
—, 16	122
54, 10	122
55, 8–9	163
58, 8	195
59, 2	192
60, 20	122
65, 17–18	123
66, 22	123

Jeremiah

1, 5–6	128
—, 8	138
—, 17–18	138
2, 8	178
5, 12	184
7, 9–10	184
—, 22–3	183
9, 23–4 (22–3)	200–2
12, 2	66, 190
20, 8–9	137
23, 24	196

Jeremiah, contd.	page
23, 36	119
ch. 28	144
29, 22–3	145
31, 3 (2)	187
32, 19	167
33, 25	154
43, 3–5	128

Ezekiel

ch. 1	42
1, 13	52
—, 26	52
2, 6	138
9, 9	201
12, 2	55
20, 25	222
20, 32	188
31, 8	52
33, 17	160
44, 21	186
—, 27	186

Minor Prophets

Joel 3, 1	129
Amos 3, 8	137
—, 8, 12	135
Hab. 1, 14–15	168
Zeph. 1, 3–4	
Haggai 1, 13	
Malachi 3, 17	

Psalms

4, 5	66
8, 5	167
—, 6	54
16, 8	189
17, 12	52
19, 8	142
25, 14	43
33, 15	167
36, 9 (10)	196
38, 21	46
49, 12 (13)	170
50, 7–9	184
58, 5	52
73, 20	52
82, 5	44
100, 3	188

Psalms, contd.	page
102, 6 (7)	52
103, 13	74
104, 21	168
119, 126	47
144, 3	167
—, 4	150
145, 16	168
147, 9	168

Proverbs

3, 15	201
5, 9	200
—, 17	199
8, 11	201
16, 4	155
19, 3	150

Job

2, 8	172
4, 19	150
9, 22–3	171
10, 10	171
11, 12	59
21, 6–8	171
—, 21	171
—, 23–6	171
25, 6	150
28, 20	59
32, 9	59
34, 21	171
37, 21	44
42, 5–6	173
—, 7	172

Song of Songs

1, 2	194
—, 6	199
5, 2	191

Lamentations

2, 9	128, 132

Ecclesiastes

1, 9	124
5, 2	196
7, 24	45, 59

I Chronicles

28, 9	188

QUOTATIONS FROM RABBINIC LITERATURE

BABYLONIAN TALMUD		Hagigah	page	Abodah Zarah	page
Berakhoth	page	11b	42, 43	3b	168
31b	79	13a	42, 43	5a	195
57b	131	15a	186	54b	124
62a	196				
63a	47	Yebamoth		Aboth	
		71a	156	I, 6	47
Shabbath				II, 17	47
30b	134	Sotah		V, 16–17	73
92a	127	10b	96		
107b	168	11a	187	Horayoth	
149a	189			8a	180
		Qiddushin			
Pesachin		31a	196	BERESHITH RABBA	
68b	154	39b	175	I	124
69b	134			V	124, 125
		Nedarim		XVII	131
Succah		20a–b	196	XXXV	201
45b	59	38a	127	XLIII	141
				XLVIII	146
Rosh Hashanah		Baba Metzia		WAYYIQRA R.	147
17b	73	32b	168	KOHELETH R.	124
31a	123			SIPHRE NUM.	43
		Baba Bathra		SIPHRE DEUT.	77
Taanith		16a–b	172	MEKHILTA EX.	129
2a	188	17a	194	MIDR. HAGADOL	45
30b	134			PIRQE R.	
				ELIEZER	134

QUOTATIONS FROM THE WORKS OF ARISTOTLE

De anima	page	Metaphysics, contd.	page	Physics	page
II, 5	224	X, 2	77	I, 9	215
		XII, 6	214	II, 3	84
De gener. and		—, 9	221	—, 7	84, 220
corr.				—, 8	152
II, 11	220	Nicomachean Ethics		VIII, 1	97, 214
		I, 8	224		215
Metaphysics		III, 10	133, 219	—, 9	105
V, 6	77	X, 6–7	224		
VII, 8	85